HEIDI'S ALP

HEIDI'S ALP

*One Family's Search for
Storybook Europe*

CHRISTINA HARDYMENT

THE ATLANTIC MONTHLY PRESS
NEW YORK

First published in Great Britain in 1987 by William Heinemann Ltd.

First published in the United States of America in 1988

Library of Congress Cataloging-in-Publication Data

Hardyment, Christina.
  Heidi's Alp: one family's search for storybook Europe / Christina Hardyment.—
1st ed.
  Bibliography: p.
  ISBN 0-87113-178-1
  1. Europe—Description and travel—1971– 2. Hardyment, Christina—
Journeys—Europe. 3. Literary journeys—Europe. 4. Fairy tales—Europe. 5.
Children's literature. I. Title.
D923.H36 1987   914'.0455—dc19   87-30742

Printed in the United States of America

First edition

The Atlantic Monthly Press
19 Union Square West
New York, NY 10003

FIRST PRINTING

To Jane, with our love and thanks

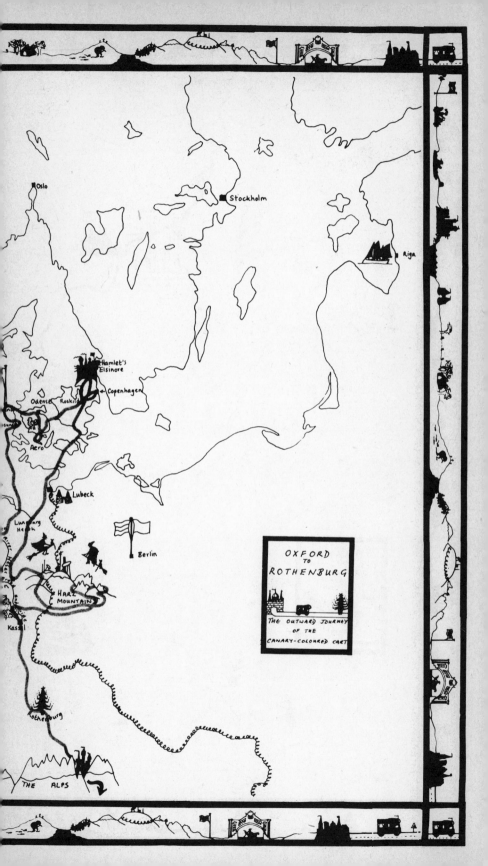

Oslo

Stockholm

Riga

Hamlet's Elsinore

←Copenhagen

Odense Roskild

Aero

Lubeck

Lune burg Heath

Berlin

HARZ MOUNTAIN

Kassel

Rothenburg

THE ALPS

OXFORD
TO
ROTHENBURG

THE OUTWARD JOURNEY
OF THE
CANARY-COLOURED CART

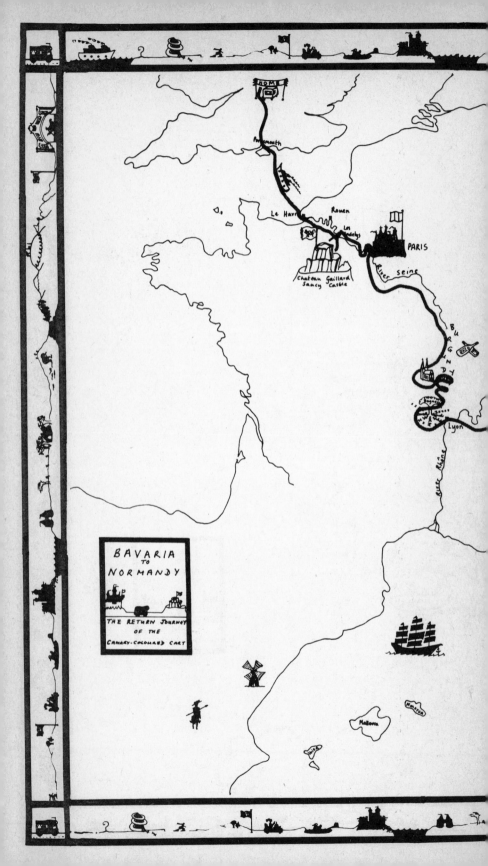

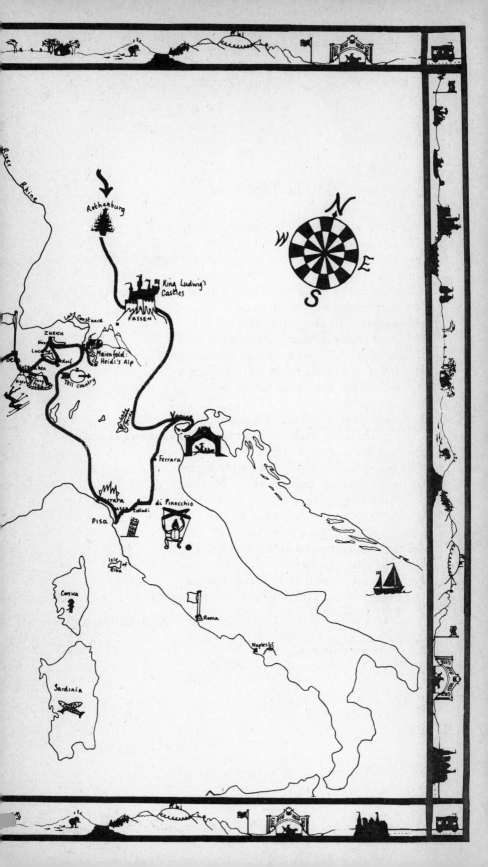

In This Time

If the myth's outworn, the legend broken,
    Useless even within the child's story
Since he sees well they now bring light no longer
    Into our eyes: and if our past retreats
And blows away like dust along the desert,
    Not leading to our moment now at all,
Settling us in this place and saying 'Here
    In you I shall continue' – then what kind
Of lives have we? Can we make myths revive
    By breathing on them? Is there any taper
That will return the glitter to our eyes?

We have retreated inward to our minds
    Too much, have made rooms there with all doors closed,
All windows shuttered. There we sit and mope
    The myth away, set by the lovely legends;
Hardly we hear the children shout outside.
    We only know a way to love ourselves,
Have lost the power that made us lose ourselves.
O let the wind outside blow in again
And the dust come and all the children's voices.
    Let anything that is not us return.
Myths are the memories we have rejected
    And legends need the freedom of our minds.

                                        Elizabeth Jennings

Contents

1
The Life Adventurous

When the virus of restlessness begins to take possession of a
wayward man, and the road away from Here seems broad
and straight and sweet, the victim must first find in himself a
good and sufficient reason for going. This to the practical
bum is not difficult.

(John Steinbeck, *Travels with Charley*, 1961)

Toad began it. Curled up by a January fire, I was reading *The Wind
in the Willows* to Ellie and Susie, our younger daughters. 'Hang
springcleaning', cries the Mole, flinging away the shackles of
routine for a day's fun on the river with Ratty. Mole is a nice
enough animal: prepared to sacrifice his cosy domesticity for a spree
once in a while, but how he revels in his return to teacup and
footstool. Toad is quite different. For all his dishonesty, his
unreliability, his incorrigible egotism, he is a true visionary – a
dream pedlar, seductive purveyor of the Life Adventurous.

'There you are!' cried the Toad, straddling and expanding
himself. 'There's real life for you, embodied in that little cart.
The open road, the dusty highway, the heath, the common,
the hedgerows, the rolling downs! Camps, villages, towns,
cities! Here today, up and off to somewhere else tomorrow!
Travel, change, interest, excitement! The whole world before
you, and a horizon that's always changing!'

Ellie stared into the red cave at the heart of the fire.
'I wish we could go for adventures,' she said.
'But we've got school, haven't we?' Susie countered with a
resignation that made me feel suddenly rebellious. Four daughters

aged between five and twelve: eighteen years of lunchboxes and swimming money, lost textbooks and missed music lessons. What had happened to my old dreams, of exploring Trebizond like Rose Macaulay, excavating in Anatolia like Freya Stark, daring the desert in memory of Lady Hester Stanhope? Was a family a ball and chain for life?

Later that evening I picked up a book I'd found in the London Library when looking for evidence that fathers were more involved with their families than the remote Victorians of myth. John Ross Browne's *An American Family in Germany* was published in 1867. The very first page drew me into a world full of revolutionary possibilities.

'Now, John,' cries the redoubtable Mrs Ross Browne, 'the dream of my life is to be realised! You are rich, and must take us all to Europe! The children must be civilised. It will never do to have them grow up like little savages. Let us start at once for Germany.'

There was breadth of vision, confidence, decisiveness. What lackeys we modern parents are in comparison, I reflected, thinking of fathers chauffeuring their children to school, mothers waiting outside the classrooms. Too timid to take an initiative, we push and prod our children through the conventional hurdles of childhood. Schooldays and homework tidy away children from adult lives – they cage up parents and reduce them to garage attendants. When the children trail home at the death of another day, we refuel, wash and service them, then post them off again in the morning.

I looked across at Tom, deep in the crossword, and a picture of content now that the hurly-burly of family supper was over. He was not by nature a travelling man, but a small voyage might tempt him. Thuds and screams came from downstairs. In our house a game of Monopoly leads inexorably to a major war. Civilisation we certainly needed, although it was possible that the children were already irredeemably savage. Gradually the idea surfaced. Why not steal a summer? Make a journey, part Toadlike, self-indulgent adventure, and part education in the old idiom of the Grand Tour. Take the children right out of school for May and June, the loveliest months, and amble unhurried around Europe well ahead of the August crowds.

'Martial would have approved of that,' said Tom. 'Aestate pueri si valent, satis discunt.' He'd had a classical education. I hadn't.

'What does that mean?'

'Children don't need to learn anything in summer if they're

healthy. I think that's right. Particularly if they're as young as ours are.'

We were not yet in the iron grip of examination syllabuses. I had finished one major project and was shilly-shallying about what to do next. But what sort of approach would appeal to the children? Every parent knows the miseries of trailing round museums and art galleries with unwilling children in tow. No one gets far up the mountain peak with an opinionated five-year-old.

Daisy wandered in with a book in her hand: *Heidi*, by Joanna Spyri.

'Enjoying it?' I asked her.

'Yes. It's brilliant. I wish we lived on a mountain and had goats. Is there really a place called Maienfeld?'

Everything fell into place. The year before we had spent half-terms and holidays exploring the places that inspired Arthur Ransome's stories about the Lake District, the Norfolk Broads and the Essex backwaters. We could spend this summer on a similar but more ambitious quest – in search of the roots of the stories that linked our children with children all over Europe in a common imaginative heritage. We could hunt trolls in the Norwegian mountains, look for witches and wolves in the German forests. In Switzerland we'd rout out Heidi and William Tell, in Italy track down Pinocchio and Punch and Judy. What sort of a man could write a book like *Struwwelpeter*? What was the true significance of Cinderella and Sleeping Beauty? Where did Don Quixote tilt at windmills? Was there a jackdaw at Reims, a hunchback in Notre Dame?

By now Tilly had given up the unequal struggle of explaining property development to her born-revolutionary younger sisters and had joined us with a cup of cocoa. The more we talked about it, the better the plan seemed.

'Let's go to Greece,' said Tilly. 'We could run a real Marathon.'

'And France,' said Daisy. 'Find Dog Tagnon and the Muskethounds.'

'But how can we miss school for a whole term?' asked Tilly. 'I'll get behind in French.'

'You can catch up in France, stupid,' said Daisy. Tilly shook her head.

'I don't think they'll let us go.' We had emphasised the legal requirement of school so much in their first unwilling days that this sudden scheme of wholesale truancy seemed criminally irresponsible.

'When would we leave?'

'How will we travel?'

'Will Daddy come too?'

Too many questions to answer in an evening – they went off to bed with their heads spinning with queries, plus a touching faith that it would really happen. In the event it was their faith which made it happen: letting them in on a fantasy that combined parental fulfilment with personal escape turned a pipedream into reality. We were badgered into admitting that really very little stood in the way of us going. A week or so later, Tom and I found ourselves in a headmistress's study. She listened thoughtfully as we sat on the edge of armchairs and outlined the plan. May and June away. Literary and cultural associations. My (brief) experience as a teacher. Tom's prowess in the new maths. Projectwork galore and regular postcards. I paused for breath. She considered for a few minutes. Then judgement fell.

'Wonderful idea. We couldn't possibly offer them anything so educational. They're very lucky children.'

Feeling like Cinderella granted attendance at the ball by her fairy godmother, I began to think about a glass coach. The Ross Brownes favoured a carriage and six, accompanied by two servants and a Red Indian slave, stopping in hotels or hiring a residence for longer halts. But unlike them we had not miraculously become rich – we couldn't afford that kind of style. One day I glanced out of the window and saw our Dutch neighbour's sleek white Dormobile with new eyes. Until then it had just been a nuisance when I made my early morning three-point turn. Suddenly it glowed with promise.

Campervans are not traditionally romantic vehicles. Around the world in a balloon, yes. Through Afghanistan on a bicycle, wonderful. Down the Mississippi in a canoe, very Huckleberry Finn. Even a train takes on a daring aspect if it terminates at a Siberian salt-mine or a North-West Frontier. By contrast campervans smack of caution, a travelling cottage approach to the unknown. Insulated from adventure, their inmates warm up own-brand baked beans and sip tea of proven quality from a familiar mug.

But we rapidly realised that for a vagrant family a motor caravan would have unique advantages. Hotels are too expensive, hostels too repeatedly unfamiliar for children's peace of mind. Tents have to be pitched when you least feel like it, and are always wet just when you want to take them down. The old horsedrawn caravans had the same advantages as campervans, but now they are towed by cars and bored children breathe down your neck as you drive. A campervan is as snug as a snail's shell: it has a car's mobility and a caravan's conveniences.

'It's too small,' said Tom, looking out of the window beside me and reading my mind. Chris and Ria had only three children, and used the van for brief visits to friends in Holland rather than long holidays.

'What about a bigger one?'

Despite a light drizzle, the next Saturday found us at a nearby motor-caravan showroom. The children's eyes lit up at the fleet of exotic vehicles. The salesman paled at the prospect of six sets of wet feet invading his immaculate autosleepers, motorhomes and Winnebagos, but he was flattered by the enthusiasm of our inspection. The more we saw, the more we wanted.

'This one's got a shower!'

'And a TV!'

'Look, bedside lights that really work!'

'Fourway stereo!'

The girls clambered into bunks, experimented with roof extensions, explored fridges and portaloos, fiddled with switches and knobs. As we retreated from the leopard-look carpeted bathroom of the largest 'recreational vehicle', I wondered if it had been wise to bring them. There was a furious argument on the way home over the respective merits of the racy Renault Autosleeper (a mere £8,000, only slightly second-hand) and the fantastical 'Enchanted Castle', a crenellated jumbo that only a good-sized ogre could have driven. All were far more expensive than we had imagined. Even to hire a van big enough for a family of six would cost between £200 and £300 a week, reasonable enough for a fortnight's holiday, but ruinous over two months.

In the end it was Ria and Chris who solved everything. They would have lent us their Dormobile, but they knew from their experiences flitting to and from Holland that it would be too cramped for long-distance travelling with six of us. The answer, they insisted, was to hire a bigger van privately – moreover they had friends with a van that might suit us very well, and who were happy to rent it at an attractive low off-peak price.

When Bruce and Clasine rolled up in Bertha it was not love at first sight. Her official description was a Bedford Supreme Motorhome, with a 2.3 litre petrol engine, a 20-gallon capacity water tank, a Calorgas-fuelled water heater and oven, and an electric fridge. She was distinctly pumpkin-like; her clumsy lines and insipid yellowness all offended against our earlier visions of sweeping round Europe in a streamlined rainbow-striped autosleeper. But the more we got to know her, the more we respected and loved her.

I discovered quite by chance that she had a romantic ancestry all her own – that yellow vehicles have traditionally carried their owners to adventures. The irascible and asthmatic Colonel Burton swept his whole family off to Italy one spring in 1830.

His wife, poor thing, who only moderately enjoyed a migratory existence, was aghast; but the young people, all three rovers at heart, were wild with delight on hearing of this exciting prospect. It seemed almost too good to be true when the yellow travelling chariot, a luxury indispensable to well-to-do folk of that period, was taken out of its coach-house and furbished up for the journey. This equipage contained all the funny old-fashioned receptacles then in vogue, some of whose very names are unfamiliar – imperial, boot, sword-case, and plate chest – a sort of miniature house on wheels.

The Burtons swept down to Italy full of pomposities and idiosyncratic judgements, leaving a trail of exhausted tutors and demoralised servants in their wake. Perhaps it was that summer running wild which set young Richard on course for his erratically brilliant career as explorer and poet, translator of *The Thousand and One Nights*.

Toad's cart too was yellow – canary-coloured, picked out in green and with red wheels, 'the finest of its sort that was ever built'. He invited Mole in to look at the arrangements.

The Mole was tremendously interested and excited, and followed him eagerly up the steps and into the interior of the caravan. The Rat only snorted and thrust his hands deep into his pockets, remaining where he was.

It was indeed very compact and comfortable. Little sleeping bunks – a little table that folded up against the wall – a cooking-stove, lockers, bookshelves, a bird-cage with a bird in it; and pots, pans, jugs and kettles of every size and variety . . .

We followed our new friends inside Bertha. Everything was a little smaller than life, trimly wood-veneered, and neatly organised. Her apple-green curtains and dark green seats were a relief after the explosive patterns that had dazzled us in the motor showroom. Bruce juggled dextrously with poles and planks and the central table at the back slid between the two bench seats to make a double bed. The berth curtained off above the cab would sleep the three younger girls sardine-wise, and Tilly could have a mattress across the cab itself. I inspected the tiny kitchen units, the walk-in shower with its pint-size handbasin and tuckaway porta-potty, the compact drawers and lockers. The girls pushed a Wham tape into the cassette player and snuggled up above the cab.

'Why not borrow her for a weekend, and see how you get on?' Clasine suggested. A few weeks later we did just that, setting off to the Malvern hills for a test-drive cum feasibility study. Successfully negotiating the hairpins of the Long Mynd did not exactly guarantee future performance in the Alps, but it was reassuring to find the engine more than capable of hauling what seemed a massive bulk up the narrow lanes. The sleeping arrangements worked out well, and during the day the girls played cards happily at the table to the companionable beat of their favourite music. No one was sick. We found that the bulwarks of the shower, wardrobe and kitchen reduced the volume of both the children and the music remarkably well. In fact Tom and I had our first uninterrupted conversation for several weeks.

The greatest relief was the ease of the driving. I had imagined that the actual steering and braking would be much heavier work than an ordinary car, and I dreaded trailing along at a snail's pace. My point of view changed radically once I was sitting high and proud behind Bertha's wheel, and I found myself sweeping round the broad bends of the A44 with a *Wages of Fear joie de vivre*. There was a pioneering thrill in leading the long illuminated caterpillar of cars behind us, and it was comforting to reflect that we were saving both their fuel and their skins by maintaining a steady 55 mph. No doubt the other drivers were relaxing, and admiring Bertha's finer points through her broad rear window.

When we returned to Oxford to clinch the van-hire, Bruce showed us how to change the Calorgas bottles, fill the water tank, drain the shower waste, check the oil, switch from batteries to mains. Head spinning a little, I listened to Clasine suggesting food stand-bys, cooking shortcuts, useful wrinkles on bedmaking and taking a shower.

'We have even had a windsurfer strapped on the roof,' she suggested encouragingly, seeing my board beside the porch. I looked hopefully at Tom. Never at the best of times a mariner, he had a determinedly faraway look in his eye. It would probably make better sense to hire a board when I wanted a sail, rather than risking its theft or damage. I remembered Ratty and Colonel Burton's wife and reminded myself that I was lucky he was coming at all.

Not that he could spare more than four weeks away from his printing presses. I would need an aide-de-camp for the first two or three weeks of our journey, and the natural choice was Jane Jones, who had braved the February blizzards on the Norfolk Broads with us when we were looking for the haunts of Arthur Ransome's Coot Club. Jane was a primary-school teacher by training, and she now lived in Holland, our first port of call. She was used to driving on the right-hand side of the road, spoke fluent Dutch and German, and had friends near Copenhagen. I had told her about the trip and she was already busy digging up traditional Dutch folktales, exploring the history of skating races, and finding out whether sailing barges could be hired for a few days. She was quite obviously the best possible person to come, and a keen windsurfer to boot. She had only one reservation. Born four months after our Norfolk trip, her first baby Sarah would be just eleven months old in May. How would she take to life on the open road?

'At seven and a half months she is incredibly sleepy,' Jane wrote in February. 'I suppose it's because she's trying so hard to walk and crawl.' That sounded fine, but three months is a long time in a baby's life. I tried to recall what one-year-olds were like. From what I remembered it was a flexible, easy-going age. Jane's letter continued: 'Please think if you can cope with Sarah too. She is a little wakeful at night. I would love to come, but I'd hate to be more of a burden than a help.' I consulted the girls. They all thought that having a baby aboard would be fun – especially Susie who had never had a little sister to practise on. I couldn't think of any plans which would exclude a baby. While Jane was with us, I would sleep in the cab, giving her and Tilly the big berth. Ideally Sarah would sleep in a basket on the floor, but she could always cuddle in with Jane. Tilly was a little dubious.

'What if Sarah cries in the night?'

'She'll wake us all up anyway if she cries in the night,' said Daisy practically. On a high of optimism I discounted such remarks and wrote back to Jane, describing Bertha's comforts and conveniences and assuring her that we could cope with Sarah.

We had one other travelling companion. By April I had done enough research to be reasonably well-informed on the obscurer aspects of the books and authors we were to pursue. One writer above all the rest had emerged as vivid, urgent, and demanding. At first I didn't even particularly like him, but like a *doppelgänger* he kept turning up at my shoulder in the most unlikely places, always with a question. Ugly, unsettled, an embarrassment to many of his friends and yet the most obsessively read and reread of all European storytellers, Hans Christian Andersen haunted me as effectively as 'The Travelling Companion' of his own macabre story. There was no confining him to his Danish birthplace Odense and to Copenhagen. After we returned I discovered that our journey had shadowed his travels even more than I originally bargained for. Like us, he admired the dikes that dried out Haarlem, stared out at Sweden from Hamlet's Elsinore and tramped along the beaches of Jutland. He visited the Grimm brothers in Germany, but he too was turned away from their door. In Venice he had been fascinated by the silence of gondolas gliding along moonlit canals. He stayed with the mad king Ludwig's parents in the fairy-tale castle of Hohenschwangau, and he had even stared down at the bears in Mary Plain's bearpit in Berne. In Paris he dined with Alexandre Dumas, and climbed Notre Dame with a copy of Hugo's *Hunchback* in his hand. A painfully nervous narcissist, a compulsive traveller, he never rested long anywhere. He drank up his welcomes with a thirst that showed he never quite believed in them, then flitted away before he saw them vanish.

I began to realise on reading his autobiography – significantly called *The Fairy Tale of My Life*, and substantially altered in the five or six different versions of it he wrote – that almost all his stories had a personal element in them. None more so than the 'Ugly Duckling', the misunderstood little bird who became the Swan of Denmark. But the sequel was not the simple triumph, public fame and recognition of that story. It was the life sentence adrift that is the true lot of the Wild Swan, hauntingly described in his *Picture Book Without Pictures*.

Twenty-eighth Evening

It was a dead calm, said the moon; the water was as transparent as the pure air that I was traversing. I could see the curious plants down under the water, they were like giant forest trees stretching towards me, many fathoms long. The fish swam over the tops; a flock of wild swans were flying past high up in the air; one of them sank with outspread wings lower and lower. It followed with its eyes the aerial caravan, as the distance between them rapidly increased. It held its wings outspread and motionless, and sank as a soap bubble sinks in the quiet air; when it touched the surface of the water, it bent its head back between its wings, and lay as still as the white lotus blossom on a tranquil lake. A gentle breeze rose and swelled the glittering surface of the broad billows. The swan lifted its head and the sparkling water dashed over its back and breast like blue flames. Dawn shed its rosy light around, and the swan soared aloft with renewed vigour towards the rising sun, towards the faint blue coast line, whither the aerial caravan took its flight. But it flew alone with longing in its breast. Solitary it flew over the swelling blue waters.

At last I put my finger on what worried me most about Hans

Andersen. It was his unquiet soul, unwilling to rest in his grave because he felt himself, with some justice, widely misunderstood and underestimated – doomed for ever to be labelled a children's writer. He wrote over 150 tales, yet today few people know more than a dozen of them. Not one of his novels is in print. Yet when the very first of his tales, 'The Tinderbox', was published, a critic advised him not to write any others because although he personally 'had nothing against fairy stories for adults', he thought children ought to be offered books with a higher purpose than mere entertainment. 'No one will allege that a child's proper sense of dignity will be stimulated by reading of a Princess who, in her sleep, rides off on a dog's back to a soldier who kisses her.' Andersen himself knew exactly what he was doing. 'I look into myself, find the idea for older people – and tell it as if to the children, but remembering that Father and Mother are listening.' Two months before his death, he was faced with what seemed to him the bitterest of evidence that Father and Mother were no longer listening. To do him honour, it was proposed on his seventieth birthday that a statue of him should be put up in the famous King's Garden in Copenhagen. But August Saabye, the sculptor commissioned to make it, proposed having a young boy leaning against him and listening. Enraged, Andersen wrote to a friend:

> Saabye came to see me again last night. My blood was boiling, and I spoke clearly and unambiguously, saying that none of the sculptors knew me, that nothing in their attempts indicated that they had seen or realized the characteristic thing about me that I could never read aloud if anyone was sitting behind me or leaning up towards me, and even less so if I had children sitting on my lap, or young Copenhagen boys leaning up against me, and that it was only a manner of speaking when I was referred to as 'the children's writer', my aim was to be a writer for all ages, and so children could not represent me. The naive element is only part of my fairy tales; adult humour is their salt. My written language is not childish but based on popular speech, that is my Danishness.

Was this just wishful thinking? Or has Andersen been unfairly banished to the nursery? He has been translated into almost every language under the sun – but very few indeed of those translations make any serious attempt to convey the deadpan subtleties, the colloquial lilt, the needlesharp throwaway lines that makes his tales so much more than stories for children. Some of them even attempt improvement – in one American version the Little Matchgirl is befriended and brought up by a generous family instead of joining her grandmother in heaven. But what could we do to right this wrong, if it was a wrong? Could people be persuaded to take Andersen more seriously? For the moment I contented myself with including the best available English translation of his tales in my travelling library, along with a copy of his autobiography and his *Romantic Rambles in the Harz Mountains*.

By March the first itinerary had been savagely pruned. There was to be no trekking across the Norwegian glaciers in search of trolls, no pacing out of Marathon, no ambling the Spanish plains on latterday Rosinantes in Don Quixote's footsteps. If we were to have only seven weeks it was better to take a neat circular route round Europe – Holland, Denmark, Germany, Italy, Switzerland and France. And it seemed wise to include some up-to-date amusements for the girls. As well as researching into the background of the classics of children's literature we planned to pursue, I had asked for lists of funparks and children's attractions from all the tourist offices. I admit that there was an element of low cunning in making the legendary Dutch fantasy world of Duinrel our first stop, but it seemed a good idea to make the children's first taste of Europe an extravagantly memorable one. They were not, after all, storybook children, and their enjoyment – or lack of it – could make or break the journey. How four such different characters were going to get on in such close quarters, I was still unsure. Tilly at twelve had an adult understanding and was impatient of babies; Daisy, individual and unpredictable, had a streak of the solitary; Ellen, once known as 'the electric baby', was incapable of staying still for long; Susanna relied too much on the privileged position of the undisplaced youngest.

And what about me? How would I manage unremitting motherhood at such close quarters when my normal impulse was to retreat as much as possible from the children? I still hadn't found my balance on a see-saw of guilt over neglecting the girls while I was working and anxiety over influencing them unduly while I was with them. I loved solitary journeys, and had always used them as voyages of discovery, flights of fantasy, and escapes from responsibility. What would it be like dragging along those responsibilities as baggage?

A few days before our May Day departure date, Bertha was

delivered. Although it was only five o'clock, Ellie and Susie instantly put on their pyjamas and climbed into the upper berth to practise going to bed. I looked round the tiny interior and tried to imagine how six people and a baby were going to live in a space this size. Where would all the clothes go? What food should I take? We needed inspiration – perhaps it was time to christen Bertha. Tom brought out a whisky bottle and we sat in state at the table looking out of the picture window and trying to imagine the next few weeks.

Passing neighbours large and small stopped to inspect our new home. The small ones disappeared aloft with much giggling, and the large ones joined us at the table. They drank to the success of the trip. We drank up the advice they gave us.

'Plug them all into Walkmans. Matthew was no trouble at all in Italy last year. He just sat at the table in the restaurant in his headphones and didn't say a word.'

'The van'll need servicing by the time you get to Italy. I know a wonderful garage near Monte Casini. When I broke down in the Dolomites . . .'

'Don't linger in Switzerland. They *despise* people with large families . . .'

'We can give you the address of our friends in Venice – they'll show you everything . . .'

I wasn't sure that I wanted to be too forewarned. A shade morose, I left Tom to learn from their experiences and began to trek backwards and forwards from house to van with armfuls of clothes, shoes, swimsuits, spare specs, nit lotion, Horlicks and other necessaries – I was as impatient as the children to be off. The travellers' tales grew more lurid on the horrors of travel in general and with children in particular. As if in illustrative counterpoint the rough and tumble upstairs suddenly turned into a landslide. There must have been a detectable weariness in the way I picked up the small bruised bodies and despatched them inside for fish fingers. Social antennae twitched. The van emptied.

Left alone, everything seemed possible. Over the next day or two I stowed an unbelievable amount of gear. By the evening before our departure Bertha had swallowed up tents, tennis rackets, five sets of waterproofs, approximately forty shoes of one sort or another, and food for the first few days. There is no furniture so charming as books, somebody once said, and on the way back from Malvern we had stopped in the small market towns that fringe the A44 and gutted the second-hand bookshops of their cheap children's paper-backs. We also found as many as possible of the old Everyman's Library editions of the classic children's stories we were aiming to track down, as these were usually unabridged and often still had the original illustrations. Once I had stuffed the ledge that ran all round the van under the lockers three deep with paperbacks Bertha's natural cosiness acquired a cultured aspect. *Pinocchio* peeped out behind *Heidi, Hans Brinker and the Silver Skates* flanked *Grimms' Fairy Tales, The Three Musketeers* jostled *William Tell*. Tapes fitted neatly above the tape recorder; heavier literary reference books stood on the shelf below it. There was space under the driver's seat for more of these and for guidebooks. Four new skipping ropes hung invitingly beside the back door – useful for exercise in inner cities. Under the passenger seat I laid down a small cellar of beer, wine and whisky.

Just as I was relaxing complacently, the girls came out with their own last-minute inspirations. Tilly had fifteen stuffed animals. Daisy carried a synthesiser. Ellie aimed her bike hopefully up the steps and Susie was puffing under the weight of a very large suitcase containing every single piece of clothing she'd ever inherited from her three sisters. That was only the first load. Tense negotiations began, involving rash promises from me about pretty summer numbers we would buy from foreign chain stores, and tearful concessions from them. At last each pushed a best-loved object into her sleeping bag, and we retreated indoors for our last night at home.

Twenty-four hours later we turned off the A12 and groped our way through a maze of neon signs to Parkstone Quay. In the darkness the maw of the Harwich car ferry gaped as widely as the giant dogfish who swallows Pinocchio. Ellie and Susie were frankly dubious about the ship's viability, nor were they convinced of the wisdom of a night crossing.

'If the front can open up like that, why doesn't it leak?'

'What if there's a great storm and it sinks?'

'What if we don't wake up in time and it takes us back to England again?'

I was in no mood for patient and comforting explanations. Clutching boarding cards and cabin reservations and stifling a private panic that had been growing stronger all day, I was concentrating on steering Bertha over the boarding ramp and into the ridiculously tiny niche that a trusting sailor was confident she could occupy. It was Tilly and Daisy who had to reassure their sisters as best they could – not that they were entirely sure themselves that the great iron shell would really float.

We locked up the van and set out to explore the ship and find our cabin. The ferry guide had advertised a disco and a cinema, so the girls were clutching glad rags as well as night-things. I had to admire their spirit, but my own energy reserve was extremely low. It had been an eventful day. An early farewell breakfast with Tom, a birthday lunch in Regent's Park with Daisy's and Tilly's godparents, a long afternoon hopelessly lost in the East End traffic with only maps of Europe to guide us, suppertime trying out the skipping ropes in Stoke-by-Nayland. When a sleek cabin steward nonchalantly told us that there was no disco out of season and the film had an 18 certificate, the neatly made-up little bunks seemed an irresistibly attractive option. The girls agreed. We drank a Coke at the rail as the *Princess Beatrix* pulled away from the quayside, watched the black water close behind her, then ducked below. The journey had begun in earnest.

2
Dutch Courage

The call to adventure rings up the curtain, always, on a mystery of transfiguration – a rite, or moment, of spiritual passage, which, when complete, amounts to a dying and a birth. The familiar life horizon has been outgrown; the old concepts, ideals, and emotional pattern no longer fits; the time for the passing of a threshold is at hand.

Typical of the circumstances of the call are the dark forest, the great tree, the bubbling spring, and the loathly, underestimated appearance of the carrier of the power of Destiny.

(Joseph Campbell, *The Hero with a Thousand Faces*, 1968)

Five o'clock in the morning. I had somehow assumed sunshine, but the jaws of the car ferry opened to reveal a drowning world. Grey rain poured down, undramatic, unrelenting. Still sleepy from a short squashed night in the tiny four-berth cabin, we looked blearily at our first Dutchman, a customs official with a flat Flemish face. Indifferent, he looked back, unaware that he was the herald at the gate of a great new world of romance and faery.

I drove gingerly along the right-hand side of the road for a few hundred yards, then turned the van into the station carpark. There was nothing to be seen of the historic Hook of Holland, the claw of land that guards the mouth of the Rhine and from which Van Tromp sailed, broomstick tied to his mast, to sweep the English fleet from the seas. Today all is Europoort: cranes and hawsers, railway sidings and flat modern warehouses. The girls stowed away their night-things while I laid out a very English breakfast of cornflakes, bread and jam, and a pot of tea. Fortified, we set off to explore the station. We had arranged to meet Jane, David and baby Sarah at seven o'clock in the buffet. I carried my copy of Mary Mapes Dodge's *Hans Brinker and the Silver Skates* as a talisman.

It had been difficult to find much enchantment in traditional Dutch children's books – Holland is a matter-of-fact country, too level-headed and sensible to deal in dreams. It took an American to find the flat wet meadowlands romantic, and even she wrote a book that was intended to be educational as well as entertaining. Mary was one of the three daughters of a freelance scientist and inventor, Professor James J. Mapes. She married William Dodge, a New York lawyer, in 1851. When he died seven years later, leaving her with two small sons, she moved back into her father's house, and fitted up a workroom in a deserted farmhouse nearby. She filled it with cast-off furniture and home-made decorations of Florida moss and leaves, and warmed it with a Franklin stove. There she spent her mornings and early afternoons writing, keeping hours as regular as clockwork. After work she played with the two boys and their friends, tramping the countryside with them to collect botanical specimens, skating in the winter, swimming in the summer – a model mother.

The stories she first told to the boys and then wrote down were snapped up by children's magazines, much commended for their high moral tone. *Hans Brinker and the Silver Skates*, her most famous work, started life as a serial, then grew into a book. The idea came to her after reading Motley's great *Rise of the Dutch Republic*, but she steeped herself in Dutch history and culture for several years before settling down to write it.

The most bizarre fact about the whole worthy undertaking is that Mrs Dodge had never been to Holland when she wrote the book. She checked all her facts with Dutch friends living in New York. It was only after it was an international bestseller that she went to see its Haarlem setting for herself. Once there she was both amused and flattered when a bookseller offered her a copy as the best way for her son to learn about Dutch life.

The plot is a good one, complex and never predictable. It centres round two children, Hans Brinker and his sister Gretel, whose father had been knocked witless some time before by a fall from some scaffolding on the Veermyk sluice while he was repairing a dike. He hovers in the background: to Gretel just 'a strange silent man, whose eyes followed her vacantly whichever way she turned', but to Hans an agonising travesty of his memories of 'the hearty, cheerful-voiced father who was never tired of bearing him upon his shoulders, and whose careless song still seemed to echo nearby when he lay awake at night'. Their mother earns a scanty living growing vegetables, spinning and knitting. In hard times she even harnesses herself to the towropes of barges, but now Hans is old enough to undertake such drudgery in her place. The children work and play in convincingly authentic Dutch style among the dikes that protect their country from the sea.

Into the story comes a light-hearted flock of young skaters, fortunate children of the rich burghers of Amsterdam, Leyden and Haarlem. Through their kindly agency, Hans and Gretel qualify to enter for the great race to win the Silver Skates. Skating also provides Mrs Dodge with an excuse for taking us for an extremely informative tour of the historic towns linked together by the local canal network. The boys skate to Haarlem and hear the great organ of St Bavo on which Mozart once played; they go to Amsterdam and inspect the paintings in the Rijksmuseum; to The Hague to see the Mauritshuis; to Leyden's Museum of Antiquities. This lengthy fictionalised geography lesson slows the action of the book down considerably, but not irredeemably. Mrs Dodge interweaves her main plot – the curing of Hans's father by the eccentric Dr Boekman (a tribute to the famous seventeenth-century Leyden physician, Dr Boerhaave) – into the skating gang's adventures, contrives a mugging and a prodigal son's return, and ends up with a fine feminist finale when Gretel wins the Silver Skates.

The door of the station buffet swung open. With heroic punctuality, David and Jane had driven nearly two hundred kilometres from Assen in the north-west and were only fifteen minutes late. Puzzled and sleepy, Sarah scanned us from the security of Jane's arms. Susie smiled at her steadily, with none of the nervous inquiry with which adults approach unknown children. Reassured, Sarah gave her one of those smiles that melt right across a baby's face and end up leaving their arms and legs wriggling in ecstasy. They were fast friends from then on.

After the Joneses had humanised themselves with coffee and trenchers of ham and rye bread, we braved the rain again. Quantities of infant kit were transferred from David's car to the van. Although I had kept a large locker under the back seat empty for Jane, I had forgotten that one baby needs about as much equipment as four children. As I considered where to put everything, David walked over with two gigantic bags of disposable nappies. I realised I had also forgotten about nappies, and all that they entailed. The only answer was to sacrifice the shower-room – it had never looked a convincing proposition, anyway. Finally, backs aching from stooping and shoving, we found a place for everything and put, for a few moments at least, everything in its place.

We strapped Sarah's pushchair to the back of the passenger seat, so that she could be tied in facing backwards, a very safe place to be. Sarah had other ideas. I trailed through the rain in David's wake, trying to change my reflexes to expect cars to hit me from the right and not the left; she howled with a determination that could not be ignored. Guiltily Jane unstrapped her and crouched amidships, holding on to her as tightly as possible. It was only ten kilometres or so to Wassenaar, but we felt every metre.

Checking into the Duinrel campsite was a simple matter, and as it was both midweek and offseason we had a small hedged enclosure almost to ourselves. I rummaged under the seat for the electricity cable, plugged Bertha proudly into the area terminal, and looked around. The rain had eased off, and the girls were eager to head for the famous amusements, most of them free to campers on the site. They dived into a deep sea of brightly coloured plastic balls, swung on pulleys across rivers into an animated world of gigantic insect puppets, scaled the highest point in Holland – all of 50 metres – to rocket down a metal bobsleigh run, and saturated each other in the bright red pneumatic bubbles of the water dodgem cars.

David, Jane and I were not feeling quite so confident. We found a beerhall and ordered a round of Grolsch, the delicious Dutch beer sold in thick brown bottles with wire and china stoppers. It cost less than the children's Coca-Colas, and was served with little paper cartons of freshly fried chips, mayonnaise dolloped on the top. From the timbered walls cavaliers laughed mockingly as David planned his route home. As he left, Jane looked distinctly insecure. We went back to the van for fast food: a quiche brought from home for us, fish fingers and frozen peas for the children. Cowardly, perhaps, but I didn't think they were quite ready for the fifty different varieties of cheese and salami on which the Dutch seem to survive. No point in overdoing the culture shock.

Then it was time for the greatest of Duinrel's attractions, the tropical wave pool. Initially, the technology was daunting. Instead of a ticket, we were given a plastic card that let us in through a magnetised gate. Once we had changed – the children completely bemused at the challenge presented by the complicated plastic hanger-cum-sack to which they were supposed to anchor their clothes – the same card had to be pushed into a locker to release its key. It stayed there until we returned, programmed to time us and charge a second entry fee if we were a second over the allotted two hours. Eventually we womanhandled the four children and Sarah, fast asleep in her buggy now, through the powerfully disinfectant showers and on to Flamingo Beach itself. Jane and I slumped in the jacuzzi while the girls explored the different pools – some hot, some cold, one bubbling like a watery volcano, another leading outside and steaming into the chilly air before winding back in again. A 5-metre high vertical chute dropped Tilly like a stone into a bottomless pool, an enormous water gun allowed Daisy to vent her spleen on Ellie, Susie could wallow under a gently weeping water-willow. Upstairs we could have sweltered in a sauna room. But the greatest attraction of all was the mighty water slide.

The girls were already at its base, looking with awe at two enormous tubes out of which people were shooting like minnows spinning through a river sluice. Together we climbed a hundred feet or so up a yellow-painted metal staircase to the top of the tower, looking out of the windows at the great blue and green pipes twisting round about and up and down. We could hear screeches and howls, see shadowy bodies swirling helplessly downwards.

Above the entrance to the blue tube was a white-fanged shark, over the green a vicious barracuda. A stream of water was gushing down them both. I donned the steady-eyed smile with which all mothers veil their secret misgivings and urged the children down Blue Shark ahead of me. One by one they disappeared into what was then the longest water slide in the world – nearly 300 metres of uncontrollable free fall.

I heard their shrieks die away. Then it was my turn. I lay back and gave myself up for lost. The slippery glass sides of the tube arched all round as I spun faster and faster downwards, screaming uncontrollably, flung up around the bends then impelled forwards into a bumpy straight like a spider washed away in a waste pipe. Even though I had left a prudent gap before setting off, my weight meant that I caught the children up. Tilly screamed as my feet came on to her shoulders, then discovered to her delight that together we went even faster. At last the pool came into sight and we were spat out into it, giggling hysterically. We forgot the sauna and raced up the stairs to try the Green Barracuda – for rapid succession of stomach-churning fear and dizzy triumph, the water chutes were unbeatable.

Time passed very quickly. Sarah woke up and had a little paddle but was not entirely sure that she liked it. Held close to Jane in the warm bubbles of the jacuzzi, she relaxed and grinned, but the trauma of getting changed was too much for her. And for us. Keys and cards got lost and muddled, towels trailed in the drain, anoraks were left in cubicles. The clock ticked inexorably on; my temper shortened as I envisaged six more entrance fees. By the time we battled through the turnstiles and got back to the van we were all tired, wet, cold and bemused.

It soon became clear that having a baby aboard was going to introduce new tensions. Sarah grabbed at the fridge controls, mashed banana into the carpet, strutted importantly at the table in front of her newfound audience of receptive older children and finally did a catapult fall on to the floor just as Jane turned her back to stop the milk from boiling over. Bed for everybody seemed the easiest solution. The three sardines overhead fell sound asleep as soon as their heads hit their tiny pillows. Tilly sat up for a little longer in her corner of the double berth reading *Hans Brinker* like a model daughter, and next to her Jane rocked Sarah to and fro. I arranged a foam mattress across the cab, padding the pit between the seats with books and the typewriter and wishing the gearstick could be unscrewed. Feeling a little old-maidish, I boiled the kettle for my hot-water bottle, poured the dregs of our evening pot of tea into a Thermos, and retired behind the curtain that divided the cab from the body of the van. Despite the repeated assurances we gave each other, both Jane and I approached the night with dread.

When I was woken in the small hours by Sarah's crying, my morale was at rock bottom. I remembered Jane's frank admission that Sarah was 'not great at night' and wondered how on earth I could have cheerfully dismissed it. Sleep, long undisturbed hours of it, seem the most necessary and desirable thing in the world at that moment. Nightmare visions of how much could go wrong in the next two weeks began to run through my head. Why on earth was I risking interrupted nights and days tyrannised by the unpredictable needs of a one-year-old just when my own children were old enough to be co-operative?

But new hope rose with the dawn. When I looked at my watch at seven o'clock I realised that Sarah had woken only once, to be quickly cosied back to sleep after a breastfeed that had more of comfort than sustenance in it.

'Officially, she's weaned, of course,' Jane had whispered across to me. 'But it's hard to explain to her that it's over.'

The others were still sleeping soundly – no one had complained of kicks, cold or Sarah's cries. Though the Thermos was a failure, my hot-water bottle was still warm and friendly. Sarah raised her head from her favourite corner of duvet and looked across at me with a king-sized grin of recognition. Disarmed completely, I grinned back. A new alliance had been formed. After a hot cup of tea and a bracing walk to the luxuriously appointed shower block, the worried zombie of the small hours was a brisk and efficient captain once again.

It was mid-afternoon before I could persuade the girls to leave Duinrel. Sheer exhaustion finally slowed them up enough for me to corral them into the van for tea and speed northwards to Haarlem. Sarah had dropped into a deep sleep in her pushchair, so Jane could sit beside me in the cab and provide a running commentary. The neatness and dapper domesticity of Dutch life struck us immediately. White-painted gables and window frames trimmed the dark brick houses like icing on gingerbread. Orange awnings curled crisply above wooden balconies. White lace fringed the windows, but the real curtains were the pot plants on the sills. We saw flowers everywhere, edging the highways, hanging from lamp-posts, perched on petrol pumps. Instead of slowing cars down by 'sleeping policemen', the Dutch have low troughs of tulips that jut into residential streets and force cars to trail through them in a slow slalom.

'Dutch towns spend more on plants than they do on street lighting,' Jane told us. 'And look out for the cyclists. They have priority over cars, and they take it. You lose your licence straight away if you hit them.'

I was having trouble with the traffic. The Dutch have a disconcerting habit of ignoring red lights completely if they're in a hurry. Even more worrying was the aggressive attitude of the cyclists. Although given generous chunks of road space both in towns and in the country, they are clearly imperialists, eager to grab even more. At road junctions they attacked from all sides, leaving Bertha crawling cautiously through them like a muddled bear in a swarm of bees. I began to wish we were on bikes ourselves. If we'd been going no further than Holland, we could well have done just that. A countrywide network of cycletracks and the flatness of the land make biking an attractively cheap and healthy way of seeing the sights.

The bikes themselves were generally heavier, more businesslike machines than our flashy chrome lightweights. They were built to carry whole families. The girls watched respectfully as a large Dutchman with bulging calves pedalled past us, a toddler strapped into a basketwork seat in front of the handlebars, his wife sitting sidesaddle on the carrier.

'It's a much more accepted thing to go out for an evening on a bike,' said Jane, pointing to a girl who was careering across our bows in an elaborate outfit, evidently party-bound. A dark-suited businessman overtook her, his briefcase strapped neatly down over the crossbar, keeping fit and saving time and money. Motorists seemed to be very definitely second-class citizens in the eyes of Dutch cyclists.

We were heading for Haarlem to retrace the footsteps of Mary Mapes Dodge's sightseeing boys in *Hans Brinker*. It was now the bulb-growing season, and a lurid patchwork of unlikely colour combinations stretched from horizon to horizon: pink by yellow, red by indigo, orange by blue. Roadside stalls were selling huge Hawaiian-style garlands of flowers – solid ropes of daffodil, hyacinth and tulip heads to sling across the bonnet of one's car or lorry.

23

'I think we should buy the van one,' said Daisy. 'It would make it look more glamorous.' Like me, she was a little offended by the staidness of our conveyance. So we stopped at one of the stalls, examined the garlands carefully, and selected the brightest of all to crown Bertha's stubby nose.

We spent the night in a national park campsite of Den Laaken at Sandvoort, deep in the shrubby dunes that edge the Dutch coast; then drove into Haarlem itself in the morning. We were heading for the gigantic organ in the Great Church of St Bavo. Tilly and Daisy had both enjoyed seeing *Amadeus*, and the news that Mozart had actually played on this organ added to its attraction. Fortunately for short legs and tempers, we managed to park literally outside the side-door of St Bavo. We walked through a low white-washed passage, dotted with old Delft tiles, and entered the church itself – strikingly tall and thin. Its coolness, the great rectangular paving slabs, and the simplicity and emptiness of the place combined to make us feel like ants crawling across the floor of an old-fashioned stillroom. The organ itself was totally incongruous – great tides of gilded baroque flourishes embracing phalanx on phalanx of silvery pipes. The main balcony, on which the infant Mozart once sat, bowed towards us like the poop of a great galleon, supported by a bosomy goddess of harmony and her attendant cherubs. Better timing would have organised an arrival coinciding with a rehearsal, so that we could have heard 'the great swell of sound' which rushes forward to meet the boys in the story.

Louder and louder it grew until it became like the din and roar of some mighty tempest or like the ocean surging on the shore. In the midst of the tumult, a tinkling bell was heard, another answered, then another, and the storm paused as if to listen. The bells grew bolder; they rang out loud and clear. Other deep-toned bells joined in; they were tolling in solemn concert – ding, dong! ding, dong! The storm broke forth again with redoubled fury – gathering its distant thunder. The boys looked at each other but did not speak. What was that? *Who* screamed? *What* screamed – that terrible musical dream? Was it man or demon? Or was it some monster shut up behind that carved brass frame – behind those great silver columns – some despairing monster begging, screaming for freedom? It was the vox humana!

Not bad for someone who had never heard it. The passage grows increasingly purple, but Mrs Dodge had boys of her own. Just as Ben's soul grows 'dizzy with a strange joy' there is a timely interruption. A friend tugs at his sleeve. 'How long are you going to stay here – blinking at the ceiling like a sick rabbit? It's high time we started.'

A small hand tugged at my sleeve.

'Is it lunchtime yet?' Susie asked hopefully. Easily, I realised, looking guiltily at my watch. We bought postcards of the keyboard at which Mozart once sat, considered a tape of the organ in action but decided nothing so big could be captured in something so small, and left in search of sustenance.

Before we could eat, we had to restock the van's larder. The grocery store which we found by a happy chance in tiny 'Baker Street' (we weren't exactly lost, just orienteering) was a very different style of emporium from the anodyne international supermarket at Duinrel. There were no impregnable plastic packets, or familiar cartons of Kelloggs. I bought ready-peeled new potatoes and freshly chopped raw vegetables for an instant lunch; big loaves of subtly flavoured bread, slices of Edam with thick yellow rind, great bars of bitter chocolate, cheap fruit juices and beer.

A contented munching, succeeded by light snores from the youngest girls, punctuated the short drive to Heemstede, just south of Haarlem. Once Haarlem Meer was an important inland sea, washing the walls of Leyden and Amsterdam. One of the best stories in *Hans Brinker* was Mrs Dodge's spirited description of Spanish galleons sailing across it to cut off Haarlem's supply lines and force the city to surrender. Two thousand of the Dutch garrison walked the plank here, where cows were meandering among the buttercups in lush polder grass. Now Haarlem Meer is a ghost sea, drained by Cornish Newcomen engines in the nineteenth century. At Heemstede there was a museum of draining history which I thought would be a good way of bringing home to the children the achievement of the Dutch in their battle against the sea – a nice anticipation of the most famous story in *Hans Brinker* – the tale of the little boy who put his finger in the dike.

We parked the van at Cruquiisdijk, and enthused over the Strawberry Hill gothic of the elegantly castellated pumphouse. Tilly and Daisy looked up apathetically – they were very happy doodling with the brush-tipped pens I'd packed for a rainy day. Fair enough, it was a rainy day. But I was feeling ambitious. One measly organ simply wasn't enough to compensate for the self-indulgence of Duinrel. This museum was just the sort of place that Mrs Jenks, Mrs Hayes, Mrs Prest and Mrs Stowe would expect to hear about back at school. We slipped Sarah still sleeping into her pushchair, then tried to rally the girls. Susie was hidden in the deepest recess of the upper berth, and had to be pulled out upside-down, a protesting dormouse.

'I can't find my shoes.' Ellie never could.

'I don't want to come.' Daisy had detected an attempt to improve her mind.

Tilly descended to low cunning: 'I want to stay here and get on with *Hans Brinker*.'

At last we sallied forth, to queue up for tickets behind a serious-minded band of German tourists. At least, I queued up. The others disappeared *en masse* into the lavatory. Since there was only one cubicle, and the novelty of a roomy lavatory after the cramped portapotty was great, this took about half an hour. Then I handed Jane an English version of the efficiently photocopied information sheets about the exhibition and attempted to proceed as recommended. Arrows pointed us firmly towards a long line of black and white photographs, each revealing marginally more land reclamation than the last.

Ellie had a better idea.

'Oh, look, Susie, a windmill. Come on, let's go and look at it!'

'No, Ellie, that's the wrong way. We've got to look at these photos first, then you'll see the point of the windmills. Now, in this one, you can see how Holland used to be. Very wet . . .' My words tailed away as Ellie and Susie ducked under the elbows of the Germans and disappeared. Cursing, not entirely silently, I retrieved them. After the first five pictures had only got us as far as the Early Stone Age, I admitted defeat. Flipping through the text and pictures like an early Chaplin movie, I gave a speeded-up account of Holland's Great Achievement and moved on to the excellent models of windmills and steam-engines.

Our bosoms swelled with national pride at the sight of the well-known names of Watt, Boulton and Stevenson. I talked of kettles. A stuffed muskrat fascinated Tilly. She refused to believe that anything so soft, sweet and furry could be as much of a pest as the diagram of its energetic burrowing through dike walls made out. Ellie was quite mesmerised by a dramatic nineteenth-century engraving of a man being washed into cascading flood waters at the breach of a large dike. She returned to it again and again. What really worried her was another man depicted as watching the accident.

'Why doesn't he jump in and save him?' she demanded. 'How can he just stand there?'

By now Sarah had woken up and decided it was time for a little exercise. Soon Susie and she were playing crawling-tig in and out of people's feet. Daisy was visibly yawning and there was a sense of lost direction. Increasingly desperate, I announced that there would be a quiz on what they had seen when we got back to the van. Tilly and Daisy brightened competitively and started following arrows and reading notices. Ellie burst into tears.

'But I haven't seen *anything*. I don't *understand* it all.'

Sarah saw an intriguing floor-level kinetic model of polder reclamation through the ages and was advancing on the water bubbling through its tiny sluices. Susie had disappeared in the opposite direction, and could be glimpsed closing in on a very frail and ancient-looking model windmill. I decided that it was time to cut and run.

'You can all choose a postcard to send to your classes when we've finished going round.' Progress became embarrassingly fast. Instead of urging on the team, I had to drag them back.

'But you haven't seen the engine room! Look at all these lovely iron levers and pivots. That is a pivot, isn't it, Jane? It looks as if it ought to move. Tilly, look out of the windows – no, Daisy, don't lean out – and you can see the – er – arms. That's how the piston things pulled the water up and down, I think.' I retreated into the stilted English text for further enlightenment, but by the time I had got my basic hydraulics straight there wasn't a child to be seen. They were battling for postcards in the hall.

'How on earth do teachers manage?' I asked Jane. We were back in the van, sipping tea in the cab. All was peace. The children were at the table writing postcards; Sarah was wedged upright between Tilly and Daisy, proudly wielding a felt-tip in imitation.

She pointed out comfortingly that children reserve their best behaviour for their teachers. That we had walked around the quaint canalside houses of Haarlem for at least an hour that morning, and that just being in a new place was pretty tiring. I began to realise the need to make major allowances for the difference in pace between children and adults. We move forward leisurely and implacably like tortoises; they dart on ahead like hares, then drop exhausted with unpredictable suddenness.

A turn-of-the-century childcare expert, Cecil Cunnington, got it exactly right in his 1913 *Nursery Notes for Mothers*. The child's nervous system is in constant fluctuation; it cannot stand sustained pressure, he pointed out. It needs frequent change – of lessons, posture, or activities. Adults, on the other hand, like to concentrate on one task for one time. 'This is why a child and an adult find each other's society irksome if it is maintained for any length of time.' His conclusion was small comfort to me and Jane. 'Women can adapt themselves better than men to this curious rate of oscillation, and Nature has arranged that the mother, and not the father, should manage the nursery.' No Virago reprint there.

Tea refreshed us all, but as soon as we drove off along the long dike, Sarah decided to fall asleep. Jane grimaced. A nap now meant routine destroyed once again, and the chances of a long quiet night reduced. But sometimes a present good is more attractive than a prospective one. As we headed north again, by-passing Haarlem and hacking through little villages, land and sea seemed to be interchangeable, a network of waterways. At one point a huge merchant ship loomed above the road, apparently gliding through the fields. Beamy barges with plump bows and curled-over sterns swanned along under full sail. Jane had gone into the possibility of hiring one to explore the northern meres, and we promised ourselves that one day we would do just that. For the moment we were concentrating on fingers.

The best-known story in *Hans Brinker* is the story of the boy who puts his finger in the dike and so saves Haarlem from flooding. Every child in Holland learns this story at his mother's knee, but people are usually hazy about the details. Mrs Dodge corrects all that. The 'hero of Haarlem' as she draws him is 'a sunny-haired boy of gentle disposition', son of one of the sluicers whose business it is to open and close the gates that regulate the canal waters. Walking back after delivering some cakes to an old blind man who lived far on the other side of the dike, he hears a trickling of water. He looked up and saw that a tiny stream was flowing through a small hole in the dike.

> Quick as a flash he saw his duty. Throwing away his flowers, the boy clambered up the heights, until he reached the hole. His chubby finger was thrust in, almost before he knew it. The flowing was stopped! 'Ah!' he thought, with a chuckle of boyish delight, 'the angry waters must stay back now! Haarlem shall not be drowned while *I* am here!'. . .
> [Night falls, his mother decides he must be staying the night

with blind Jansen; the chubby cherub grows chillier and chillier.]

How can we know the sufferings of that long and fearful watch – what falterings of purpose, what childish terrors came over the boy as he thought of the warm little bed at home, of his parents, his brothers and sisters, then looked into the cold, dreary night! If he drew away that tiny finger, the angry waters, grown angrier still, would rush forth and never stop until they had swept over the town. No, he would hold it there till daylight – if he lived! He was not very sure of living. What did this strange buzzing mean? And then knives that seemed pricking and piercing him from head to foot? He was not certain now that he could draw his finger away, even if he wished to . . .

[Luckily a clergyman happens along at daybreak.]

'In the name of wonder, boy,' he exclaimed, 'what are you doing there?'

'I am keeping the water from running out,' was the simple reply. 'Tell them to come quick.'

My Dutch friends, in Oxford, the Schuellers, had been a little embarrassed when I asked them about this story.

'Of course, it is just a symbol. No one in Holland believes it is actually true,' they had said.

After the dramatic picture she had seen in the pumping-station museum, Ellie certainly didn't. No childish finger could ever have stemmed the fury of those rising waters. It is probably significant that Mrs Dodge has it read out in an English school, and she is careful to get one of her Dutch boys to explain that it symbolised 'the spirit of the country . . . Not a leak can show itself anywhere, either, in its politics, honour, or public safety, that a million fingers are not ready to stop, at any cost.'

But I heard a rumour of a statue to the memory of the heroic little boy, and the Dutch Tourist Office had confirmed that this was true. It was at Spaarndam, a tiny village just north of Haarlem. It was put there early this century in response to the demand from American and English tourists who had read their *Hans Brinker* and wanted to see where it all happened. Well-informed after my spirited reading of the story the night before, the girls were very amused to read in the tourist guide that the statue was of Hans Brinker himself. We decided to make a small pilgrimage to see it.

Bertha rumbled along the single main street of Spaarndam late in the afternoon. As the road bridged two small meres we saw the statue – a puckish bronze urchin crouched with finger extended over a small mound. In the background on either side of the road were boats, moored or pottering along on some small business. The rain had eased off. A huge sky tumbling with billowy clouds dwarfed the flat landscape. Masts were the tallest things to be seen. We jumped out, eager to scoff, but found the legend, engraved in both Dutch and English, sublimely evasive. 'Dedicated to our youth to honour the boy who symbolises the perpetual struggle of Holland against the water.'

It was a peaceful place, and well worth the detour. We did the decent thing and photographed ourselves around the plinth, just like proper tourists. The sun shone out suddenly, approving our homage.

Our original plan at this point was to camp a little further north at Alkmaar, a small town with a legendary cheese market where every Friday traditionally dressed cheesemakers trundle deep yellow cheese footballs around on their carved barrows. Jane's researches had discovered a skating museum at Molen de Eendragt, close to Alkmaar station in Prins Alexanderstraat, part of it the Hans Brinker Museum that had once been in Schermerhorn. She had phoned up to discover that it was mainly concerned with skating history, and that special arrangements had to be made to visit it, except on every fourth Saturday of the month – which this wasn't.

Alternative attractions were the world's largest flowershow at Keukenhof, or the early-morning flower auction at Aalsmeer. Dolphins beckoned from Saandvoort, windmills from the open-air folk museum at Zaanse Schans. The prevalent mood in Bertha was not receptive to any of these schemes. We did get to Alkmaar, but as it was Saturday the cheese market was over and the skating museum not yet open. The skies had darkened once again. Slowly and indecisively circling a small roundabout near the town's pedestrian precinct, we glimpsed enticing gables, an ancient square. Alone one might have nipped out for a cup of coffee and a dash of atmosphere, but the prospect of finding shoes and jerseys, packing up spare nappies, bottle and biscuits for Sarah, and turfing five sleepy children out into the drizzle was not an attractive one.

Haarlem had been a success. They had admired the ornate houses, enjoyed the freshly made doughnuts, the great baroque organ, the shops. A tourist should avoid promiscuity, I told myself primly. Let Haarlem remain uncluttered by afterthoughts, a fine simple picture of a traditional Dutch city.

The roads were broad and empty. Looking at the map for somewhere to camp, I suddenly realised that it was only 220 kilometres, between three or four hours, to Jane's house in Assen. Although Sarah was thriving, and the girls, particularly Susie, who had never had a younger sister to baby, were all enjoying her, the last three nights had not been altogether peaceful. The weather had failed us. A pit-stop for a refit and sort-out would refresh us all. We had planned to stop at Assen anyway on Sunday night. Why not use it as a base for exploration of the Dutch scene? Jane talked of traffic parks, where the girls could learn the continental rules of the road in vintage pedal cars, of cheesefarms and clogmakers. I thought of long hot baths and solitude. I had always predicted that we would need a break from the close quarters of the van. Maybe it was better to have it sooner rather than later. Bertha took wing and flew northwards across the Afluitsdijk.

We had chosen the road across the Afluitsdijk rather than the southern route to Assen because it looked, on the map, such a dramatic drive: half an hour of watery horizons. The old Zuider Zee was finally reduced to lake status as the Yssel Meer in 1932. Building the 30-kilometre-long dam that reclaimed it from the North Sea was the fulfilment of a very old Dutch dream. In 1667 Hendrik Stevens drew up a plan to link the whole chain of islands off the Friesland coast, but it wasn't until 1891 that a feasible plan was finally drawn up by Cornelius Lely. He witnessed the beginning of his scheme in 1920, but died in 1929, three years too soon to see it completed. At a stroke the Afluitsdijk (literally, the closing-off dike) cut down that stretch of coastline from 300 to 45 kilometres, making flood damage within the new Yssel Meer a far less frequent problem, and enabling polder reclamation within the Meer to increase dramatically.

'When they reclaimed one of the largest polders, they found an aeroplane settled on the mud,' Jane told me. 'It had crashed during the First World War. You can still see it now, set in the middle of a grassy field.'

We passed the statue of Cornelius Lely gazing out at the fulfilment of his vision, and set out across the dike itself. All we could see just then was a dead straight road narrowing into infinity, and lots of water. Far away on the Meer Jane and I could see the white wings of sailing barges, distant birds of passage. Bertha suddenly seemed suffocatingly sedate.

'This doesn't look very safe,' complained Ellie, as we drove along between a high wall that only just hid the North Sea and a grassy bank that ran down to the shore of the Yssel Meer. 'There isn't even a fence.' The repeated references to flooding had unsettled her. I don't think she ever really trusted Holland, despite, or perhaps because of, my efforts to explain the wonder of it all.

Nearly seven o'clock – suppertime. We parked the van at the first of the stopping points that punctuate the Afluitsdijk, climbed the observation tower and looked eastwards. The wind was whipping across the dike and the sea had a mean, steely look. At close quarters the Meer looked equally unattractive. The sailing barges were heeling hard. Perhaps at this time of year we were better off in Bertha, now pungent with the smell of frying bacon and deliciously warm after the keen wind outside.

Over supper we looked at dramatic aerial photographs in the guide to the dike which we had bought in a souvenir kiosk halfway up the tower. They showed the sea swirling greedily through ever-shrinking gaps until at last, to a salute from hundreds of ships' hooters, the dike was ceremoniously completed on 28 May 1932. Just here, where we were parked. Ellie shifted uneasily. Sarah, wrestling with her first whole green bean, nearly choked. It was time to move on.

Further across the dike we passed a restaurant and a garage; at the next halt there was even a campsite. Tempted, I looked back at the crew. They had tired of dike-watching and were deep in their books and drawing. Sarah had dropped off to sleep in Jane's arms. Jane too was dozing. I remembered the wind and the rain and decided not to draw their attention to it. In warmer weather and with a windsurfer on the roof, it would have been a wonderful place to halt for the night and sail in the sunset or the dawn.

I drove along the empty road, with only the seabirds for company. That suited me fine. I was already finding the continual compromise between my ambitious plans and the children's needs wearing, and this was only day four. At the same time, I was also beginning to appreciate their realism. My desire to see everything there was to see in any given place was in fact an absurd one. We might indeed see the sights, but what would remain of them except a muddled memory – like the old tourist joke of 'Where are we? If it's Friday it's Paris.'

When the pencil-thin horizon of Friesland came into sight, a low dark streak under leaden skies, Ellie crept out of the mound of sleepers and wedged herself companionably behind my seat. She offered to while away the time by telling me the story of Little Claus and Big Claus. She told it very well, but I was a little disconcerted by her familiarity with it. I'd just been reading Bruno Bettelheim's theory in his *The Uses of Enchantment* that children find a great deal of satisfaction in fairy stories that express their unconscious wishes and fears. What was it about Big Claus and Little Claus that fascinated her? The gory dispatch of the grandmother (obviously a mother-symbol, Bettelheim would say) or the triumph of the weak over the strong? Such a materialistic tale too – why couldn't she have a simple and understandable affection for Cinderella?

Two hours later we stopped at the Joneses' canalside house in Assen. David came out to welcome us and Jane thankfully handed Sarah over to him, then shepherded the girls inside. Their house was once gutted by a fire, and its former owners took the opportunity to play with its space in a completely new way. Outside it looks like the neat Dutch version of a 1930s semi. Inside we felt as if we were in an eggshell. All was open plan, with a spiral stair down to David's computer room and up to the bedrooms above. A low sofa curled round the wall, below the bay window and up to the hearth; the back wall was simply glass. Leaning back on the sofa, toasting my toes in front of the fire and with a glass of Glenlivet in my hand, I had to admit that it hadn't just been Jane who had been feeling the strain.

Sunday was a leisurely day. Jane and David took the girls off to the promised traffic park and gave them lunch in a pancake house – fat Dutch pancakes, stuffed with savoury fillings. I sorted out the van and processed laundry, revelling in the complete silence lapping me round. Then at last there was time to read. How had Hans Andersen reacted to Holland? 'The people live half in water, like amphibians,' he noted as he passed through Amsterdam. 'We passed over a kind of bank between the open North Sea and the sea of Haarlem, and I wondered at the great enterprise of pumping out a sea.' A country he respected then, but not one he dawdled in. Within a day he had taken a Dutch steamer, 'a true snail of a ship', to England, where by contrast his imagination was quite set alight by the self-important bustle of London, 'the city of cities'.

Next day we meandered around the large modern shopping precinct, amused to explore the Dutch versions of C&A, Etam and M&S Modes. One of the major attractions of the trip as far as the girls were concerned was our issuing them with an outrageous £5 a week pocket money each. Normally they got slightly less than that between them. But we felt that they needed some degree of financial independence, so that they could both enjoy the security of silver jingling in their pockets and be able to be generous. It would also make them conscious of foreign currencies and improve their arithmetic. We dictated that the money could be used for drinks and ice-lollies, but not for sweets – the normal ruling of 15p sweet money on Saturday morning would be maintained. On the whole this system worked very well, although I think they were all a little saddened not to find themselves millionaires in Italy. Two thousand lire had sounded so much more than 8 guilders.

Their reactions to wealth were quite different. The two older girls spent almost all their money on carefully chosen presents for their schoolfriends, but Tilly spent hers fast and joyfully, then wondered if she had bought the right things, while Daisy hung on to hers, only parting with it when she saw something that was exactly what she wanted. Ellie established a happy medium between small treasures and ephemera, but found the whole business an agonising exercise in decision-making. Susie was a disappointment. She developed an unerring eye for Taiwan tat and I had to retire hurt from several ill-starred confrontations in supermarkets. She was right. The money had been given to her and I had no business to dictate the spending of it. But I couldn't help trying.

There were so many snappy goodies in the Dutch shops that failures in taste and style were few. Ellie and Susie bought gaily painted clogs, a little nonplussed to see that they were stamped 'made in Italy'; Tilly and Ellie found white-framed sunglasses with Snoopy and Mickey Mouse perched archly at the corners. Jane let them each choose a hand-painted tile from Delft in an Aladdin's cave of a china shop. I picked up a comfort object, a small yellow mug painted with a sketchy green and brown farmyard scene and a bold black cock. It stayed close at hand for the rest of the journey, miraculously unbroken.

In Miro, a gigantic Assen supermarket, the children sat in a row in front of a cartoon video while Jane and I mooned along the aisles like Stepford Wives. Basic essentials and a few treats. Twenty packets of good cheap Douwe Egbert coffee. Handfuls of rainbow-coloured garden flares. Lots of biscuits. I tried to buy the wooden children's skates that Jane had told me were still worn there by beginners, but such an enterprise in early May was looked on as lunacy.

'Never mind – I'll get the boy next door to show you his,' said Jane. Later that day Peter brought round a pair of wooden skates – metal blades set in wooden frames which can be strapped with long woven red ribbons over any boots. He also brought his speed skates, which he handled as reverently as Gretel must have treated her hard-earned prize. The gleaming silver blades were extraordinarily long, the boots highly polished black leather. In skates like these Dutch champions achieve speeds up to 30 miles an hour. Jane asked Peter a question in Dutch; he nodded and talked rapidly to her for a few minutes.

She explained that he had been telling her about the Elfstedentocht, the Eleven Towns Race. It sounded like a good parallel to the *Hans Brinker* race, although the prize is a gold medal, not silver skates. It dates from a mid-eighteenth-century Friesland tradition – the young farmers used to skate to the eleven main towns of Friesland by canal and have a drink in each. In 1909 it was formalised into a 125-mile-long race. Competitors set out before dawn and the last skaters arrive late at night. The winners are usually home for lunch.

The problem with the Elfstedentocht has been its popularity. Since over 16,000 participants are expected to take part these days, the ice has to be very thick for the race to take place at all. There have only been twelve races since 1909. But this year, after a tantalising will-it-won't-it few weeks, the frost bit deep enough for the first race in twenty-three years to take place. Jane and David, like everyone in Holland who wasn't on the ice, had spent the day watching it on television, and luckily for us had made a video of the highlights.

The girls and I sat on the long sofa and watched the five o'clock start at which 16,000 pairs of shoes were abandoned – no one attempted to find their own afterwards. Then we saw the urgent chaos of the checkpoints, the clowns young and old, and the real racers, the champs in their bright skintight skating suits. Bent forward one behind the other to cut down the wind-resistance, hands clasped behind their backs, legs pushing sideways with long gliding strokes, they mesmerised us; we found ourselves swaying to the rhythm they set up. Making the race competitive is a modern idea, resented by many of the participants. In 1940 and 1956, the first five skaters held hands as they crossed the finishing line in protest, only to find themselves disqualified. The country needed heroes, in the opinion of the 322-strong organising committee, and certainly today the winner of the Elfstedentocht has rather more status in Friesland than Queen Beatrix herself. The 1929 winner lost two toes through frostbite – he had them pickled and kept them on the mantelpiece as a trophy.

Whether it was the effect of the race or a restlessness of their own, I don't know, but as we switched off the television Tilly and Daisy turned to me with a concerted determination.

'It's nice here, but it's too like England. We want to see more foreign places. There doesn't seem to be much magic in Holland.'

'I thought we were supposed to be camping, not living in houses.'

They were right, of course. The Dutch are so neatly and intelligently organised that there seems little room there now for the old legends and stories that Mary Mapes Dodge chronicled so lovingly. Hans Andersen hadn't lingered there for long, and nor should we. It was time to move on. One way of ensuring Sarah slept was to drive during the night. We talked things over and decided to set off after supper, drive into the night through the inconvenient spur of Germany that interrupted our intended progress to Denmark, and stop when I felt sleepy.

We threw ourselves into a frenzy of packing. Jane had so many good children's books that we could solve the problem of running out of reading matter by moving all our books into the boot of David's car, to rejoin us at Hamelin, and filling Bertha's shelves with Jane's instead. As alternative occupations Jane produced knitting wool and needles, black paper to cut out in Andersen-style silhouettes, and a Dutch variety of Happy Families – trolls instead of butchers and bakers. David, who has a fine intuitive grasp of essentials, pressed the rest of the two-litre bottle of Glenlivet into my hands. After a very English feast of beef and roast potatoes, we got the children into their night-things, settled them down in the van, and took off into the unknown once more.

3

The Ugly Duckling

Hans Andersen died before I was born, yet I have the feeling that I know him well, and that he has been a friend of mine.

(Karen Blixen, 1962)

Waved across the frontier without formalities, we stormed across northern Germany unnoticed and unnoticing. Motorways are always a powerful disincentive to exploration – there is something about the endless ribbon ahead which makes the foot push down on the accelerator, the eyes set in a blinkered forward glaze, the mind concentrate on a far-off objective, oblivious to the tempting distractions signalled off down the slip-roads. To exit seems a defeat. My concentration was intensified by the darkness. Once I got used to the German juggernauts sweeping past with their massive trailers, leaving Bertha tossing from side to side in their slipstream, I found I was enjoying the regular pace, the night-lit cities we passed, the slumbering silence behind me. Tilly was sitting up in the cab that evening, guardian of my Thermos of strong black coffee and the chocolate biscuits. It was a good chance for a gossip – we don't get enough time alone together at the best of times, and it takes a little while to switch to talking person to person instead of using my normal mother-of-four public address system.

'Bremen,' she said suddenly. 'Off at the next junction. Weren't we going to go there?'

It was only ten o'clock. I felt ready to tackle several hundred more kilometres. All there is to commemorate the Grimm Brothers' Four Musicians of Bremen is a modern statue in the town's main square. Nor was it a story that had much seized our imaginations. Motorway mania drove us on to the distant new horizon of Denmark.

By twelve thirty the coffee was finished, and Tilly had dozed off. Although I still felt wide awake, I decided that the macho thrill of getting places ought to be tempered by responsible thoughts about my cargo. The autobahn lay-bys in Germany are roomy, set well back off the road, and equipped with every convenience. It seemed a waste of time and money to go off in search of a proper campsite, so I drew into the next lay-by and followed the arrows away from the lorries and towards the cars. A welcoming sign suggested we made ourselves at home, and we did. I picked Tilly up and tucked her in beside Jane and Sarah. It didn't seem worth hauling out the mattress that night, so I just rolled myself up in my sleeping bag, curled round the gearstick, and fell asleep more quickly than I had thought possible.

Sarah gave the alarm at four thirty, and since dawn was breaking, I took off again while the girls slept on. Past Hamburg, black-etched against a gold and turquoise sky, under the Elbe, and north to the Danish border. We stopped at a high-tech motorway café which offered showers as well as breakfast. The girls spent most of their time trying out taps that turned on magically as they walked up to the hand-basins. Sarah gave the automatic doors a brisk workout. Jane and I drank third-rate coffee and munched the foamy factory-baked rolls uncritically.

Denmark, Hans Andersen's own country, made a fine entrance into the story. The sun shone out as we crossed the border, and a patriotic line of red and white flags waved a welcome. A lean, tanned Dane looked into the van and gave the girls a blue-eyed smile, a happy contrast to the Flemish indifference at Hook. Soon we were spotting other national differences. The road signs told us to forget the Dutch problem of slender-legged roe-deer scampering in front of our wheels – instead fully antlered stags would walk purposefully forward. School children too were clearly more dignified than in Holland – there they were drawn as racing pigtailed pellmell across the road; here they would walk calmly, briefcases in hand. Perhaps this sedateness of approach was due to the very low traffic density – Denmark has only a third of Holland's population spread over a slightly larger country. Driving was getting easier – my left-right reflexes had switched themselves over, and now being on the wrong side came naturally. I had realised that there were two ways to drive such vehicles as Bertha: timidly, a large white rabbit at the mercy of motorway wolves and cut-in city stoats, or with confident panache, using our size to discourage lesser vehicles from taking liberties. We had graduated to the second technique by now, and were careering along in fine style, the flower garland still looped raffishly across the bonnet. Given the long straight Danish roads, the van could be nursed up to a thrilling speed, and with the wind behind us we occasionally touched 60 miles an hour.

The children were already eagerly leafing through the Legoland brochures we had been sent in England. But Billund is 120 kilometres or so from the frontier, and we decided to investigate the coast on the way. This was the best weather so far – there might even be the chance of a sail. We turned east off the E3 motorway at Haderslev because the map showed a promising-looking little island close to the coast. The Danes are a sea-faring nation, their country a pattern of islands – nearly 500 in all, and I wanted to extend the children's vision of Denmark beyond pastries and bacon. We found ourselves driving through lush, rolling farmland. The houses were longer and lower than the hump-backed Dutch barns, with rows of windows flanking the front doors and thatched roofs, not unlike the halls in Norse Sagas. They were painted surprising colours – terracotta, ochre, a rich green, with window-frames dark in contrast.

The gateway to the island of Åro was the port of Årosund. It boasted a small and smelly smoked-fish factory, a tiny harbour mole curling round to a bright white lighthouse, and not much else. The ferry that crossed to the island every hour held only a dozen cars, and there was no competition for places. The grey-bearded captain, clearly a retired Viking, was surprised to see us. Were we sure we didn't think he was sailing for Funen, the much larger island to the east beyond Åro? That was more common for foreigners. Reassured that we were not lost, just exploring, he invited us up into his wheelhouse. It was a well-varnished, brass-trimmed eyrie with a proper helm to turn as well as a modern electric sounding device. The fifteen-minute voyage was not a taxing command, but we felt he presided over it with dignity. He picked Susie up and sat her high on the console so she could see every detail of our approach to Åro. Only two hundred people lived there, he told us, even fewer in the winter. All it has are flat fertile pastures, lakes running into the sea and rambling farmhouses where the Ugly Duckling might have started life.

I told him about our quest for fairytales and he nodded approvingly.

'You know of Andersen, then? Nowadays every Dane is proud of him – the most famous writer our country has produced. Things weren't always like that, though – people used to make a lot of fun of him. They said he didn't write proper Danish. He was rather an embarrassment, with his openness. All his feelings were on the outside. Most Danes are more – hidden, less vulnerable. And I don't think they understood what he was trying to do very well.' The captain picked Susie off his console and checked a reading, then popped her up again.

'But Andersen was more sophisticated than most of them, even though he came from a very poor home. That's why he never stayed in Denmark for long – he got more admiration abroad. Now of course, we all think a lot of him, but it was a long time before he was as respected in his own country as he was in Germany, for example – or in your England. But now I think he is only read by children in England·and America – now it is us in Denmark who take him more seriously.'

I knew that he was quite right. Most of the sophisticated literary criticism now being done on Hans Andersen is in Danish or German. In England and America he is Disney-fodder, rarely read in respectable translations, although not to do so means we lose as much sublety and wit as we would if we read Jane Austen in comic-strip form. But I thought there was more to Andersen's travelling than escape from his unappreciative fellow countrymen. He travelled to furnish his mind with ideas, to become a citizen of the world instead of an accepted inmate of the Danish duckpond. He had the same 'virus of restlessness' that drove John Steinbeck on across America, the same wanderlust that was sending us off on our travels. And his journeying was the essence of his art – it gave him the perspective and distance that makes his stories so hauntingly international.

We drove off the ferry and took the van as far across the island as we could, ending up on a sandy seashore edged with low grassy dunes. Within minutes the girls had donned their swimsuits, grabbed towels and rushed out to swim. Although the wind was bracing and the sea recently melted ice, they were soon prancing in and out of the low breakers. All it needed to make life perfect in Jane's and my eyes were a couple of sailboards.

As if in answer to a matron's prayer, two vivid sails dipped and rose at the other side of the lake that almost met the sea just behind us. I dashed into the van and unearthed my wetsuit, just to hint at our oneness with the windsurfing fraternity. Then we stationed ourselves casually on the shore line. The sails came closer and closer, skimming across the water to where we were standing. A blond man and girl stepped off them, German visitors, who spoke good English. They nodded in a friendly way, and we started the sort of sailing small talk common to all countries – the epic carve jibes, the failed water starts, the benefits of battens and double concave hulls. But that was all. The hoped-for invitation to try out their boards never materialised. With a gay wave, they flitted away to continue their honeymoon. Oh well. The boards had been bulbous beasts, probably pigs to turn, and unreliable on a beat. Or so we decided later, like foxes sourly reflecting on grapes. At least the wetsuit made the Baltic waters almost bearable.

Meanwhile the girls had spread themselves out in fine style on their brightly striped towels, complete with Snoopy-trimmed sunglasses to give a Miami air to the whole. I got out the camping table, some red and white folding chairs, a can of lager and my typewriter and began to record our impressions of Denmark so far. Sarah sat under the table fingering the wetsuit's ankle-zips and fumbling for mouthfuls of the deliciously salty sand. Jane sank back in the cab with her knitting and a beer. Tilly and Daisy decided to make the lunch, and disappeared into the back of the van. A little later they emerged with warmed-up French sticks split in half and stuffed with paté, lettuce, hardboiled egg, cheese and mayonnaise. Clearly the continent was firing their culinary imaginations. They would never have mixed up anything so radical at home.

All was good humour until I took my plate into the van to wash it up.

'Why did you decide to fill the rolls on the seat cushions instead of the table?' I asked in as neutral a tone as I could manage. It seemed a shame to criticise such a good effort, but the sight of the smears of yolk and butter all over the upholstered seats was somehow lowering. Tilly sniffed.

'Well, we can't put the table up – it always collapses on my foot. And we wanted it to be a surprise. Oh well, it you don't *want* us to help, we won't!'

Chores were a problem in the van. A sudden stop used to send everything hurtling to the floor, and we had become accustomed when in motion to wading through books, food, shoes, pens and paper as if they were slurry in a cowshed. There wasn't enough space for more than one person to clear up at a time, so tasks like sweeping out the constantly crumb-laden floor, or washing up in the minute sink were impossible to do simultaneously. Susie made more mess than the other three put together, but I yelled at them all equally – so offending the sensibilities of Tilly and Daisy, who were the best at tidying up. It was in fact far easier and quicker to do everything myself, but that seemed immoral. So I would find myself suddenly and unpredictably exploding into wrath at the unfairness of it all, then contritely apologising for my unreasonableness. Still, we were learning. Lunch had been delicious, and next time I'd make sure the table was up before operations began.

The wind moved rapidly up the Beaufort scale. As soon as the breeze freshened, the sailors had abandoned the lake, giving Jane and me a comfortable feeling of superiority about what we would have done had we only had sails. The gale increased. We watched a schooner ploughing into the wind, its masts bare poles. We began to wonder if the ferry would make it back to the mainland in a force 8, and decided to pack up quickly and cross while it was a mere 5 or 6. Our ancient mariner was unperturbed. Nothing short of a hurricane delayed his sailings, he assured us. Where were we off to? Legoland? Wonderful place. More visited than Tivoli, these days, he'd heard. About an hour's drive, perhaps a little longer in the van. A paradise for children. Have a good time! *Farvel!*

We headed north to Billund, once just a small market town, now a major industrial centre sporting the second largest airport in Denmark. All because a toymaker's son had a bright idea for an improvement on the oldest toy in the world – building blocks. Gottfried Kirk Christiansen started work with his father at the age of twelve. They made wooden toys until the 1940s, when they bought a plastic injection moulding machine which made, among other things, 'Automatic Binding Bricks'. Soon the bricks were given a snappier name, one which became synonymous with the company. LEGO came from the Danish words LEg GOdt, play well. In the later 1950s the unique Lego stud-and-tube coupling system was patented, and their export markets have now spread all over the world.

Legoland was originally intended as a static showplace home for the complex Lego constructions used in publicity campaigns, but it rapidly became a shrine for Lego-freaks in its own right. Half a million people came to Denmark last year for the novelty of walking around in a true toytown world, a nursery come to life.

Susie looked in awe at the red-coated steward who ushered us in. 'His buttons are bits of yellow Lego!'

'So are the doorhandles,' Daisy pointed out. 'Giant Lego.' The curtains in the reception office had the letters 'Legoland' woven diagonally into the fabric, the ceiling of the special Legoland post office had lights shining through the tube couplings of black mega-Lego blocks. We walked through a huge Legobutik, and the girls rushed from pack to pack covetously. I thought about buying them enormous sets of Lego to provide happy occupation over the next few weeks, then thought about it underfoot in the van and reconsidered. It was just as well I did. Legoland is no bargain basement – £50 trickled effortlessly through my purse that day. But we were after all six, not counting Sarah, and four of us tireless riders of cars, trains, monorails, roller-coasters, boats, round-abouts and ponies. And everything – except the ponies – seemed to be made of Lego. The effect is to feel your own scale reduced, as you charge round in cars, boats or trains which seem identical to the little models made on the playroom carpet back at home.

The ponies were part of Legoredo, a reconstructed wild west town for the benefit of the Legosick. Like a Hollywood film set, it has stores, saloons, sheriff and riding stables, and a small contingent of good-natured Red Indians, who howed us politely through their head-dresses, and invited us to toast twists of dough over a real campfire. Over all looms an enormous grey Lego model of the sculpted presidential heads of Mount Rushton, the American Mount Olympus. In the saloons, American visitors can eat apple-pie just like mom used to make, and pour out generous quantities of coffee from red enamel pots. Though Ellie returned several times for a pony ride, on the whole we avoided Legoredo as a distraction from the real point of it all – quantities and quantities of Lego in every conceivable form.

Legoworld illustrates different styles of town life in minute detail. There are Lego dresses in the Amsterdam shop windows, Lego geisha girls in the shadow of a Lego pagoda, Lego ships nosing round a Lego Copenhagen harbour. According to the park brochure, a Norwegian schoolteacher from the Lofoten Islands was 'quite overcome' when she recognised her home-town, correctly reconstructed in every detail. 'That's the school I teach in,' she exclaimed in disbelief. We were a little less impressed by the slice of old England, an odd amalgam of York, Chester and Stamford, but the general impression of architecture worldwide was excellent.

'We could save a lot of time and money by just staying here,' Jane suggested drily. 'See the world on the spot. There's a good baby-changing room at this campsite.' The bright colours and cheerful shapes and faces of Legoland were keeping Sarah very contented, and she watched with absorbed interest as the girls swept past her in one bizarre vehicle after another.

Children's traffic parks are as much a feature of Danish life as Dutch, and Legoland has a challengingly intricate layout, with garages, traffic-lights, level crossings, and hairpin bends. The girls were issued with Legomade Union Jacks to attach to the front of their Legolook electric cars, and then set off to master driving on the right-hand side of the road. The controller could hail them in the language of their flag through his loudspeaker if they drove through a red light or failed to make a handsignal in time. At one point whistles blew, lights flashed and the level crossing gates closed so that the Legoland Express, crowded by now with sightseers, could trundle through the scene. Poor Susie was exiled from this little paradise because she was two years too young. But she was comforted by the Duplo Dodgems next door, unpatrolled by policemen, where she could achieve breakneck speeds of up to 4 miles an hour. We lunched extravagantly in the Legoland restaurant, then digested it on the stately Duplo monorail that offered a bird's-eye view of Duploville. At least Sarah, Jane and I did – the girls preferred the insanely swirling speed of the Legocentric Caterpillar.

By now jaded with Lego, Jane and I wandered into the toy museum to look at Titania's Palace, the most incredible doll's house in the world. It was built by an Englishman, Sir Neville Wilkinson, for his daughter Gwendolen, because she believed in fairies. Even with twelve skilled cabinetmakers to help him, it took twenty years to build. Did Gwendolen still believe in fairies as she turned thirty and took final possession? We doubted it somehow – this was a home for manikins, not magic, although startlingly beautiful and complete down to the tiniest detail: nursery friezes in the style of Aldin and Hassell, a mother-of-pearl paper-knife on the inlaid Queen Anne secretaire. Legoland bought the palace at Christie's in 1978 and spent three years repairing and restoring it. But the contrast between the strict cubic structures that Lego dictates and the exquisite craftsmanship of Titania's Palace was not altogether a happy one. I began to feel the limitations of Lego as a medium, the hard edges it puts on the imagination.

Although the girls love to recall their day in Legoland – like Duinrel, it remains a highlight of the trip – by five o'clock they had had enough. We walked out through the Legobutik, but there was no demand at all to buy Lego sets. Maybe future engineers are demoralised as well as impressed by the sophistication of the exhibits. What Ellie and Susie did spend twenty minutes pondering over was which of the doll's-house miniatures on sale they would buy. In the end they each bought the same – an inch-long chest bound in brass to hold the tiniest of treasures.

Prominent beside the gates of Legoland we saw a bronze statue of a seated man – Hans Andersen, of course, reminding us of the real point of our journey. It was a copy of the very statue about which he wrote so indignantly in the last year of his life – the statue that he felt should show him as a poet for all ages – not just a teller of children's tales. In the end Saabye did him justice: there isn't a child in sight. A cloak is slung around Andersen's shoulders. His face is long, bony and ugly, with a large but gentle mouth, and the hooded eyes of a visionary. He holds a book in one hand, and raises the other in emphasis as he tells a story to an imaginary audience.

That night we drove to his birthplace, Odense, now the second largest town in Denmark. We arrived too late to check into a campsite, so we parked discreetly in a back street for the night, then moved to the central carpark beside the townhall for breakfast. As well as space to park there was space to play – a scarlet-painted castle with rocking-horse steeds outside had been thoughtfully built there for the benefit of bored children. Jane and I bought hot fresh bread for breakfast from a nearby baker, then sipped coffee peacefully while the Bastille was being stormed outside the window.

Our first visit was an undramatic one: a low-eaved, one-storey house in Munkmollestrasse, now almost swamped by the modern buildings that run down to it from the town centre. Most people bypass this small shrine, known to be Hans Andersen's childhood home, in favour of the better-known museum on the other side of the town. When we rang the doorbell, a thin elderly lady opened it and showed us into a narrow room, empty except for an upright iron stove at the back. Its bareness was disappointing at first, particularly as we had expected to find it unchanged from Andersen's own description of it in his autobiography:

One single room, nearly all the space filled up with my father's shoemaker's workshop, the bed, and a bench where I slept. This was the home of my childhood: but the walls were covered with pictures; on the chest of drawers there were cups and glasses and ornaments, and over the workshop, by the window, there was a shelf with books and songs. In the kitchen, over a cupboard where we kept the food, there was a rack full of plates; the little room seemed to me big and wonderful. The door itself, with its landscape paintings on the panels, was as much to me then as a whole art gallery. From the kitchen we could go up a ladder into the attic, and in the pipes between our house and the one next door, there was a little box of soil with chives and parsley. This was all the garden my mother had; in my story 'The Snow Queen', those plants are still growing.

But our guide was inspired, a conjuror of atmosphere, waving her hand to create a ghostly cobbler's last, a child's seat beside the stove, a weary mother sitting in the corner with a pile of darning on her knee. She led us through to what had once been the house next door, and is now an Andersen reliquary.

'Here a family of six children lived, also in one room,' she told us. 'Compared to them, Andersen was generously lodged.' Perhaps the memory of a friendship with one of them was Andersen's inspiration for Kay and Gerda in 'The Snow Queen', the 'two poor children' who 'weren't brother and sister, but . . . were just as fond of each other as if they had been', whose 'parents were next-door neighbours, living in attics' with boxes of roses growing in the gutters between the two roofs.

She pointed out the pictures on the walls showing Odense as it once was: a low-lying city, rich in curved tile roofs and wide cobbled streets. The most touching exhibit of all was a small pincushion, shabby now, but once bright satin, painstakingly made by Andersen as a boy for a parson's widow who lived in the almshouses opposite, Eilskow's Dwellings. It was she who first gave him a respect for poetry – her husband had written popular verse. She also introduced him to Shakespeare. Apparently he was most enthralled by the melodramatic scenes – the three weird sisters on the heath, the ghost on the ramparts of Elsinore. One of his favourite occupations as a child was his homemade puppet theatre, for which he made and dressed a legion of characters – he was evidently extraordinarily neat-fingered.

Far more significant than the poverty of this little Odense household was the character of Andersen's parents. His father was a freethinker and a romantic, who nourished his son's literary imagination with such books as the *Arabian Nights*, La Fontaine's fables, and the satirical comedies of Ludvig Holberg, 'the Danish Molière'. Those three works alone could go a long way to summarising the combination of fantasy, dry moral wit and social satire that characterises Andersen's best work. His father loved the theatre, and passed on his enthusiasm, taking the small boy to the local playhouse whenever they could afford it. When they couldn't, Hans used to beg a poster from the theatre and make up a plot to suit it all by himself. Andersen senior was also extremely politically aware. His hero was Napoleon, and his final quixotic gesture was to join the Danish forces that set out to support the French just before their disastrous defeat at Leipzig in 1813. Health shattered, he returned home and died in 1816, still raving of Napoleon.

Although she was barely literate, and highly superstitious, Anne-Maria Andersen behaved towards her son in a way that modern psychologists have calculated would be bound to nourish a powerful sense of self in a child. Much more important than her casual sexual morality or her alcoholic tendency was the deep and protective love she showed towards him. She never forgot his father's advice: 'No matter what the boy wants to be, if it is the silliest thing in the world, let him have his own way.' So Hans was never forced to stay at a school or in a job which he disliked; he developed a feeling of his own specialness which ended up with his setting off to seek his fortune on the streets of Copenhagen aged only fourteen – for all the world like Dick Whittington. He acknowledged his debt to his mother in many of his tales. 'The Story of a Mother' idealised that totally generous love; 'She was Good for Nothing', the story of a washerwoman betrayed by her aristocratic lover, excused her weaknesses.

After Munkmollestrasse, we walked across the centre of Odense to find the Andersen Hus, the well-known museum devoted to Hans Andersen. Here he is supposed, though not guaranteed, to have been born, on 2 April 1805, and here are preserved the enormous quantities of letters, diaries, papers and accumulated ephemera he left behind him.

Wary after the Haarlem pumping-station fiasco, I was prepared to compromise, to split the party between the excellent little playground in the main square and the museum itself, but there was no need to worry. The museum is beautifully planned, built around a duckpond with a fine nesting-house complete with wooden gangplank. In one large room, stuffed with hundreds of thousands of foreign language editions of Andersen's tales and lined with illustrations for his stories in every imaginable style, visitors can sit down on a comfortable sofa, pick up a telephone and hear a story read in their own language. Tilly tried hearing French and English versions of Thumbelina simultaneously; Sarah talked back into her receiver, delighted to find a captive audience.

Andersen, it appears, never threw anything away, and the girls found the rich hoard of relics engrossing: his school reports, the letters he illuminated with rough ink sketches, the train tickets and trivial receipts, hundreds of fan letters with exotic stamps, even a correspondence with Anna Maria Livingstone, daughter of the famous African explorer. Best of all were the sentimental mementoes, love letters, dried flowers, locks of hair and the battered leather pouch containing a letter from his first love which was found round his neck when he died.

One part of the museum is full of drawings, collages and papercuts made by Andersen himself. He was famous for the intricate papercuttings which he tossed off for the amusement of the children he met, but which were evidently so much more than that. Charles Dickens' son Henry, who was eight when Andersen visited his Kent home at Gadshill in 1857, recalled them in his memoirs. 'He had one beautiful accomplishment, which was the cutting out in paper, with an ordinary pair of scissors, of lovely little figures of

sprites and elves, gnomes, fairies and animals of all kinds, which might have stepped out of the pages of his books.' More than 1500 survive, a weird world of disturbing visions made solid. A great-niece of the Copenhagen Collin family was more perceptive about them than young Henry.

They were, so to speak, little fairy tales, not illustrations for his written tales, but expressions of the same imagination . . . As in his writings, he was essentially concerned with a limited series of motifs which he went on repeating. There were castles, swans, goblins, angels, cupids and other imaginary characters, many hearts, a dead man hanging in a gallows, a chamberlain with his key hanging on his back, a windmill in the shape of a man.

Other more bizarre motifs were snarling devils, naked witches with four or more breasts, and bleakly desolate pierrots. Again and again the same two turned up; a stork, the embodiment of the daddy-long-legs image he had of himself, and a ballerina, as if he could never shake off some childhood image of a graceful little girl. Andersen himself, I believe, was always haunted by a shadow, the image of his lost half-sister Karen.

Karen was his mother's illegitimate daughter, farmed out to her grandmother six years before Hans himself was born. At first she lived a strange half-concealed existence at Bogense, a two-day journey from Odense, but in 1802 registers show her living with the same grandmother in Odense itself. Considering how frank Andersen appeared to be about most of his childhood, his direct references to her are oddly rare. In 1822 she too went to Copenhagen to seek her fortune, but her fate was a far more predictable one than Andersen's – she joined her Aunt Christiane, a prosperous brothel-keeper. Like Mozart's sister, she vanished from history. But not from Andersen's dreams, or his stories. The thought that she might reappear in his life filled him with a mixture of hope and dread and three tales in particular, 'The Snow Queen', 'The Red Shoes', and 'The Girl Who Trod on a Loaf', seem to sum up his relationship, real and imagined, with her. Little Gerda is Karen as she never was, devoted to her brother and prepared to risk any danger for him. The proud pretty little girl in 'The Red Shoes' came closer to her true character, but the respite Andersen created for her in that tale was never achieved. She sank into the mire of a prostitute's life just as the girl who trod on the loaf to save her pretty feet sinks into the Marshwoman's swamp, a black bubbling pool full of damp toads and fat snakes.

She did in fact reappear in his life, but only once or twice, and Andersen's references to the occasions are laconic in the extreme.

1842, 11 Feb: Sent letter to Karen, expecting her husband to call.
1842, 12 Feb: Karen's husband Kaufmann called, he looked honest and decent. I gave him four rixdollars: he was very happy, so was I.

1842, 30 Sept: Visit by Karen this morning. She looked quite
well-dressed and young, I gave her one rixdollar.

A year later the last reference to Karen occurs – '1843, 30 Sept:
My sister announced herself at the porter's lodge.' Whether
Andersen saw her or not is not known. The official registers of
Copenhagen show that Karen Marie Andersen was sharing a room
with a Peter Kaufmann, an unmarried labourer of twenty-nine, in
1840. She was described as a washerwoman, and gave her age as
thirty-two, although she must have been at least forty. The
registers also show that she died in 1846, leaving no children, and
was buried in a pauper's grave. No one attended the funeral.

There are three more small pointers to the truth about their
relationship, although of course the truth will never be known.
Karen Marie's surname was not Andersen at all but Rosenvinge.
Why then did she take her brother's name but not seek publicity
about their connection? And why did Andersen always call her his
'mother's daughter' rather than his sister when his favourite
compliment to his many women friends was to describe them as
sisters, himself as their brother? Finally, what relationship did
Karen bear to the heroine of Andersen's novel, *Only a Fiddler*,
written in 1837? As Andersen's biographer Elias Bredsdorf points
out, Naomi is a complete opposite to the book's hero Christian:
'daring where he is timid, sensual where he is puritanical and
ascetic, cynical and sophisticated where he is naive and prone to
tears'. Although a musical genius, Christian is too pedestrian for
Naomi – she elopes with a wastrel, and ends up miserably married
to a dissolute marquis. She passes through her home town just in
time to see her childhood sweetheart being carried to a pauper's
grave. The end of the novel is an ironic reversal of the brother and
sister's actual fates; its moral, though, is appropriate enough:
'Genius is an egg in need of warmth, in need of the fertilisation of
good fortune, otherwise it will only be a wind egg.'

In the museum we discovered a reconstruction of the room in
Copenhagen which was Andersen's base in his last years. It was
unexceptional, quite characterless, except for the leather luggage
which was heaped casually in the centre of the room, as if its owner
had just arrived, and had gone to ask cook what was for dinner.
There was a hatbox and a length of thick rope on top of the
suitcases, an umbrella and a walking stick leaned against them. The
rope reflected Andersen's characteristic nervousness: it was a

makeshift fire-escape in case he was ever trapped in the upper room of a hotel when it caught fire. A pair of high square-toed boots, worn into the shape of their owner's feet, stood forlornly at attention at one side. I could almost hear a story beginning to unfold: 'A pair of boots that had given good service once asked their master's umbrella which of them it considered as the most useful . . .' The luggage had all the personality that the room lacked – not surprisingly, since it, rather than any set of furniture, was Andersen's constant companion. 'To travel is to live,' he once said. 'Then life takes on vitality: you do not feed on your own blood as the pelican, but on nature in all its greatness.' The metaphor is an odd one – half Christian, half masochistic. It was clear that if he stayed in any one place too long he was seized with self-doubt – he travelled for distraction from some inner dæmon as much as for inspiration.

For despite his profound confidence in his own genius, the legacy perhaps of his parents' faith in him, he was wracked with self-doubt. He evidently found his physical appearance loathsome, and one unkind contemporary nickname the Danes gave him was that of 'our beloved orang-utang'. Was he really as ugly as he feared? As a small boy, he claimed to have been pretty enough to be mistaken for a girl, so it must have been a traumatic experience to grow into a tall gangling stork of a man, with a mouth like a toad and nose that was not only prominent but askew. In *Picture Book without Pictures* he draws himself as Punchinello, hideous to look at, 'but the inner man, the soul, ah, that was richly endowed. No one had deeper feelings or greater elasticity of mind than he. The theatre was his ideal world. If he had been slender and well-made, he would have been the first tragedian on any stage.' As it is, Punchinello loses his adored Columbine to the dashing Harlequin – 'It would have been far too comic in real life if Beauty and the Beast joined hands.'

Perhaps this sense of beauty lost was what lay behind his constant search for admiration. He loved being photographed, and in his comment on one picture taken when he was fifty-six – an age at which most people have become resigned to their appearance – he could still sound as excited over a flattering picture as the ugly duckling felt on seeing its swan image reflected in the water.

I was completely surprised, amazed that the sunlight could make such a figure of beauty out of my face. I am incredibly flattered, and yet it is only photography. You shall see, it will be the only portrait which my vanity will wish to be left for later generations. How the young ladies will say, 'Fancy him never marrying?'

But when, aged only fourteen, he left Odense for the golden city of Copenhagen in 1819, it was with none of these later doubts. He was out to make his fortune, and, by sheer force of personality as much as by evident talent, he did so.

4
Of Tivoli and Travellers

Accidents will occur in the best-regulated families.

(Charles Dickens, *David Copperfield*, 1849–50)

Legoland and Odense were both well-known tourist stamping-grounds. Before we pursued Andersen to Copenhagen, we decided to see a little of the humbler, more rural Denmark that he loved so much – to get off the beaten track a little, explore the byways of Fyn, and cross over by ferry to another little island, the appropriately 'fairytale world' of Ærø. So we turned Bertha southwards, and found ourselves bowling along empty roads, through fields bright with the fresh grass of spring and hedgerows budding into blossom. The trees were barely in leaf – well behind Oxfordshire. We had if anything gone backwards in the year by driving to Denmark: my prediction of warm summery weather once we crossed the channel had been far too optimistic.

We decided to camp on Thuro, a long narrow island linked to Svendborg by a roadbridge, and a very pleasant place as far as we could see. That wasn't very far, because the rain had returned, hammering on the roof of the van like a hundred demented woodpeckers. Still, the campsite, right by the sea, was extremely well-equipped, and the girls decided to cook a feast – baked beans, sausages and mash – in its roomy kitchen. Jane disappeared with Sarah to the grandest baby-changing room she had enjoyed so far – located in fashionable shared parenting style between the male and female washrooms, so that either fathers or mothers could handle the baby. Sarah was still coping magnificently with the many changes foisted upon her. She did occasionally take against a particular style of basin, and her insomniac tendency persisted, but on the whole she seemed to be thriving on the gipsy life.

I sat in the cab with a glass of whisky and Susie on my knee, reading her 'The Snow Queen', my favourite of all Andersen's tales. She liked the cheeky gutsiness of the robber girl. Perhaps that vivid character was more like the real Karen Andersen than virtuous little Gerda. The other girls came roistering in with steaming bowls of supper, crowing over the fact that Jane and I would have to wash up for once, as they had done the cooking. And we did, too, enjoying the opportunity for a private gossip, while they gave Sarah a late-night gym lesson on the big bed.

We were all getting comfortably campwise. In our early innocent days we seemed to head unerringly for the only basin with no plug, the shower that was a feeble trickle, the loo with no paper. Incredible manœuvres accompanied the mere boiling of an egg (stop van, switch on gas from outside, pump water, fail to get any, find water bottle empty, drive on to garage for more, put on water to boil, get out egg and drop it, step in egg, swear, decide to go out to restaurant). After nearly a fortnight we had all sorts of sharp tricks up our sleeves. Damp sleeping bags were tumbledried into delicious warmth in the site laundry; the girls took the watercan to fill when they headed off to brush their teeth, precautionary pieces of kitchen roll stuffed in their pockets. No matter how small and unstable the surface, Jane could whip Sarah's mercifully disposable nappies on and off her with elegant sangfroid. Washing was done en route – we left it sloshing around in detergent inside a large insulated box intended for cold food storage.

This idea, and other cunning gambits on life in a campervan, I lifted from John Steinbeck, who once spent three months travelling round America in a converted Ford truck called Rocinante with his giant poodle Charley. Jane and I owed his book – *Travels with Charley* – more than tips on vanhold management. In the early hours of the morning I used to read bits out to distract her as she tried to lull Sarah back to sleep. It was like having a friendly late-night visitor – Steinbeck had the knack of putting himself and his thoughts across as casually as if he was sitting beside us in an armchair. One observation in particular struck a chord. 'A journey,' Steinbeck warned, 'is a person in itself; no two are alike. And all plans, safeguards, policing and coercion are fruitless. We find after years of struggle that we do not take a trip; a trip takes us.

Tour masters, schedules, reservations, brass-bound and inevitable, dash themselves to wreckage on the personality of the trip.'

The ferry left Svendborg for Ærø at 7.15 in the morning. Confident that Sarah, definitely the personality of this particular trip, would wake us at her usual unearthly hour, I didn't bother to set my so-far completely redundant alarm clock. But you never can tell. That was the first (and last) night she took a civilised stretch of sleep. I opened my eyes at twenty to seven, tossed on some clothes and got the van lumbering across the camping field and down the winding lanes back to Svendborg. It was a peach of a morning – pearly blue sky, little boats as still at anchor as if painted on a looking-glass sea, swans motionless beside them. Valiantly the girls rose to the occasion, and struggled into their clothes as Jane packed a huge picnic and a large sack of swimming things. The camp director had predicted a scorching day, and we were still under the delusion that summer had arrived. We caught the ferry with ten minutes to spare, leaving the van illicitly but conveniently parked alongside the embarkation office. The port authorities turned a blind eye – perhaps they were family men themselves.

The hour-long crossing was a smooth one, in a much grander, more expensive and less friendly boat than the Årosund ferry. By the time we arrived at Ærøskøbing, the island's capital, the promise of sunshine had evaporated. A tentative drizzle started as we forced Sarah's pushchair over the gangplank and on to the cobbles. As we strolled along the objectively enchanting streets of Lilliputian houses the rain gained in confidence, and was soon pouring down the children's parkas and down Ellie's and Daisy's rashly unprotected legs. The picnic and the sack of swimming costumes hung leaden on our backs. We looked for a café, but this was pre-season Ærø, and at 8.30 in the morning only one lacklustre postcard stall had opened. We peered into the windows of an odd little museum, apparently devoted to ships in bottles. But it wasn't due to open until 10.00. Morale ebbed.

Then the museum door opened, and the curator, an elderly man with pouchy cheeks and sad spaniel eyes, beckoned us in.

'It's raining. And I am here anyway. So why not?'

This special treatment put the children on their mettle. We left a dripping mountain of wet-weather gear and beach bags in the hall and prepared to enjoy ourselves. There were around five hundred ships of various sizes cunningly inserted into impossibly shaped bottles, and about as many more models of every sailing craft imaginable. They were the work of an Ærø craftsman known as Bottle Peter. He worked with a seaman's knowledge rather than an artist's skill, but the children loved his careful attention to detail. Susie, who now felt herself experienced in the ways of the sea, started looking for wheels like the one she had seen on the ferry to Åro. The fleet of tea-clippers appealed most to Daisy, who began to count their scores of sails in disbelief. Ellie coveted an Eskimo canoe, made of tightly stretched skin, and Tilly hunted for the best embottled harbour scene. Sarah had a warm floor to crawl on, and discovered a glass-fronted cabinet full of beady-eyed Staffordshire china dogs. She tried both English and Danish barking noises on them, and found they went down equally well.

Time passed rapidly and pleasantly, even instructively. Our new friend sketched his life history – a successful industrial career in Copenhagen, three children, now grown-up, a beautifully restored old farmhouse just outside the town – and illustrated his talk with photographs. Then he showed the children the trick of rigging ships in bottles. Flattered by their interest, he turned away again and came back with real magic: a red ball that appeared and disappeared from a yellow goblet with mysterious suddenness. He did it again and again, then pocketed it with a magician's legerdemain.

After postcards had been written to each school, addressed, stamped and posted in the hall, some watery sunlight was glinting through the window panes. Perhaps we would get a swim after all. Jane wrapped up Sarah again in her plastic envelope, and my girls burrowed into their damp anoraks. We set off, courage high and hearts aglow, to explore more of the town. Our friend waved goodbye from the window through which he'd beckoned us in.

We agreed that he must have been a friendly wizard. Certainly, most of the houses in Ærøskøbing could have been built for Hansel and Gretel. They were painted in bright blues and ochres, terracottas and greens, clashing and blending under uneven red-tiled roofs. Doorways were curiously carved, windows edged with red geraniums, chimneys bulbous and crooked. We stopped where a twisted gold sign signalled a traditional baker, and fortified the inner girls with warm spicy buns. There wasn't much sign of the camp director's sunshine, but an optimist might have detected a lightening of the clouds that were massing overhead.

'What about hiring some bikes?' I had read in a brochure from the Odense Tourist Office that this was possible. The children, for once united in a desire, whooped with excitement. The local information office sent us to a garage at the back of the town. Attached to it we saw a bike shop. One side sported shiny new models – featherweight racers, BMXs large and small. The other was heaped with shabby but stout basic bikes. Needless to say which the children rushed up to. Not without bitterness, their mistake was corrected, and the vision splendid faded. We were equipped, after much trial and error and shifting of rusty steeds, with two adult and three smaller bikes. There was nothing remotely Susie's size. Tears welled in her eyes. Firmly quelling an idiotic urge to buy a brand-new little BMX, I tried to console her.

'You'll be much better off behind me. Look, the man's putting a seat on Jane's bike for Sarah – you can have one too.'

Sarah, ever ready for novelty, was amiably allowing herself to be strapped into a high-backed babyseat. Susie was deeply insulted. By *force majeure* I got her into a similar seat behind me, but the first five minutes of our journey were silent ones.

Fortunately Susie's sulks never last long. Tilly, Daisy and Ellie pedalled ahead with gusto, and once the strange continental custom of backpedalling to stop had been mastered, and the rules of the road acquired in the traffic parks recollected, we made good progress. There are very few cars in Ærø, especially in early May. The road dipped and rose across the fields, and we could see the sea on both sides, as we were at the narrow neck of the island. This was the comfortable settled farming country of Andersen's 'Dad's Always Right'.

> Of course, you've been in the country, haven't you? You know what a real old farmhouse looks like, with a thatch roof all grown over with moss and weeds and a stork's nest perched on the ridge – we can't do without the stork – and crooked walls and low-brow windows, only one of which will open. The oven pokes out its fat little stomach; and the elder-bush leans over the fence where there's a little pond with a duck or some ducklings, just under the wrinkled willow tree. Yes, and there's a dog barking at all and sundry.

We had not set out entirely haphazardly. I had looked at a map and seen that a small village, marked with a store and an inn, should appear about a kilometre after we left town. However, after two or three very pleasant kilometres, there was still no village to be seen. We must have started out on the wrong road altogether. The clouds were now making no pretence of lightening; instead a drizzle began. At first it was rather refreshing.

'I'm singing in the rain, si-i-inging in the rain!' I yodelled, to the children's huge embarrassment. 'Let's just get to the top of that next hill, and see what we can see. The Grand Old Duke of York, he had ten thousand men. . . .' Jane, unusually silent, pedalled ahead, Sarah's red-capped head bobbing behind her. As the hill got steeper, the girls were reduced to pushing their bikes, and I walked beside them. We saw Jane stop at the top of the hill, look ahead, and then turn round.

'No village at all,' she called back to us. 'And Sarah's getting awfully wet.'

We turned back again, and biked a few hundred yards along a side turning that did at least have a signpost. As we topped another rise, by now in pelting rain, I caught a glimpse of Jane's set face and realised that rapid retreat to known territory was the only course. Visions of critical doctors bent over a small white-swathed body and diagnosing infantile pneumonia were clearly running through her head. We hotpedalled it back to Ærøskøbing. Susie had sunk into a dejected heap behind me. Ellie was wailing as her sundress flapped wetly against her thighs, and even Tilly and Daisy were low-spirited. Sarah, trusting soul, still looked patiently and uncomplainingly out at the strange wet world all around her, but a stream of snot trailed from her tiny red nose.

This was no time to count the pennies. We headed for the jewel in the crown of Ærøskøbing hospitality, the Ærohus Hotel, and begged refuge. Without batting an eyelid at the soggy horde, a cheerful waitress took our wet clothes, showed us to a long table and lit its candles, then disappeared into the kitchen. Within minutes she was back with a jug of steaming hot chocolate for the girls, and hot coffee for Jane and me. As we thawed gently, she returned with plates of chicken and chips for the girls and some exquisitely arranged open sandwiches for us. We wound up with icecream sundaes, smiling faces, and a sizeable bill which I paid without the slightest regret.

For the rest of the afternoon, fate and the sun smiled on us. The three older girls left us to find their own adventure. Jane and I biked around the town with Sarah and Susie behind us. Warm, dry and full of lunch, they chuckled together over some game they'd invented. We stopped in at the church, an airy little place where models of ships hung as sailors' prayers from the rafters. The pews were deep slate blue, and at the end of every one was painted a different wild flower, framed by cream, light blue and navy blue lines: ideal distraction from the sermon.

The girls were waiting for us at the bike shop, full of their discoveries – bathing huts along the strand, lots more little islands that we could have swum to if it had been warmer, a bookshop full of postcards that we could buy to send home. We paid a last visit to the baker's shop, admired the extremely elaborate duckpond – it even had a church for Sunday nesting – and boarded the ferry. Everyone was looking forward to getting back to Bertha. Even a day without her had shown us how adrift we could get. We tucked ourselves under her plump comforting wings, and let her cluck disapprovingly all the way to Roskilde.

Roskilde lies at the head of the deepest and most sheltered fjord in Denmark, and five perfectly preserved Viking ships have been recovered from it. We arrived too late to book in at the campsite, a spectacularly beautiful one, spread along the shores of the fjord among beech woods and clumps of silver birches, but as we planned to spend the next day or two there I parked Bertha at the gate and fell asleep in the cab. Sarah did quite well that night, but Jane looked in no state to be amused by her favourite six o'clock rise and shine routine. I like early mornings, so I took Sarah off with me to explore. Together we admired the hundetoilet, a square of sand neatly edged with logs and signposted with a doggy silhouette. Sarah produced a small interrogative bark, and I nodded. Across the fjord we saw the graceful spires of Roskilde Cathedral, traditional burial place of Danish kings. Downstream the sails of a small sloop were shivering in the wind: perhaps it was making an early start for Copenhagen. We had decided to make a late start ourselves; to use Roskilde as a daytime base, and to visit the famous Tivoli Gardens in the evening.

If it had rained, we might have visited both the ship museum and cathedral, but the next two days were brilliantly sunny and what we needed was wide-open space. The girls raced around the grassy slopes, swung under the beech trees and dangled their toes from a little wooden pier just like Carl Larssen children. We hardly saw Sarah during her waking hours – she was taken off by one or more of her four nannies for pushchair rides, walking practice, or rides on the little wooden rocking elephants down in the sandpit. If it had been later in the year there would have been windsurfers to hire, said the camp director, a kindly man who made a special trip into Roskilde to fetch some milk for Sarah. Jane and I sorted out the van, hung long virtuous lines of washing between the birch trees, and used the camp kitchen to cook more ambitiously and leisurely than was usually possible. Jane finished a marvellous seascape jersey which Daisy wore almost continuously for the rest of the trip. And I caught up a little on Andersen's progress in the literary world of Copenhagen.

I hadn't realised how casually the fairytales had been written – that they were originally just a sideline, begun almost by accident, and not intended to be his main claim to fame. When Andersen first came to Copenhagen, his sights were set on the theatre: his plan was to be a poet and a playwright. Through dogged persistence, charm of personality and good luck, he endeared himself to enough influential people to be adopted into Copenhagen life, first singing in musical productions in the theatre, then sent to be properly educated at Dr Meisling's grammar school, finally granted a pension from the king himself to finance the travels abroad which he believed were necessary to his genius. His gratitude was infinite, his letters and diaries almost embarrassingly fulsome in the praise of his patrons. Equally extreme was his sensitivity to criticism. When he heard that the Copenhagen production of one of his most ambitious plays, *Agnete and the Merman*, had been a failure, he fulminated against the ingratitude and obtuseness of his country-men – 'the streetboys spit on my heart's best creation'. But he recovered – and it was then that he began to think that his future might lie in his tales rather than in the plays, novels and travel writings for which he was at first best known.

'I believe – and I should be happy to be right – that the best thing I can do is to write these tales,' he wrote to a friend. 'The first ones were of course mostly some which I had heard in childhood and retold, but then I found that those which I created myself, such as "The Little Mermaid", got the most applause and that has given me a new start.'

So arguably it was with the story of 'The Little Mermaid' that Andersen found his true *métier*. That evening, on our way to the Tivoli Gardens, we went to pay our respects to the famous statue. She sits forlornly on a rock just off the Angelinie promenade, looking out across Copenhagen harbour at a confusion of cranes and warehouses. I think I would have preferred a view of the open sea if I'd lost my prince. The children scrambled down to the rock to stroke her poor little feet, shiny from the attentions of thousands of other devotees. Although it was half-past seven in the evening, there were still worshippers of all nationalities waiting their turn to be photographed beside her. What was the attraction of the story of her selfless devotion, the ultimate in sacrificial love? It was evidently too much for some people – in 1964 some students performed a most unDanish act of disrespect and cut off her head – international uproar saw to it that she was restored in record time. I looked with interest to see if there was any evidence left of her sad decapitation but the restorers had done a fine job.

We climbed into the van again and drove through the quiet central squares of the city to Tivoli itself. The pleasure gardens were laid out in 1843 by Georg Cartenson, in imitation of the famous Vauxhall Gardens in London and the Bois de Boulogne in Paris. Neither of these survives, but Tivoli has gone from strength to strength. We had decided to come on Saturday night because of the fireworks that close the show on summer Saturdays and Wednesdays. What I hadn't realised was that the rest of Copenhagen would think along similar lines. Every year on Tivoli's First of May opening night over 50,000 spring flowers bloom to welcome visitors. This was only the second Saturday of the season, and cheerful, semi-inebriated masses were swarming towards the gates.

With some qualms we formed a defensive square around Sarah's pushchair and made our entrance: a small wagontrain beset by benign Sioux. As the children were below the eye level of most of the revellers, they were constantly jostled. The whoops and warcries grew louder as the evening progressed, and the danger of being trampled underfoot greater. Jane was nervous, although she had done everything possible to make Sarah secure and comfortable, wrapping her up in a small duvet and putting the plastic rainbubble over the pushchair itself to keep off the cold wind. Fortunately, one of the original rules when Tivoli was laid out, that only 25 per cent of the park should be covered by permanent structures, has been rigidly maintained. We soon realised that the crowds were only in certain places: pushing in and out of the gates, thronging round the favourite rides and commiserating beside the roulette halls.

Our immediate purpose at Tivoli was to see the classic pantomime of Harlequin and Columbine which is still played out there every day. Andersen himself had often watched it, and the pierrot was one of his favourite characters. Infuriatingly, our detour to see the mermaid meant that we missed the mime – it plays only once an evening at seven thirty. We could only admire the magnificent peacock tail curtains of the theatre and stare forlornly into the sad empty eyes of the masks on the pantomime posters that were stuck up on every lamp-post. It also turned out that many of the children's free amusements, slides, swings, and so on, were closed off in the evening.

But as dusk fell and the lamp glowed more brightly we stopped regretting our evening visit. Tivoli can only be seen at its best at night; its lights are its special magic. The trees were spangled with lanterns, pagodas and palaces glittered in the distance, great striped balloons glowed above the seats of the Big Wheel. Streams and waterfalls bubbled over lights cunningly hidden under rocks; the great central lake mirrored terraces full of flickering candles and laced with garlands of flowers; against the black sky a Taj Mahal and a Teahouse of the August Moon glowed invitingly.

There were entertainments to suit all tastes – a concert hall and a knockabout comedy show, dancehalls and haute cuisine, popcorn at a couple of kroners the coneful, and the Tivoli speciality, an icecream wrapped in a freshly-toasted waffle and laced with chocolate sauce. But the real business of the evening as far as the girls were concerned were the rides: the Flying Carpet, the Tunnel of Death, the Big Wheel, the Rocky Mountain Express. Tilly and Ellie were hellbent on the most suicidal of all, a circle of whirling cars that reduced the people inside them to a long yellow streak, then snapped a hood shut over their heads to throw them into blackness. It produced louder screams than any other ride at Tivoli, a sure testament of its quality. Daisy eyed it with distrust.

'There's a very long queue,' I warned them. 'What about those sweet little ladybirds? They look better for children.' Tilly and Ellie were adamant – the Whirling Vortex or nothing. They queued up among the other enthusiasts while Jane and Susie took a gentle turn on the Ladybird Rollercoaster. Daisy was not sure she wanted to commit herself to anything, but eventually made a stately circuit with Susie on some small Viking ships. They had very fetching dragon figureheads, with flashing eyes and long red tongues lashing amicably from side to side. I feel queasy just watching fairground rides, so I took charge of Sarah – not a demanding task, as she had been sound asleep ever since we tucked her into the pushchair.

Tilly and Ellie not only relished the agony of the Vortex but started queuing up for another turn. Unnatural children. By the time they had satisfied their urge to spin around with sickening speed and unpredictable motion in a dozen different ways it was nearly eleven o'clock, and getting decidedly cold. Danish hot chocolate, with a thick frothy head, a dollop of cream and a sprinkling of cinnamon, cheered us up; then it was firework time. We found a good vantage point halfway up the stairs of one of the terrace restaurants. Susie insisted on climbing right to the top of the stairs and sitting there in solitary state. Stewards were hosing down the stage where the comedians had been horsing about an hour earlier, and a huge expectant crowd hemmed it round. The lights dimmed and disappeared – only the ghostly finger of the Raadhus Clock tower, Copenhagen's Big Ben, remained. Then the fireworks began – streaking upwards, bursting into stars, dropping down in golden showers with unpredictable explosiveness. Susie, who had sat wide-eyed and silent for the first few, suddenly rushed down and into my arms, pushing my hands over her ears. Sarah stayed fast asleep, much to the amusement of the well-upholstered Americans who came out of the restaurant to watch the fun.

The final flourish of iridescent colour tumbled from the sky. It was over. Time to go home. A great tidal wave of drunken humanity washed us towards the high flight of steps up to the exit gates. Jane and I quailed at this last hurdle, but a tall blond Dane took in our predicament, lifted up the buggy and Sarah bodily, and carried it up the stairs ahead of us. That left us with enough hands for everyone. Buffeted but unbowed, we reached the pavement at the top, regrouped, thanked St Christopher, and staggered off towards the van. Sarah simply slept on; Jane and the girls pulled on night-things and got straight into bed. The drive back to Roskilde was swift and peaceful, with the motorway lights echoing the splendours of Tivoli and the city misty in the distance. There are times when the night is friendlier than the day. Without a decent town map, I did get a little lost in Roskilde itself. Giggling conspiratorially to myself, I bumped over sleeping policemen and executed careful five-point turns in a smart residential quarter at one o'clock in the morning. The crew remained oblivious. At last Bertha lurched up the campsite hill to the same fine patch with a view on which we had parked ourselves the day before. Roskilde's spires were just visible against the night sky and the fjord lay dark and mysterious in the moonlight. It felt like a homecoming, even after only one day there.

After another day and night at Roskilde we headed north-east to

Helsingør, hacking across country on minor roads through a paradise of beechwoods, their leaves still transparent enough to let the sun light up the drifts of tiny white anemones lying beneath them. We spent the middle of the day at a small deserted north coast resort called Hornbaek, paddling in the sea, scaling sand dunes, damming a stream and picnicking in the marram grass. The sand was the best of the entire holiday – deep and dry, silver white, soft as silk. After lunch we reached Helsingør and the Kronberg, Hamlet's castle.

No one knows why Shakespeare chose Elsinore as the setting for Hamlet. Amleth, the tenth-century Jutland prince whose history is set down by the chronicler Saxo Grammaticus, never went there at all. But in 1585 some English actors were invited over to Denmark to celebrate the completion of the great Renaissance palace which became Frederick II's favourite residence. Perhaps they talked to the company at the Globe about it on their return. Genuine Hamlet-territory or not, Elsinore has a spectacular site, looking across the Øresund, the narrow strait that divides Denmark from Sweden. Eric of Pomerania built the first recorded castle there in the fifteenth century, to collect tolls from traffic in the sound. Though there are no 'cliffs beetling over their bases into the sea', the place does have an extraordinary atmosphere, the legacy of its strategically vital position. Cannons still bristle from the great ramparts that face the sea, and a huge Danish flag waves above them.

We walked right round the castle and down to the shore in the lee of the castle walls. It is covered with boulders of all shapes and sizes, so we perched on rocks like little mermaids to eat our picnic tea, and watched the fishermen excitedly culling a shoal of dogfish which had just appeared off shore. On the way back the girls were busy with their skipping ropes along the paved rampart walks that hem in the green roofs and Byzantine towers and turrets of Elsinore itself. Somewhere deep in that castle, claim the romances of Charlemagne's time, lies Ogier the Dane, Holger Dansk, ready to awake in the hour of his country's greatest need, just as surely as King Arthur will return to Britain's aid when the time comes. A comforting thought. Much more use than Hamlet's introverted indecision.

Around four o'clock we left to meet some real Danes. They were related to a Dutch friend of Jane's, and they were coming to our aid right there and then with the offer of supper and a night at their house. One of the limiting factors of travelling *en famille* in the campervan was that we were so closed off from the ordinary people of the countries we were speeding through – sometimes we felt we were just ticking off the sights visited without really touching on the country itself at all. A family tended to be seen as a self-contained unit, less approachable than the solitary traveller. I had originally considered following up the Danish Tourist Office's offer of a contact with a Danish family to any visitor to Denmark who applies at one of their information bureaux. They have a register of host families, and every year hundreds of successful introductions are made. But thanks to Jane we had no need of this thoughtful service – we had a date with Connie and Kjell Poulsen and their family at their hometown of Hillerod, just west of Copenhagen.

We drew up outside a low, old-fashioned house with a long row of windows across the front, and a wild, much-played-in garden. Several children, all rather larger than ours, came out to greet us, and the girls tensed at the social challenge to come. When they discovered that the Danish children spoke good English, they relaxed, and soon disappeared to play with them and their friends. Connie, small, dark-haired and sharply alive, beamed a welcome and asked after her sister. Jane and I walked with her into the comfortably messy house, very unlike the style-conscious Danish life I had been expecting after reading a eulogy of the Danes I had bought in Ærø – *Danish Quality Living: The Good Life Handbook*. But it turned out that the mess in the house and the garden was not typical – the Poulsens had returned only a fortnight earlier from a year away to find that their tenants had turned it into a pigsty. Most of their furniture was in store while the floors were resanded, the kicked-in cupboards repaired and the walls repainted. Connie found some toys in the attic for Susie and Sarah to play with, then made a big pot of tea and sat down to talk.

I showed Connie my guide book to the Real Dane, and asked her if she and Kjell qualified. She giggled.

'I think most Danes are more conservative than us. You see, all we want to do is to travel, to see the world.' Magical names rolled off her tongue as she described their travels in the past year – through Europe to Asia Minor, Arabia, and India in the big blue Mercedes bus we had seen parked outside; then by air to Hong Kong and Australia. In comparison to their journeyings our quest was no more than a short sprint to check out the bottom of the garden for fairies.

'It makes your children very strong, travelling like that. In some places we were really frightened – in Baluchistan for example, parked in the wilderness, knowing that there were wild tribesmen about, and listening to every sound we heard in the night. But we got through all right. And now the children are so interested in new experiences – so good at getting on with whoever they meet.' I looked at the window to see Daisy crawling through the under-growth behind Martin and hoped some of his bush skill was rubbing off on her.

Later Kjell joined us and began talking of the next trip. He works as an architect, but only to save up money to travel again as soon as possible.

'We discussed it with the children, and they are so keen to go again that they have agreed to cut down on pocket money and new clothes so that we can go sooner. We want to spend the whole time in India this time. We have a wanderlust, you see.' Was there a fanatic gleam in his blue eyes? I remembered the Vikings at Byzantium and Novi Novgorod, Amundsen at the Poles and Eric the Red on the Atlantic. All this Nordic talk confirmed my suspicion that I had my own Norwegian forefathers to thank for this first exploratory adventure of ours. What a concept wanderlust was: an instant invitation to adventure. Not a native English idea at all – the word, dismissively branded with a G (German), was only grudgingly slipped into the supplement of the *Oxford English Dictionary* in the 1930s. That night Jane took Sarah indoors to enjoy a spacious night alone in a bed. As the girls and I settled down in

Bertha we looked out of the window and saw the Poulsen children, evidently insatiable young wanderlusters, hauling sleeping bags and pillows into their own van. I took their gesture as I think it was meant – a token of solidarity among travellers of all ages and ambitions.

Next morning a historic event took place. As we lounged on the grass in the Poulsens' garden thinking about packing up Bertha and taking off towards Germany, Sarah revealed how deeply affected she had been by all this talk of travel. She did her tiny best: she took her first unaided step. The girls cheered. Jane reacted first with delight then despair – David had missed it.

'Never mind,' said Ellie. 'We'll teach her to say "Hello Daddy" for you.'

Connie escorted us out of town, and showed us where we could buy the neatly designed fjällräven knapsacks which we had admired on her children's backs when they came home from school. They are the standard school and travelling kit of Danish and Norwegian children, strong, comfortable to wear, and double-zipped for convenient opening. No more heavy sacks of bathing things or two-ton picnics; now we could share the load around with ease. They were the perfect souvenir of Denmark, very useful over the next few weeks, and today, hanging in the hall at home, they hold a silent but secure promise of journeys to come.

5

Lübeck to Lüneburg

This part of the life, the halting for sleep, seemed to be enjoyed by all. When the kettle was put on to boil over the roadside fire every one cheered up and got talkative.

(Hugh Lofting, *Dr Dolittle's Circus*, 1925)

In April 1831 Hans Andersen wrote to a friend that he had been feeling 'sickly and sentimental of late', and that travel would be the best cure. 'I have decided to go at the beginning of May via Hamburg and Brunswick to the Harz mountains.' Although he claimed that he would be writing a new sort of travel book, it seems probable that he had his hero Heinrich Heine's *Travels in the Harz* in the back of his mind. Not only because Heine was a poet, and a seeker like Andersen after the romantic and fantastical legends of the Harz, but because he too was escaping from the misery of an impossible love affair.

Cynical commentators have suggested that Andersen fell in love hopelessly to be more like Heine, but this seems harsh. Whatever the truth of the story of his brief encounter with Riborg Voigt, it left a permanent legacy of bitterness in his heart. Arguably it was the first time he had to accept that, talented and able as he was, he could not have everything that he wanted.

Riborg was the twenty-four-year-old sister of a student friend of Andersen, Christian Voigt. Andersen called at their Faaborg house one day to find Christian still in bed. Riborg received him 'with great kindness, blushing every moment she spoke to me'. He was flattered that she had read his first fantastical account of his daily walk across Copenhagen (*A Walking Tour from Holmen's Canal to the Western Point of Amager*) and that she knew his poems. That 'tickled my vanity and immediately made me interested in her,' he wrote two years later in his autobiography.

> She had a very lovely face, with much childishness in it, but her eyes looked clever and thoughtful, they were brown and very much alive. She wore a simple grey morning dress which was very becoming; in fact, her entire simplicity and this face of hers won me over for her immediately . . . She made jokes about her brother's sluggard manners, proved herself possessed of so much spirit and humour that I, too, felt a desire to make myself interesting – I don't know why, but it was almost immediately as if the two of us had known one another for a long time, and it gave me a tremendous pleasure the whole day to please the young girl.

The 'young girl' was actually only two years younger than he was, and engaged to the son of a local apothecary. Andersen did not know this until he confided his feelings for Riborg to her brother. He left the house immediately, but a few weeks later he met her several times more in Copenhagen. Having failed to arrange a private meeting with her, he was forced to put his feelings on paper. 'You are my one and only thought, my everything, and a poet's heart beats stronger than any other heart.' He admitted that on hearing of her engagement he ought to withdraw, 'but – I think you have already sensed my feelings, I am not enough of a man of the world to be able to conceal my heart, and I dream of a hope, without which my life is lost. DO YOU REALLY LOVE THE OTHER MAN? I do not know him at all, cannot have anything against him, and I dare say he has his good sides since you have chosen him, but do you really love one another?'

To write a letter as frank as this at a time when the conventions governing relations between the sexes were extremely strict was extraordinarily brave, not to say rash. Andersen's postscript is apologetic: 'If you really love the other person, then forgive me! Forgive me for having dared this, which will then be an effrontery. I wish you will both be happy . . . Bless you! Maybe good-bye for ever!' Did he love Riborg just because she was unobtainable? I don't think so. It seems more likely that she did love him, but that the conventions he was prepared to flout were too strong for her. Andersen wrote in his autobiography that he had heard that she burst into tears when she read his letter, and said that it was her duty to stay faithful to the other man. He saw her in the Royal Theatre on the same evening, sitting in the audience with her family. 'Her eyes sought mine, she was deathly pale and very beautiful, extremely beautiful.'

Later Riborg wrote to her brother. 'I cannot of course give him my love since it has for a long time belonged to someone who fully deserves it; but my friendship he can have. I shall be pleased to be his sister, his friend, if he considers me worthy of it.' Although Andersen's most recent biographer quotes this as proof that she was not 'an unhappy girl unable to marry the man she loves', there are enough loose ends to make the truth of the story a matter for debate. There is something distinctly chilly about that 'who fully deserves it'. What else, after all, could a conventional girl say to her brother? It has the same flavour of protesting too much as Andersen's letter to Christian, written a few months after the wedding:

> Every time I think of her I feel an unspeakably profound pain, but I cannot cry, and I do not love her any more, *that is certain,* but now I am suffering *more* at the memory of her, I am feeling an emptiness – Oh God, Christian! I hope you will never feel what I am feeling now.

Andersen wrote to a friend a few months later: 'We never write to one another, it would not be right, and yet, I know that she thinks of me often, that she really loves me, though I cannot understand how she can then MARRY someone else – I could not do it.' Perhaps he did not reflect on what a poor proposition he must have seemed to Riborg's parents, who would undoubtedly have put a great deal of pressure on the girl to keep to her engagement.

Much quoted as evidence of the short-lived superficiality of Andersen's feelings is the bitter-sweet fairytale 'Sweethearts, or The Top and the Ball', which he wrote after he had met her twelve years later, a matron now, not unmarked by the passing of time. The Top is deeply in love with the Ball, but she rejects him for a dashing swallow. While the Top assumes that she is lording it in the swallow's nest, he pines forlornly for her. When he discovers she had merely been rotting in the gutter, it is all over.

> Nor did the Top ever again boast of his love for her; such a feeling must have passed away. How could it have been otherwise, when he found that she had lain five years in the gutter, and that she was so much altered he scarcely knew her again when he met her in the barrel among the rubbish?

But to me that 'how could it have been otherwise?' is a taunting echo of the letter he wrote to a friend just after he had met Riborg for the first time. People, he wrote, were reading his latest poems and guessing that he was in love – there were six or more candidates for his affections. 'The last guess is rather foolish, as she is engaged, and I dare almost take my oath, that she is no more to me than I to her. We have only seen one another for a few days, and she will soon be a bride. Oh, it is a foolish world!'

How could it have been otherwise? Riborg certainly preserved the mementoes he gave her well enough for them now to rest in the

Odense Museum. The letter from Riborg that might provide the key to the truth of the whole story hung around Andersen's neck in a battered leather pouch for the rest of his life. Jonas Collin removed it on his death, and obeyed Andersen's instructions by burning it – unread. When she wrote it, and what was in it, no one will ever know.

Also in the museum was a picture of the ship Andersen boarded in Copenhagen on 16 May 1831, 153 years to the day before we left Denmark in pursuit of him. It was a sail-assisted paddle-steamer called the *Prinz Wilhelm*, with bunting flapping from its shrouds, passengers in elegant travelling costumes posed on the deck, and crew lined up in fine style. On his voyage from Copenhagen to Lübeck, Andersen slept three to a divan in his steamer cabin, 'one with his legs against the head of the other. I happened to be in the middle, and now one of them would ask me to move my legs, the other to move my head; I was too long for them.'

'Just like us in Bertha,' said Daisy feelingly. 'I wish Ellie didn't kick so much.'

'I wish we could have had a cabin again. And gone by ship all the way to Lübeck too,' said Tilly. 'Much more fun than that long wait for the ferry.'

Despite much measuring and pleading Bertha had been classed – only just, by 16cm excess height – as a long vehicle by the port authorities at Rødbyhavn. So we had to wait in a very long queue of lorries, watching cars sweeping by into ferry after ferry. I discovered later that we should have telephoned and booked a

passage in advance to avoid such inconvenience. But the voyage itself was smooth and comfortable, the ship the best we travelled on, with carpeted passageways, excellent food, and a dutyfree shop bursting with temptations. We played cards in the cafeteria, refreshed at intervals by lemonade and lager, and – why I'm not quite sure – Susie still regards that late evening episode as one of the high points of the whole seven-week journey. Perhaps it was because she was not relegated to baby status, but allowed to sit up in the night with us, joking and laughing, watching the lights of passing steamers through the rain-splashed windows of the saloon. One effect of the holiday was to lessen differential treatment in the family. If Tilly occasionally suffered the oldest child's frustration at having to sink down to the level of the youngest, Susie benefited overall by her promotion, and came home much less babyish than she left.

Andersen's steamer chugged down the eastern Danish coast past the white cliffs of Mon to the fashionable bathing place of Travemunde with its highbacked cane beach chairs. Then it wound sixteen miles up the river to Lübeck itself, 'a very odd-looking and antiquated town'. Our approach was in conventional modern fashion, along the motorway, after another of our lay-by nights. The money we saved by these was usually spent on breakfast in a café the next morning, but the illusion of thrift was a fine feeling. Moreover, at seven in the morning city parking is never a problem, and we found an idyllic spot beside a small lake right in the heart of Lübeck, under the shadow of St Anne's Abbey.

Old Lübeck, like all the best cities, is virtually an island, surrounded on three sides by rivers and canals. Seven bridges link it to the surrounding suburbs, seven towers mark its skyline. The most engaging of these are the twin towers of the Holstentor, a dumpy gatehouse that was once the principal entrance to the city. Today it looks a little bemused to find itself in the middle of a busy traffic roundabout, an odd survivor of the grand old days before the cutting of the Kiel canal, when the port of Lübeck was an important gateway from the Baltic to Europe, as strategically important and prosperous as Hamburg or Bremen.

Happily for the antiquarian, little rebuilding took place after its decline, and the seventeenth-century streets are full of ornate façades and small cloistered gardens. We had elevenses on soft green grass in one of them, now an almshouse, in Glockengieser-strasse. From small windows in the eaves old ladies peeped hungrily at the girls. Witches? Not at all. One even came down and offered us more chairs and a bottle of lemonade.

Lübeck is not altogether the city that Andersen saw, and in which he could easily fancy himself 'carried a century back'. We discovered why when we headed through its new central pedestrian precinct (buying four new swimsuits and four pairs of brightly coloured rubber boots in Woolworths on the way), past students playing *Eine Kleine Nachtmusik* on their violins, and ranks of tempting craft stalls, to the stark gothic bulk of the Marienkirche. We were looking for the famous Dance of Death cycle of paintings, round which the lovelorn Andersen had spun a macabre fantasy.

It appeared to me as if the painter had placed an ironical smile in the dancing skeleton's faces, that seemed as if it would say to me and the whole company of spectators who were there, and made their remarks on it, 'You may imagine, now, that you are standing still, or at most walking about in St Mary's Church, and looking at the old pictures. Death has not yet got you with him in the dance, and yet you already dance with me; aye, altogether! The great dance begins from the cradle. Life is like the lamp, which begins to burn out as soon as it is lighted. As old as each of you are, so many years have I already danced with you: every one has his different turn, and the one holds out in the dance longer than the other; but towards the morning hour the lights burn out, and then – tired, fatigued – you all sink down in my arms, and – that is called death.

The series was famous all over Europe. It was painted by Bernt Notke in 1463, and at least one copy may still be preserved at Reval, in the Niklaikirche. But when we walked into the Marienkirche there was no ancient gloom, no tombs with battered effigies of knights and ladies or long epitaphs to past glories. Scaffolding spanned the choir, dustsheets were draped over the pews, the organ was restrained and modern. The astronomical clock which Andersen had also mentioned looked brand-new. There was a Dance of Death, in its own way a splendid one, in the tall stained-glass windows of the northern aisle. Susie liked the rainbow in the topmost corner, Ellie admired the flames that lapped the doomed dancers' feet. But no paintings. I asked a verger for enlightenment, showing him Andersen's description. He shook his head.

'That was before the war, you see. The bombs in 1942 destroyed everything.'

He led us behind the scaffolding and showed us the photographs kept there to illustrate the incredible reconstruction that Lübeck has been working at ever since the war. Ellie was electrified. Her class had been working on a project about the effect of the war on ordinary people's lives, and she knew all about the bomb alerts, the all-clears, and the debris that had to be cleared away afterwards. But I don't think she had imagined anything on the scale of this cathedral's devastation – or for that matter had thought about the other side of the coin, the effect of our bombs on Germany as well as the effect of theirs on us.

Feeling confused, embarrassed, idiotically guilty, I heard myself muttering 'I'm very sorry' to our guide. We wandered round the church with a new respect for it. There was one small compensation. I discovered at the postcard stall that they were still selling the old pre-war black and white strip photograph of the original medieval dance of death that Andersen had admired. I bought a copy and we studied it ourselves later on. In the background is a fine view of Lübeck at the height of its prosperity, the Holstentor clearly recognisable. In the foreground is a long string of figures – 'every rank, every age, from the Pope to the child in the cradle, is here invited to take a part in Death's cotillion'. Every other figure is a grimacing spectre, swathed in a tattered shroud and cavorting in wild triumph. It was an appropriate enough memento.

After a lakeside picnic lunch, Jane disappeared for a spell of solitude. Sarah and I studied the habits of the Lübeck duck. Ellie and Daisy arranged themselves in striped canvas chairs at the lakeside, fishing for sharks with the wooden handles of their skipping ropes. Susie tried on everybody's swimming costume in turn and decided that hers was the nicest of all. When Sarah dropped off to sleep, Tilly asked me where we were off to next. We got out the map of Germany and studied it. In comparison with Denmark and Holland, it looked dauntingly large.

'Well, Hans Andersen went to Hamburg, then Lüneburg, then Brunswick. He got very lugubrious in Brunswick watching a wedding. I think he was trying to say something to poor Riborg again – read this.'

> After church-service, there was a marriage. They were a handsome couple, but what struck me particularly was the singular expression of joy and sorrow depicted in the bride's eyes: she appeared to be looking for some one as she went up to the altar. 'He is certainly in the church,' whispered two women, who stood by the side of me.
>
> 'Poor Edward! – yes, that he certainly is.'
>
> A light broke in upon me; but I was certain he was not there. Had it been a novel of Johanne Schopenhauer's he would assuredly have stayed, deathly pale, behind a pillar, and witnessed the marriage ceremony: here on the contrary, it was reality; he was not there, but where — ?

Riborg had been married shortly before Andersen left for Germany, I explained.

'I think he went on and on loving her,' said Tilly, loyal romantic soul. 'Anyone could get fed up after twelve years and write a sarcastic sort of story. But wearing a great lump of leather round your neck must have been really uncomfortable. Are we going to Hamburg and Brunswick?'

I had decided to do some by-passing. Andersen had paused in Hamburg, dutifully admired swans gliding on the Elbe, the fashionable crowds thronging the Jungfernsteig, the flower girls and the busy monied men. But his heart wasn't in it. He sat 'like a pale hermit' in a theatre box, wandered in the Botanical Gardens, watched a pauper's funeral and made up a sad, rather bad, love poem about a little bird who saw the choice blue blossom he fancied plucked and taken to the breast of a comely young sportsman. Wandering alone and unacknowledged in a great city was not Andersen's idea of fun, nor of ours. Much more attractive was the prospect of Lüneburg Heath, where a campsite acquaintance had told us we could still find carriages and horses for hire, and so travel for a short time in proper nineteenth-century style.

Undeloh is 30 kilometres south of Hamburg, just west of the autobahn E4. It lies deep in beech woods, surrounded by the massive black and white timbered barns typical of Lower Saxony. As we drove into the village early on Ascension Day, a large diligence (it may not have been a diligence, but that seemed the right word for it) drew out of a turning, full of holidaymakers. We stared sadly after it, but in no time at all a smaller carriage swung out of the nextdoor farmyard. Its flaxen Saxon driver waved cheerfully at us, and reined in her horse. The girls climbed aboard, Jane and I followed with baby necessaries, packets of biscuits and cameras, and we were off. The ambling pace of her Rocinante suited Sarah's dozemode perfectly, and she made up for another bad night by sleeping on Jane's shoulder all the way to Wilsede.

We found the silence, the slow pace and the emptiness all around an immense relief after the huggermugger throb of the van. The drive took about an hour, across a flat, bleak land, the horse's methodical plod occasionally improving to a trot or canter up an incline. It was perfect riding country – a group of men on huge high-spirited hunters caught up with us and trotted urgently past, filling the air with hoofshocks, whinnies and hurried breathing. Wilsede itself would make a good setting for a Wagnerian opera. Among its ancient oak trees loomed dark timber barns, the finials of their crossed roofbeams carved with dragon snarls or horses' heads.

Nothing modern was in evidence at all – no motor traffic, no new buildings. Even the telephone kiosk and the postbox were shrouded under dense thatch.

Our driver, friendly enough, but not an English speaker, pulled up beside a restaurant, indicated that we would stay there for about an hour, and disappeared to talk to an rosy grandmother in another waiting cart. Life without cars was remarkably restful. We strolled about, found Sarah a wall to crawl along, explored the ancient barns. Later in the day the horse-traffic would no doubt thicken up – a few bicycles were appearing already, and well-breeched and stoutly shod Hamburgers were striding into the unknown with determination. The children disappeared into the restaurant to buy ice lollies; Jane and I sat over cups of black coffee and selected a few of the less garish postcard renderings of sunset over the heath. Why all of sunsets? I wondered.

When I wandered off with my own camera, I could see the photographer's problem. Huge stretches of rough grass, flocks of grubby brown sheep and a few plaintive pines are hard to organise into any sort of framing; nor could a single shot do justice to the harsh, scanty wildness of it. Lüneburg Heath was notoriously ugly in Andersen's time, but he too found it had a certain charm: 'The monotonous grinding of the wheels in the sand, the piping of the wind through the branches of the trees, and the postilion's music, blended together into a sleep-bringing lullaby – one passenger after another nodded his head.' One of his companions in the post coach from Lüneburg to Brunswick stretches himself sleepily and sums it up. 'One can, after all, dream here.'

Luck was with us when we reached Hamelin later that afternoon. We had arranged to meet David at the station at six, and were an hour early. Stopping to ask the way, we became aware of a kerbcrawler behind us, a bearded presence looming up – David himself, equally early, and by a fortunate chance lost in the same obscure corner of the town. Within half an hour we had unpacked Bertha and his car at the comfortable little campsite right beside the River Weser itself, put up the Joneses' super-luxurious tent, and ordered three pints of beer and five orange ice lollies at the friendly onsite bar.

The prospects were bright: a day to unwind and reorganise Bertha, a weekend to look into the mysterious affair of the Hamelin Rats, and then a rendezvous with Tom at Hanover airport on

Monday. David, who had his campsite priorities absolutely right, refused to let us go and fuss over supper and sleeping arrangements until we were well-oiled enough to function on automatic pilot. By that time we decided that it would be a shame to leave the restaurant at all, so we dined upon chips, with slices of ham, and talked hesitant German to the regulars. David earned the children's lasting respect by his dexterity in juggling with beermats. Jane and I found it unutterably relaxing just to say and do nothing at all. Sarah, at long last, decided to call it a day and fall asleep. The girls and I all crawled into the tent and did the same.

Next day was positively slovenly – late to rise and late to bed, with much relaxed non-achievement in between. We had time to look around us and take stock of campsite life a little. Certain stereotypes were emerging, international rather than national characters whom we would encounter and re-encounter all over Europe. Each evening a ritual dance of arrival and establishment plays itself out. First cyclists arrive, hot and sweaty with tents in rolls on their panniers, makeshift hats shading their raw red necks. Within a few minutes their Everest-style tents are pitched in a wagon train circle, and the riders are lounging beside them with a long wurst or two and a bottle of schnapps. Someone is tuning up a pearly guitar; his friend clears his throat to yodel an accompaniment.

Then a lowslung Citroën roars up. With rather more fuss an exotically shaped tent with a porch incorporated into its flysheet arises from the grass. A table clicks into place with a sharply striped chair on each side. A candle is lit, avocado and prawns appear, a bottle of rotwein, a Bach partita tinkles in the background. The cyclists observe it all sidelong, glance at each other and sniff, yodel a little louder.

Next us. The bulbous campervan, compact, complete, overflowing. It tries too hard to achieve mod cons – the sink gets blocked, the shower dribbles. Within minutes a litter of books, boots and bedlinen spreads across the neighbouring grass, a washing line is hung and furnished, a bowl of unfinished washing-up is carried away to the showerblock. The children race off to explore, come back loud with enthusiasm or disgust. Their mother slumps lifelessly in the cab, trying to think of something other than fish fingers for supper.

She peers enviously at a sleek cream Mercedes that purrs past the van to a patch well away from all signs of juvenile activity. It tows an equally sleek, colour-co-ordinated cream and brown caravan. An elderly couple creak out of the car, carefully place a step in front of the caravan door and disappear inside. Inside China tea is brewed, poured into Meissen cups and enjoyed from the depths of heavily upholstered Dralon armchairs, but a frilly blind has been coyly drawn down to hide the plastic roses from covetous gazes. A television aerial is clamped on to the roof, the air is scented with something subtly lemony – breasts of chicken broiled in milk. Just the thing for ulcers. He's retired now, having made it in a small way – she has always supported him and deserves to be supported herself now.

The grandees of the campsite world never move at all. Their gardens are properly planted, at the moment with tulips and pansies, later begonias and pinks, finally chrysanthemums. Kneehigh fences guard miniature windmills and personal latrines from the common herd. Plugged in for electricity, wired for TV and radio, conveniently close to the water-tap, they are second homes, the equivalent of a duke's shooting lodge in the Grampians, or a stockbroker's timeshare in Tenerife. Here in Hamelin we found the most settled of all the permanent vans we had seen on our travels. A fair imitation of a Tyrolean cottage, it had wooden shutters at its leaded windows, miniature alpenstocks and elk antlers in its magnificent wooden storm porch. Its occupants were absent, poring over leather-look ledgers in nearby Hanover no doubt, so we could safely peer in and admire its cabinet-built wood veneer interior, the thick velvet pile on the chairs, the infra-red oven, the tiny dishwasher stashed away under the fridge.

In the end we turned away a trifle sickened. How absurd, after all, to recreate all the complexities and responsibilities of modern life just when they were supposed to be away on holiday, escaping, recreating themselves. Given a choice I would settle for the sleek Citroën now; a few years earlier it would have been the bikes. Given the children, Bertha was best. We went into Hamelin, had an extravagant brunch in the swankiest of all its ancient cafés, found a swimming pool with a water chute on the same lines as the great Duinrel Barracuda, and bought enough steak, salad, fruit and chocolate for a farewell barbecue. And a set of German Monopoly to make Bertha even more of a home from home.

On Saturday morning we waved goodbye to Jane, David and Sarah. Had taking a baby along been madness? Despite such occasions as the saturated cycle ride on Ærø, I didn't think so.

Normally we could always make adjustments to our schedule because of the flexibility that being self-contained in the van gave to the daily planning. In principle I think we proved that travel with a baby in a campervan is not only possible but pleasurable. To the girls, Sarah was a positive asset – easy to humour and endlessly amusing. And I think that Sarah herself found her four handmaids an inspiration. With us she chewed on her first french bean, choked on her first curry crisp (and demolished the rest of the packet), took her first unaided step. For a little while at least she enjoyed that rich resource, the legendary extended family.

6
Rats!

Hamelin Town's in Brunswick,
By famous Hanover city;
The river Weser, deep and wide,
Washes its walls on the southern side.

(Robert Browning, *The Pied Piper of Hamelin*, 1842)

Summer, it seemed, had at last arrived. After Jane and David left, we moved to a campsite in the hills south of Hamelin at Elbrinxen because it had a swimming pool. The girls swam while I lazed in the sun, sipping a bottle from the case of Dutch beer that David pushed into Bertha as a farewell present. After lunch diaries had to be brought up to date ready to show off to Tom on Monday – Susie's had only got as far as 'In Holland a baby joined us . . .' With only five of us aboard, Bertha seemed positively palatial. We ate at a table outside the van, fraternised with other holidaymakers in the playground, sipped Cokes on high stools in the cheerful and welcoming camp bar. Even when Susie sent a glass crashing to the floor with an expansive gesture, the goodwill persisted. Back in England the children would have had to shiver outside or be corralled up in some shabby 'games room'. Here in civilised Germany we could sit together sociably to consider the still unsolved mystery of the Pied Piper of Hamelin.

Was he the devil in disguise, a medieval moonie, or a gay transylvanian adventurer? Were the rats really dormice? Is the whole story separation anxiety of nightmarish proportions? I decided to offer the girls a few of the different answers and see what they made of them.

In the first known version, recorded by a Dominican friar called

Heinrich von Herford in 1450, the disappearance of the children is simply a mystery – no explanation is offered for the odd conduct of the 'handsome and extremely well-dressed' young man who piped on 'a silvery pipe of an unusual sort' and enticed away one hundred and thirty children on 26 June 1284. But haunting evidence of the traumatic sense of loss suffered by the citizens appeared in the system of double dating used in the ancient Hamelin townbook, the Donat. This fourteenth-century manuscript recorded events with

two dates, one the usual Anno Domini, the other the number of years 'since the children left'. Similarly, on the so-called Neu Thor, one of the four city gates, an inscription in the stone once read: 'Centum ter denos cum Magus ab urbe puellos Duxerat ante annos 272 condita porta fuit' – This gate was built 272 years after the Magician led away 130 children from the town.

When did the rats creep into the story? A sixteenth-century chronicle by Aelarius Erich tells the story of 'an adventurer in a gaycoat of all sorts of colours (without doubt an evil spirit in the said form)' attracting the children by playing on his pipe, adding in brackets that 'some folk say that he gave himself out for a mousecatcher, and had piped together in the town many great rats'. Aelarius' son Samuel Erich went to Hamelin himself to do some personal detective work, and found a manuscript in doggerel Latin. In it the Pied Piper was said to have been revenging himself on the townsfolk because they had refused to pay his price for destroying the rats. At this point the legend changes its message entirely from an event of purposeless devilry to a moral tale of justified retribution.

Robert Browning got his story from an encyclopaedic work on human nature in all its variety called *Wonders of the Little World*, written by a seventeenth-century clergyman, Nathaniel Wanley. He must have browsed through it in his father's study when he was a boy – and his ballad is faithful to its version in every detail.

At Hammel, a town in the Duchy of Brunswick, in the year of Christ, 1284, upon the twenty-sixth day of June, the town being grievously troubled with rats and mice, there came to them a piper, who promised, upon a certain rate, to free them from all: it was agreed; he went from street to street, and playing upon his pipe, drew them after him out of the town all that kind of vermin, and then demanding his wages was denied it. Whereupon he began another tune, and there followed him one hundred and thirty boys to a hill called Koppen, where they perished and were never seen again. This piper was called the Pied Piper, because his clothes were of several colours. This story is writ and religiously kept by them in their books, and painted in their windows and churches, of which I am a witness by my own sight. Their elder Magistrates, for the confirmation of the truth of this are wont to write in conjunction, in their public books, such and such a year of Christ, and such a year of the transmigration of the children, etc. It is also observed in memory of it, that in the street he passed out of, no piper is admitted to this day. The street is called Bungelosenstrasse; if a bride be in that street, till she is gone out of it there is no dancing to be suffered.

Robert Browning's contribution to the Pied Piper canon was not intended to be taken too seriously, although the details he worked into his story are impressively accurate. He wrote the poem for the benefit of the small sick son of a friend of his, Willy Macready, recalling no doubt the facetious ballad on the same subject which his own father had written for him when he was a boy.

> There is at a moderate distance from Hanover
> A town on the Weser of singular fame.
> A place where the French and the rats often ran over
> But tho' my tale varies
> Yet sage antiquaries
> Are all in one story conceiving its name.

'Tis Hameln (but you had better perhaps
Turn over your atlas and look at the maps)
Which without flattery
Seemed one vast rattery . . .

When Robert Browning's much-improved version first appeared, in an 1842 collection he called *Dramatic Lyrics*, little critical notice was taken of it. One reviewer did comment kindly that 'Mr Browning is a genuine poet, and only needs to have less misgivings on the subject himself.' By the end of the century it was the most popular of all children's ballads. Why? Did it tap some deep source of anxiety, pick up some ancient mythical thread, or was it just loved for its robust, bouncing metre? 'Sage antiquaries' who have studied the legend have generally concentrated on its historical truth – there have been dozens of more or less convincing attempts to explain it in rational terms.

One theory is that 'children' is a changed form of 'young people' – interestingly, Wanley only mentions boys. This suggested that the exodus from Hamelin might have been a mere migration, and Herford's finely dressed young man an agent of the Count of Schaumberg, who at around that date was commissioning such young noblemen to raise colonists for his new lands in Moravia. But it seems odd that a story full of so many specifics – the pipe, the number of children, and date – should have lost the critical fact that it was an optimistic jaunt in search of new horizons rather than a doomladen loss.

Dr Franz Jostes, investigating the matter in the 1890s, did some very clever mathematics to prove that the exodus had been confused with losses of young people at the well-authenticated battle of Sedemunde in 1259. There were apparently two dates on the Neu Thor inscription quoted above – 1531 and 1556. Suppose, he suggests, that the earlier date marked the erection of the gate and the second the setting up of the inscription just as one might date a letter on the day it was written. Then the true meaning of the inscription would be that the children left 272 years before 1531 – that is, in 1259 – exactly the date of the battle of Sedemunde! The weakness of this story is that it doesn't explain a perfectly clear reference to the battle of Sedemunde in a chronicle which goes on to describe the exodus 25 years later. Moreover the chronicler Fincelius, writing before the Neu Thor was rebuilt in 1556, also mentioned the story.

Rats!

Another scholar detective, Dr Otto Meinardus of Hanover, believed that there had been some skulduggery and interference with the ancient Hamelin manuscripts. He claimed that the references to the exodus and the double-dating system were added in an early sixteenth-century handwriting. The plot thickens. Was the whole legend a brilliant effort by the town's first tourist board to entice visitors to Hamelin? Did they paper neighbouring towns with junkmail, broadsheet ballads and maps showing the Piper exiting from the walled city of Hamelin towards the gruesomely gibbet-hung Koppenburg?

Certainly several of these survive. One is illustrated in Sylvanus Thompson's very authoritative monograph on the subject, published privately in 1895 by an eccentric bibliophile society called The Sette of Odde Volumes. Their motto, repeated solemnly thirteen times on every possible occasion was 'We are odd, we are odd, we are very very odd.' The first president of the society was Bernard Quaritch, whose renowned antiquarian bookshop still flourishes in Mayfair. Members were known as Odd Fellows, and perhaps the oddest of them all was the polymath Sylvanus Thompson, styled the Magnetiser because of his work as a physicist.

After exhaustive researches Thompson offers two more plausible options. The first is that the seed of the story was a particular plague, epidemic in the Middle Ages, which took the form of a dancing mania, perhaps St Vitus's Dance. An Erfurt chronicle records a plague in 1236 when a thousand young people fell into such a mania and danced all the way to Amstadt, swooning and dying along the road. The date of the exodus, the feast of St John the Baptist, was a traditional night for dancing, which could account for it being attributed to that particular day.

Thompson prefers his final theory, a connection with the notorious Children's Crusade of 1211, when thousands of children all over Europe set off in the touching hope of reclaiming the holy places of Palestine through their innocence. Perhaps the Hamelin story is symbolic of a hundred similar tragedies for parents who lost their children then. Personally, I think this thin – the discrepancy in time is far too great, and there are references to the Children's Crusade in manuscripts which also deal with the Hamelin affair. But the children's historical writer Henry Treece has woven this version of the legend into his excellent book, *The Children's Crusade*. His piper is a subtle mixture of magician and villain, his music surely exactly what those ill-fated little children must once have heard.

A man was standing beside the wild rose-bush watching them, his thin dark face twisted in a strangely mocking smile, his black eyes glimmering, half-closed, beneath bushy brows.

Had the girl seen only this face with its deep lines and twisted expression, she might have taken to her heels without delay, assuming that no-one but a lordless man, an outlaw, could possess such a mask of evil. But, as the man came forward from behind the rose-bush, Alys saw that he was dressed in a livery which proclaimed him harmless, and at the same time provided him with an excuse for travelling the countryside unhampered by the tools of his calling.

For the stranger was dressed in a long ragged gown of parti-coloured fustian, red on one side, yellow on the other; his sleeves hanging almost to the ground. About his thin waist he wore a narrow belt of blue leather, into which was thrust a silver-mounted flute of ebony. On his head danced a red cap in the shape of a cock's comb, from the sides of which hung two asses ears, on the points of which dangled little bronze bells, which jingled with every movement he made . . .

Then he set the flute to his thin lips and blew down it softly, his slim fingers moving up and down the holes as nimbly as a company of dancers.

At first it seemed to Alys that the music was weird and uncouth, but then she suddenly thought that it was the most beautiful sound that she had every heard. The sweet dull notes seemed to weave in and out of each other like a coloured tapestry, and in those sounds the girl heard the story of creation, of the richness and complexities of Nature. Yet, to Geoffrey, the music meant something else; it was glory in battle, with the scarlet banners waving in the wind, and the jingle of harness and armour, and the thundering of hooves at the charge . . .

'I think that sounds quite likely,' said Daisy. 'I'd go on a Crusade if I could. Specially to a nice hot country with deserts and Arabs.'

'They wouldn't be very friendly Arabs,' Tilly pointed out. 'Only an idiot would believe that they could convert them just by turning up and looking sweet. I think that story about the settlers in Transylvania sounds the most likely. Didn't you say that they even found people with German surnames living there?'

That was apparently true – but after all, I argued, they could have been settlers from anywhere in Germany. Transylvania, now part of Romania, was full of immigrant Germans, a fact eventually used by Hitler as an excuse for claiming the country for the Third Reich. I wanted some mystery to remain.

'I think the dancing sickness is the best story,' said Susie, twirling absentmindedly on her stool (this was the moment of the crash of glass, the quick and kindly attentions of the barman, the restoration of face by a second round of drinks).

'But perhaps there really was a ratcatcher – like the snake charmers they have in India,' suggested Daisy, still unwilling to lose the romance of the tale. 'And perhaps he did manage to magic the children away, for revenge, because the people were too mean to pay him. Perhaps it was all true.'

'It's certainly possible to charm animals with music,' I agreed. 'They've been testing that with very high-pitched sounds, the sort of noise those dogwhistles make – or rather don't make.'

On Sunday morning we went to see what we could find out for ourselves in Hamelin. Tilly was map-reading, with a puzzled frown on her face.

'The river Weser deep and wide seems to have moved,' she said. 'In the poem it's supposed to be on the south, but on our map it goes round the eastern wall. Browning doesn't seem to have known much about the place.'

'I don't think he ever came here,' I said. 'He got the idea of writing the poem from his father, and from the Wanley book. He was in England when he wrote it.'

Although the old gate-studded walls are now flattened under a ringroad, we found most of the inner city of Hamelin still recognisably the orderly circular medieval town of an old map I had copied from Sylvanus Thompson. The Neu Thor had disappeared. Roughly on its site was a Tourist Information Office, already bustling with activity in anticipation of a busy day ahead. We crossed over the ringroad and entered the old town – now mainly a pedestrian precinct. The third house on our left had a delicate wrought-iron sign, a silhouetted Pied Piper with curlytailed rats leaping around his feet. It is known as Rättenfangerhaus – the Ratcatcher House – because on one side of it is an ancient wooden inscription, high above the street and running the length of the house. In close Gothic script picked out in gold is written: ANNO DOMINI 1284 AN DAGE JOHANNIS ET PAULI WAR DER 26 JUMII DORCH EINEN PIPER MIT ALLERLEI FARVE BEKLEDET GEWESEN 130 KINDER VERLEDET BINNEN HAMELN GEBON TO CALVARIE, BI DEN KOPPEN VERLOREN.

The old story, repeated once again. Daisy pointed to the name of this sidestreet: Bungelosenstrasse – the street of the silenced drum. An odd shiver ran down my spine. It had seemed funny enough to guy all the contradictory explanations of the legend, but here in Hamelin itself, still a perfectly preserved medieval city, the tragedy had an undeniable reality. I remembered the vivid words of one of the earliest chronicles: 'And the parents ran pell-mell to the gates, seeking diligently and with sore hearts for their children, and there rose amongst the mothers a pitiable howling and crying.'

We walked speculatively down Bungelosenstrasse, but no piper appeared.

'They aren't allowed down here,' said Susie knowledgeably. 'There aren't any in Hamelin now. Horrible pied pipers.'

'Yes there are,' said Ellie, contradicting her with an elder sister's relish. 'They're allowed in every Sunday. So the visitors can see what happened. And it is Sunday.' Susie gripped my hand tightly.

'"All visitors say 'Ooooooh' when they enter the old town of Hamelin for the first time". Come on, Susie, say "Oooooh",' said Tilly, who was reading the glossy brochure in four languages which we had picked up as we passed the Tourist Information Office. Actually, only English, German and possibly Japanese visitors said 'Oooooh'. The French ones exclaimed themselves, conquered by its charm. It was a very interesting brochure. I hadn't realised that after the Seven Years War between France and England Hamelin had come under English rule. George III rebuilt its fortress in 1784, and it was nicknamed 'the Gibraltar of the North'. The first of the paddle-steamers, whose successors still puff up the Weser deep and wide, was called the *Duke of Cambridge*.

Tourists were arriving in force, guided round the town by chic girls in red blazers and skirts who took them from one piper-memorable sight to another, settled them down under the jaunty parasols of the street cafés and directed them to the souvenirs in the ever-open shops. There were still millions of rats peeping malevolently out of windows and doorways, but happily all were made of shiny bread dough or marzipan. Off the main thoroughfares we

Rats!

could wander in peace, forgetting the rats and enjoying instead the extraordinary excesses of the Weser Renaissance houses. The façades are like coloured wedding cakes, thickly embellished in wood or stone with every imaginable flourish and grotesque.

Returning to the town centre, we sat down for elevenses in a street café which had a fine view of the Glockenspiel, a complicated carillon which plays a five-minute overture at noon to the weekly replay of the dreadful events of 1284. After a fat bunch of postcards had been despatched back to England, Tilly and Daisy disappeared on a secret mission connected with Tom's arrival the next day. Susie and Ellie skylarked about on the narrow walls of a nearby fountain. The square began to fill up with visitors of all nationalities, photographers, and television crews. The broad steps outside the church were a natural stage, and a gang of brightly clad burghers was already earnestly setting the medieval scene. We took our seats. As the bells stopped ringing, one of them stepped forward and began to intone importantly. The girls grabbed at me anxiously, all clamouring at once.

'Why isn't he speaking English?'

'We aren't going to understand *anything*. How long will it take?'

'What's he saying? You didn't tell us it would be in German.'

'Is he the Pied Piper? He doesn't look like the Pied Piper. Where is the Pied Piper?'

I shook them off.

'Shut up. You know the story perfectly well. Just WATCH.'

They subsided with dark and doubting looks. But once that initial speech was over and a troupe of bewhiskered children in baggy grey flannel rat costumes came scampering on to the stage they grew more interested.

> Rats!
> They fought the dogs and killed the cats,
> And bit the babies in the cradles,
> And ate the cheese out of the vats,
> And licked the soup from the cook's own ladles,
> Split open kegs of salted sprats,
> Made nests inside men's Sunday hats,
> And even spoiled the woman's chats
> By drowning their speaking
> With shrieking and squeaking
> In fifty different sharps and flats.

'This is all wrong,' objected Ellie. 'The Pied Piper didn't turn the children into rats.'

'They're not *meant* to be children,' said Tilly helpfully. 'They *are* children, but they're *acting* being rats.'

'They look like children to me,' persisted Ellie. 'Why don't they use real rats? You can train rats, can't you? I think it would be better to have real rats.'

'And drown them every Sunday, and train up more by the next week, I suppose?' said Daisy cuttingly. 'Anyway, I think they look quite good. I'd like a costume like that. But the heads are too small for the bodies.'

Heads were turning towards us. I made myself into a buffer state between Daisy and Ellie, pulled Susie on to my knee and shushed them firmly. The burghers' wives were screaming and panicking realistically, the mayor trying unsuccessfully to calm them. Then a hush fell. On strode the Pied Piper himself. His costume was resplendently red and yellow, long pheasant feathers waved from his hat, and his shoes curled upwards with vigour. Small, a shade stout, benignly apple-cheeked, he smiled at the audience through a wispy beard and made his offer to the assembled corporation. This wasn't Henry Treece's enchanter by any means, nor did he have the veiled menace, the devilish quality of Browning's vision.

> His queer long coat from heel to head
> Was half of yellow and half of red,
> And he himself was tall and thin,
> With sharp blue eyes, each like a pin,
> And light loose hair, yet swarthy skin,
> But lips where smiles went out and in;
> There was no guessing his kith or kin:
> And nobody could enough admire
> The tall man and his quaint attire.
> Quoth one: 'It's as my grandsire,
> Starting up at the Trump of Doom's tone,
> Had walked this way from his painted tombstone!'

Siegfried Sacher, Hamelin's piper for the last 24 years, is a family man, a mild-mannered musician who works as a builder when he isn't piping. He plays a clarinet rather than a pipe, but he plays it well, and the old mystery of music quivered on the air. Off went the rats obediently to their watery Weser grave. The last and tiniest pair were obviously making their stage debut, and looked anxiously

round at one of the burghers' wives. She stepped forward and shepherded them off in the right direction.

'I expect she's their mother,' said Tilly.

'That's rather mean, then,' objected Susie, who clearly fancied a part as a ratling herself.

Back came the townsfolk in triumph, the piper expectant. Mirth and rejection. Disappointment and dejection. The girls had given up interrupting; they were as taken up in the ancient tale as the intent and silent crowd all around us.

> Once more he stept into the street
> And to his lips again
> Laid his long pipe of smooth straight cane;
> And ere he blew three notes (such sweet
> Soft notes as yet a musician's cunning
> Never gave the enraptured air)
> There was a rustling that seemed a bustling
> Of merry crowds justling at pitching and hustling,
> Small feet were pattering, wooden shoes clattering,
> Little hands clapping, and little tongues chattering,
> And like fowls in a farmyard when barley is scattering,
> Out came the children running.

With a cheerful farewell wave, the piper negotiated the steps and disappeared behind the church. The townschildren swung after him towards the street of the silenced drum. We could hear the strains of the clarinet getting more distant, then dying away all together. Silence of mourning. Beating of breasts and repentance – too late. Sonorous moralising in dense gutturals, bows and applause, mêlée of photographers, and it was all over, barely half an hour after it had started. A free gift from the town of Hamelin to the visitors who make them as prosperous today as they were before the coming of the Pied Piper.

'Served them right, really,' observed Daisy as we drove back to Elbrinxen. 'They did break their promise.' Since the play, and the undeniably cuddly quality of the piper as played by Sacher, their sympathy had shifted from the townsfolk to the thwarted magician. Browning agreed with them.

> So, Willy, let you and me be wipers
> Of scores out with all men – especially pipers!
> And whether they pipe us free from rats or mice,
> If we've promised them aught, let us keep our promise.

Rats!

But all this talk of promises and rats, the stress on the benign righteousness of the piper, seemed to me to conceal the most ancient message of the story – what those earliest chronicles described as loss – and loss through devilry at that. Wasn't the real moral of the tale the much older and arguably more useful one put across by a German pastor in 1590 in a sermon inspired by the sight of the old window in Hamelin's St Andrew's church?

> Oh you dear Christian parents, do not behold or gaze upon this glorious painting merely as a cow or some other unreasoning beast gazes at an old door: but ponder it in your hearts in a truly Christian manner, and do not let your children run astray, so that the Devil may get power over them, as he so quickly and easily can do.

After the heat of the town square, the dark pinewoods that fringed our campsite were enticing. We packed our knapsacks with supplies, and set off to put the new boots we had bought in Lübeck to the test of the Everest that rose up behind the swimming pool. The girls picked up long sticks to use as ice, or rather pine-needle, axes; we strode upwards womanfully, and eventually made base camp in a hollow tree. Tilly shot a buffalo, Ellie collected rare herbs and mixed them into a tasty salad. Then onwards to the top. We looked down over the tops of the trees like conquistadors and saw the brave new world of the campsite below us.

'There's Bertha!' said Daisy. 'I think it's teatime.'

Down again. So far the novelty of her yellow rubber toes had kept Susie unflaggingly up with us, but now she had run out of both energy and good temper. So had Ellie and Daisy, and all the imaginative games in the world couldn't stop the expedition degenerating into an idiotic feud between the three of them. Baffled by their unreason, I always become hopeless in this situation: bullying and doctrinaire or bitingly silent. We trailed back to the van, and had tea. Then I announced a series of unattractive chores to be completed before supper and disappeared into the laundry block to vent my spleen on some dirty clothes.

The world looked no less bleak half an hour later, and suddenly, scrubbing away at some potatoes in the van's silly little sink, I found myself dissolving into tears. I still don't altogether understand why. Loneliness mixed with a sense of maternal inadequacy, I suppose. Daisy nudged Tilly, and they both came up and hugged me. That made it worse.

'What about a cup of tea?' said Daisy. 'I expect you're tired after that long walk.'

'Or a whisky. Isn't it time for your whisky?' said Ellie. This was terrible – this was just what one isn't supposed to impose on one's children: a hopelessly immature feebleness instead of the serene smiling background lap of one's childhood dreams. But I let myself be babied up to the berth above the cab and cosseted with a cup of tea and a glass of whisky, then ducked out of the performance altogether by pretending to be asleep.

'Let's give mum a surprise – let's spring-clean the van,' I heard Tilly whisper. Through my eyelashes I watched as they tidied out drawers, sorted through shoes, wiped out the fridge, arranged a little mug of buttercups on the table.

'It's really fun this, isn't it?' I heard Daisy say as she scratched away at the grime round the edges of the van's carpet with a stiff brush. When Susie began washing down the seat cushions, humming happily to herself, I began to realise how completely I underestimated them. Why did I race round trying to do everything instead of letting them take on some responsibilities? When I did eventually clamber sleepily down – after a real nap – the atmosphere was as light and clear as a summer's day after a thunderstorm. We forgot home cooking, ate chicken and chips in the camp restaurant, then cuddled up together on the big berth at the back of the van and told a running story: everyone makes up as much as they can, then passes on the thread of the narrative to their neighbour.

'And the moral was . . .' they end. I'm not sure how much of a moral there was to the day's adventures. Except to make me see my children with respect as well as love – and to sympathise more than ever with a parental bereavement which has survived seven hundred years of mourning.

Later that evening, when all the girls were sound asleep, I discovered a completely different approach to the Pied Piper legend in Sabine Baring Gould's *Curious Myths of the Middle Ages*. Baring Gould was a bizarre character – vicar of a remote marshland village on the East Coast. He seems to have spent more time poring over books of wizardry and writing darkly passionate novels about his parishioners' emotional lives than in saving their souls. Instead of looking for later historical proof of the tale, he had hunted out its earlier antecedents in folklore and myth – he wanted to set the tale in a quite different context, to extend it to universal relevance. At first the idea seemed absurd, but in the end I was almost convinced.

Gould began by considering the plague of ants that devastated Lorch, and the white-clad hermit who spirited them away, didn't get paid, and piped the town pigs into the water in revenge. Unrepentant, the people of Lorch accept a charcoal-burner's offer to destroy the next year's plague of crickets and then renege on that deal too. The charcoal-burner promptly pipes all their sheep into the lake. Next year there is a plague of rats, and a little old man pipes them into the Tannenburg for a 1000 guilders. He doesn't get paid either, and this time it's the children who are spirited away. Lorch is an interesting parallel to Hamelin, as it seems to have given Browning the 1000 guilder pricetag that he puts on to his ballad's ratbane.

Gould, shifting his ground cunningly at every step, touched lightly on the Isle of Wight Jongleur and the Enticer of Belfast, then moved on to the Harz mountain piper who pipes away girls' souls as they sleep, and souls in the form of mice slipping out of the mouths of the dying, to the 'pagan' Wesleyan supposition that angels pipe away the souls of the blest. 'From my experience of English dissenters,' he observed tranquilly, 'I am satisfied that their religion is, to a greater extent than any one has supposed, a revival of ancient paganism which has long lain dormant among the English peasants.' On he went to the singing of Mother Holle's elves deep in the dark German forests, and to the sirensong withstood by Ulysses. Singing becomes by analogy the wind, and just as nothing can but dance if the wind blows it, so a whole orchestra of magical instruments trails back through folk memory keeping feet jigging and leaping. Perhaps the most memorable of all Gould's examples are the fish whose tails are set tapping by the blind Irish piper Maurice O'Connor.

> John-dories came tripping;
> Dull hake by their skipping
> To frisk it seem'd given;
> Bright mackerel came springing,
> Like small rainbows winging
> Their flight up to heaven;
> The whiting and haddock
> Left salt-water paddock

This dance to be put in,
Where skate with flat faces
Edged out some odd plaices;
But soles kept their footing.

Other instruments send their hearers to sleep – we are off on to a
Balkan trail for the origins of the magic harp in *Jack and the
Beanstalk*. For a moment Gould recalled himself – 'I very much fear
that I am leading my readers a sad dance like one of these strange
pipers; I only hope that I shall not, like the Slavonic demon harper,
send them to sleep.' Unrepentant, he continued for another ten
pages. Apollo once delivered Phrygia from a plague of rats,
Orpheus charmed all living creatures and was split by the Christ-
ians into St Francis and St Antony. Through Sanskrit legends and
the Aryan *Rig Veda*, the wind takes us back at last via the Tartars to
Odin's rune-chanting. Odin was nicknamed Galdner, the songster,
from which we get both the word gale meaning a wind and
our nightingale, a night-songster. Had Andersen read Keats? I
wondered, thinking of the faery lands forlorn conjured up by that
particular 'dryad of the trees'. Were both the Pied Piper and
Andersen's Nightingale really part of the same charmed thread?
Too fanciful by half, I decided, and fell asleep myself, charmed into
oblivion by an eccentric Essex parson.

7

Picking up Gold and Silver

Thus the current of conversation ran rapidly on, whilst the vehicle moved slowly forward in the sandy road. The mountains came gradually forward from behind their misty veils, like strong proud masses, overgrown with dark firwoods; the cornfields wound picturesquely between them, and Goslar, the old free imperial city, lay before us.

(Hans Andersen, *Romantic Rambles in the Harz Mountains*, 1848)

We had managed mere rats alone. To face the witches on the notorious Brocken, the dwarves and giants that are reliably known to frequent the Harz, we needed reinforcements. Monday morning saw us scurrying out of Hamelin at the summons of our personal Pied Piper. Tom was landing at Hanover airport at 1.15, and I had badly miscalculated both how long it would take the girls to complete their mystery shopping and how far it was to Hanover. Bertha responded nobly to flat-foot pressure on her accelerator, and we stormed along the autobahn at a record 65 mph. So far, so good, but the fuel gauge was winking a warning that we were travelling on borrowed time. I called on the whole pantheon of motor gods – Ford, Morris and Benz – to help us, and decided to risk running out. It worked.

Quarter to two: hardly late at all. I parked Bertha in a convenient cab rank and raced into the smoked glass sepulchre that is Hanover airport. Lulling music washed around me, soft voices announced the rising and falling of airliners, huge screens clicked soothingly through neverending arrivals and departures. Where in all this superterrestrial world was Tom? Suddenly I saw him, gliding weightlessly down an escalator, looking remarkably grim: the Beast before he gets to kiss Beauty. Half an hour is a long time at airports. I grovelled hastily, and turned him into a handsome prince.

We walked out to the van together, and climbed in. The children were momentarily struck quite dumb. I think they were overwhelmed with relief at the sight of him. I realised then what a brave front they had all been maintaining during our hectic journeying from place to place, what an act of faith it had involved to let me carry them off over land and sea in our frail canary-coloured cockleshell, what continual adaptations they had made to the different languages, campsites, currencies, washrooms, food and drink. Now that their father had been spirited up in front of their eyes they were probably wondering if he would suddenly change into a frog and disappear with a croak.

Tilly broke the hiatus with a hug, then Ellie hurled herself into his arms. Susie wasn't quite sure that she had finished her presentation drawing, so she stayed in the background, but Daisy soon crept out of her nest aloft and wrapped round his neck. All this affection and a bottle of Grolsch turned forgiveness into enthusiasm, and we set off along the autobahn to find first a garage and then a quiet place for lunch.

Sitting back on a bench in the sunshine, Tom and I began to catch up with each other while the girls arranged their surprises at the remotest picnic table in the lay-by. Genial lorry drivers, munching wurst high in their cabs, looking down on their secretive toing and froing with interest. Then we were led to the spread. Garlands had been draped over the flowering elder trees, balloons bobbed sportively in the sunshine. A small bottle of sparkling Rhineland wine was the centrepiece; beside it was a large marzipan pastry topped with strawberries. Kiwi fruits, grapes and pears were set around it. Yellow cheeses, herrings soused in purple Madeira, pale pink shrimps exquisitely set in aspic, a heap of crisp lettuce. Each guest had a bright pink paper plate, beaker and matching napkin. We settled down to feast. Susie settled down on Tom's knee.

Dawn next day found us waking up in the ancient pinewoods that clothe the upper slopes of the Harz mountains just west of Goslar. Tattered balloons hung from Bertha's wing mirrors and our heads ached after an evening's carousing. But the mood in the van was an excited one. We were back on Andersen's trail, and this time it was leading us into the wilder regions of faery.

Today the Harz mountains rarely feature on international itineraries of English-speaking travellers; they have become a mere Peak District – much loved locally, but little known abroad. This is partly due to the ease of modern travel. Once the English, the Danes and the Dutch made frequent trips to enjoy the health-giving heights of the Harz; now they can as easily flit down the motorways to the Alps or the Dolomites. But the principal reason for the modern decline of the Harz is the unlucky chance that the Iron Curtain slices it in two. Its geological structure is roughly that of a great wave – a high muscular back lies to the west, a crashing drama of cliffs and tumbling waterfalls to the east. Although the old mining towns, thick pine forests and broad summits of the Upper Harz have their attractions, the real heart of the Harz, the dramatically picturesque castles, chasms and caves, the ancient forests of beech and oak, are all in the Lower Harz, east of the border. Few holidaymakers can be bothered to go through the tedious formalities of arranging a visa to cross into the Eastern bloc. But it is possible – and we found it one of the most fascinating parts of the entire holiday.

Andersen's journey to the Harz was probably a tribute to the German poet Heinrich Heine, whose *Travels in the Harz* he admired very much. Heine's book was a little frowned upon by strait-laced English readers – even George Eliot, reviewing it in the *Westminster Review*, declared that there was 'need for a friendly penknife to exercise a strict censorship' before Heine's works were 'put within reach of immature minds.' Heine, it emerged on reading this supposedly risqué work, might have been a far more cheerful companion than the love-lorn Andersen; although he too claimed to be mourning a lost love, he was evidently close to recovery. Early English translations carefully excise his frequent references to pretty passing maidens and draw a prudent veil over his boasts of conquests. Still, on the whole I found Andersen's sharp observations more attractive than Heine's hypersensitivity towards the picturesque. Consider this:

> The stream murmurs and rustles so wondrously, the birds sing snatches of yearning song, the trees whisper like a thousand girlish tongues, like a thousand girlish eyes the quaint mountain flowers stare at us, and stretch out their wonderfully broad, drolly jagged and cut leaves. The joyous sunbeams glance playfully here and there, and thoughtful little

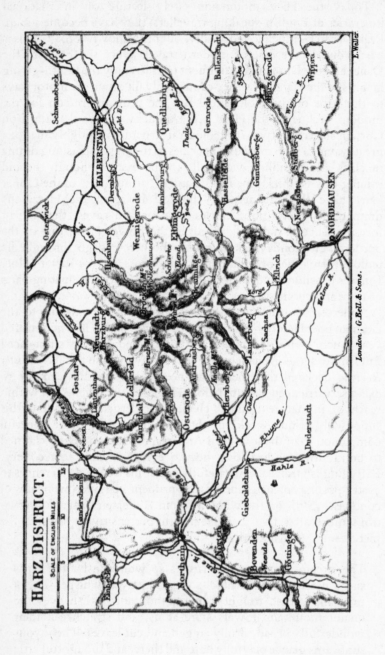

HARZ DISTRICT.

SCALE OF ENGLISH MILES

London ; G. Bell & Sons.

E. Weller.

herbs tell green lovestories one to another; everything is enchanted, and it becomes more and more mysterious; an ancient dream come to life . . . If, in response to the invitations, one bends down, then the secret growing stories of the plants may be heard and the quiet heart-beat of the mountain.

But both poets were equally interested in bringing to light the rich hoard of ancient Teuton folklore that still survived in the remote recesses of the Harz, and purple as the worst of Heine's prose is, he has some interesting things to say about the origins of German folktales. One passage in particular could have been Andersen's personal credo. Heine pictured an 'ancient palsied crone' who might have sat in her chimney corner for a quarter of a century, doing nothing more than gaze at the well-loved old objects around her.

It is only the quiet privacy and retirement of such a life of contemplation which can give birth to those German 'Märchen' – fables whose peculiarity consists in making not merely animals and plants, but also apparently lifeless objects, act and speak. To these sensitive and harmless people, in the still seclusion of their humble forest or mountain huts, the inner life of the objects is relived, and they are endowed with a necessary and consequent character, a pleasant mixture of fantastic wilfulness and purely human disposition.

Thus in these tales we see, with wonder and yet without astonishment, pins and needles coming from the tailor's workshop and losing themselves in the dark; straws and cabbages that want to cross the brook and come to grief; shovels and brooms that stand on the stairs, and fall out and kick each other; the looking glass questioned, showing the face of the most beautiful woman in the world; drops of blood even beginning to utter timid dark words of anxious compassion.

For the same season our life in childhood seems of such infinite significance, everything is of like importance, we see everything and hear everything, and all our impressions are of equal value, whereas in later life we become more purposeful and concern ourselves exclusively with particulars. We laboriously exchange the pure gold of intuition for the papermoney of book definitions, and gain in breadth of life what we lose in depth.

Goslar, although still 'a nest of narrow, crooked, labyrinthine streets', has none of the sinister and oppressive atmosphere that Andersen remarked on in 1831. The mines of Rammelsberg, medieval source of Goslar's prosperity, no longer spew out their sulphurous fumes 'like a whiff of the devil'. The gold and silver has gone too, but lead and zinc are still being extracted. We drove into town very early, and bought hot sweet plaited bread from a market stall. Other stalls, selling flowers, fruit, vegetables, or a thousand and one varieties of sausage, were opening up. All around were intricately carved houses, with oriel windows, and stepped storeys that made archways of the smaller lanes. Their roofs, Goslar's most peculiar feature, were clad in dark grey overlapping slates that fitted as trimly as the scales on a mermaid's tail.

Tom, eager to make up for lost paternal time, suggested that the girls deploy themselves around the arcaded market square and find something to draw. On inquiry the evening before, he had found their formal education sadly neglected. The notebooks and diaries so enthusiastically begun, and lovingly kept up to around day three, had been languishing in the activities drawer for far too long. Maths had been practical rather than theoretical – deft currency dealings rather than the nitty-gritty of fractions and graphs. They had, I pointed out in self-defence, learnt a lot about babies and collective living. And a mother's limitations. He patted me understandingly on the shoulder and suggested I went off to reconnoitre Andersen's Goslar on my own.

Andersen had stayed at the Kaiser von Rusland hotel. It was tempting to think that this might have been the present Kaiserworth Hotel, which flanks the town hall. But the Kaiserworth was clearly the building Andersen mistakenly described as the town hall, 'dark and antiquated, with all its mighty emperors disposed outside: they stand on the first floor, with crowns on their heads, sceptre in hand, and all strongly illuminated like a Nuremberg image.' I turned to Heine for clarification. He called the same building the Guild House, and irreverently described the statues, 'smokily black and touched with gilding' as looking like 'well-roasted university beadles'. This was not to be the first time I would find Andersen weak on accuracy, but he took us to so many unforgettably romantic places that I didn't grudge him his embroideries and omissions.

One potentate on a corner looked particularly exhausted, rolling his eyes up to heaven as if asking for deliverance from his long vigil. Perhaps his expression had something to do with the awkwardly posturing little mannikin which some medieval joker had carved in the plinth he stood on. Known as the Dukatenmännchen, or ducat dwarf, he is Goslar's favourite mascot; as the guidebook primly put it, 'a symbol of luck and a scatological demonstration of Goslar's right to mint coins'.

'A new version of the goose that lays the golden eggs,' suggested Tilly, who had worked her way round the square to where I was standing. She had just sketched the great bronze fountain which Andersen claimed was a direct gift from the devil, a frequent visitor to the Harz if its many legends were to be believed. Daisy and Ellie were waiting for the town clock to strike again. Dusty puppets wielding first mattocks and then modern drills revolve round it whenever it strikes the hour, giving a five-minute exhibition of mining techniques through the ages. Susie was perched on the broad stairs of the real town hall, making a fair attempt at drawing a little shrine set into its wall. Trust her to find another baby. They all seemed happily occupied; Tom has a quiet genius for organising them.

'Shall we go and look for Matilda's tomb?' Tilly asked. She had been fascinated by a strange tale which Andersen included in his book. He said that he visited a chapel which was the only surviving vestige of the ancient cathedral church of Goslar. In it he saw a female figure, carved in sandstone, lying in an open coffin.

It is said to be that of the beautiful Matilda, a daughter of the Emperor Henry the Third. She was so handsome that her own father fell in love with her; therefore she prayed to God that he would at once make her very ugly. The devil then appeared to her, and promised that he would change her father's love for her to hate if she would be his for ever. She agreed to the contract, on condition that if he did not find her sleeping the first three times he came to her, she should then be free of him.

In order to keep herself awake, she took her needle and silk, and embroidered a costly robe, whilst her little dog Qvedl sat by her side. Every time she fell asleep, and the devil approached, the faithful dog barked, and she was again awake and actively at work. As the devil now saw himself duped, and obliged to fulfil his promise, he passed his ugly claw over her face, so that her beautiful arched brow was pressed down, and the royal nose made broad and flat: her little mouth he extended till it reached her ears, and he breathed on her beautiful eyes, so that they appeared like lead and mist. The Emperor was now disgusted with her; and she then built an abbey, which, after her faithful dog Qvedl, she called Qvedlinburg, where she herself was the first abbess.

We asked at the Tourist Office, but nobody had heard of Princess Matilda. There was a tomb of the Emperor Henry III in Ulrich's chapel, the only original part now left of the great Imperial palace built in 1050, but not of his daughter. We were disappointed, especially Tilly who had taken a personal interest in the fate of her namesake.

'Let's go and see the chapel anyway,' said Daisy. 'The statue might be hidden somewhere there.'

We left the market square and crossed over the Abzucht, a woodlined aqueduct that runs all round the town, to the broad expanse of grass in front of the Kaiserpfalz, a formidable riot of pseudo-gothic grandeur. The Michelin guide describes it, with distinct lack of enthusiasm, as 'reminiscent in outline and plan, if in nothing else, of the old eleventh century palace'. Andersen would not have seen it at all. It was Kaiser fever much later in the century that inspired the complete reconstruction of this ancient symbol of Imperial might. Today it is an uncomfortable anachronism, unsure what to do with itself. The vast first-floor banqueting hall is lined with gigantic frescoes tabling imperial triumphs since Charlemagne.

They culminate in a khaki-clad Kaiser William flanked by his generals gazing ambitiously out of the arched windows but seeing nothing to command but a regiment of coaches.

We crept past a shrill guide who was lecturing a large party of listless tourists on the merits of the florid historic scenes. At the far end of the hall a winding passage and a steep stair lead to Ulrich's chapel. Built to last, with five-foot thick walls of golden stone, with a soft, glowing light filtering through its stained-glass windows, it had all the atmosphere the palace lacked. But there was nowhere that Matilda could be hiding. The only tomb was the central sandstone slab clearly labelled Emperor Henry III in four languages. Then Ellie tugged at my arm. She was pointing at a curved shape curled at the imperial feet.

'Look, there's a sweet little dog at this end. Perhaps it's Qvedl.'

We all came over to look more closely at the tomb. Sandstone – an open coffin. There was no hoary imperial beard of the sort that fringed the Kaiserworth statues. Instead a smooth, oddly flat face stared peacefully up at us. What had Andersen said? 'The old woman who showed us this image knew not rightly if it were intended to represent her in her days of beauty, or in the following time, when the devil had laid his fingers on her: I was most inclined to the latter opinion.'

Clutched to its breast was the model of a building – assumed no doubt to be the Imperial Palace. But suppose this was Matilda. There was Qvedl, and there was the Abbey of Qvedlinburg, her sanctuary. The more we looked at the effigy, the less masculine and imperial, the more feminine and filial it appeared. None of us doubted for a moment that we had indeed rediscovered the poor wronged Matilda and her faithful dog Qvedl.

But there are two postscripts to this story. One, a week later, confirmed our theory. Over the border in Qvedlinburg, we climbed a steep hill to the Colditz-like bulk of the ancient Abbey, set on a crag in the centre of the town. With our usual genius for mistiming things, we found it closed. But on the very door that barred us from investigating further we found another sign. The doorhandle, polished bright by a thousand years of handling, was again in the shape of a dog. Qvedl again. And high above in the decorative arcading among the beasts and birds and monstrous men disporting themselves, again and again was the same image – a slim little dog with a rampant curly tail.

The second may be ignored by romantics. Possibly only pedants will be interested in it, although it could be just the tale for those who enjoy the tangled family webs and powerful matriarchs of *Dynasty.* Back home in Oxford I decided to find out what sort of a man Henry III was. Sensitive, pious, and musical, the authorities assured me. He preferred moral to brute force, and lost popularity by sending the wandering troubadours who traditionally entertained wedding guests away from the feast at his own marriage to Agnes of Poitou. Agnes was a powerful character, and highly involved politically. She and Henry had five children, one of them the Henry IV who was given such a hard time by the pope in the legendary confrontation of Church and State at Canossa. Henry III did indeed have a daughter Matilda, born in 1045, but she married Rudolf of Swabia when she was 14 and died only a year later in childbed. There was no hint of incest or devilry, and no connection of Qvedlinburg with her name, although Goslar was her father's favourite residence. But she had a sister, Adelheide, and Adelheide did become abbess of Qvedlinburg when she came of age at 14. Perhaps Andersen's guide had got the name wrong.

Then, right next to the index entry for that Matilda, I discovered not one but two other Matildas – both, it appeared, closely connected with Qvedlinburg, and both redoubtable figures in their own right. As I read about their careers, I began to wonder when women lost their political influence. The first Matilda, 895–968, was a Saxon princess and wife of Emperor Henry I. She was noted 'for her intelligence, humility and piety', but then so were most noblewomen at the time. What I liked about her was the chronicled record that she never stayed in a town during winter without causing fires to be lit in all homes, and even in the streets. It was she who founded a monastery at Qvedlinburg, and persuaded Henry I to found a convent there. Far from being a timid virgin, however, she had five children, one of them the next Emperor, Otto I.

His daughter was the third Matilda (955–999) – and she did become Abbess of Qvedlinburg. But she was only ten at the time, and had already been living with the nuns for some years. This Matilda, a formerday Mary Warnock, was as highly gifted and politically active as her grandmother. One chronicler criticised her for continuing to wear the imperial purple in the cloister, but this was not unusual at a time when a cloistered life was not necessarily a quiet one. It was in fact the most legitimate way in which an intelligent woman could opt out of the deadly obstacle course of childbearing and pursue a career in her own right. The nuns of

Qvedlinburg vowed chastity and piety but not poverty, and moved freely between court and cloister. They were mainly noblewomen, and the abbey was a well-known cultural centre with its own poetess, Hrothsuitha of Gandesheim.

Matilda was born within a year or so of her brother Otto, who succeeded to the imperial throne in 973, aged only 18. Otto was almost constantly absent from court, at war with rebellious vassals, and the regency was held jointly between his mother Adelheide, Matilda and his Byzantine wife Theophano. When Otto was killed, aged only 28, this powerful triumfeminate held together the empire for eleven years until Otto's 3-year-old son Otto III reached his official majority. In gratitude, Otto III endowed Qvedlinburg extremely generously and by the time Henry III's daughter Adelheide became abbess it was one of the most renowned abbeys of the empire.

Where did that leave Andersen's strange story? Lots of Matildas, lots of abbeys, but no little dog, no devilry. Browsing onwards, I came across another Matilda in Henry III's life. Matilda of Tuscany, daughter of the rebellious vassal Geoffrey of Lorraine and his wife Beatrice of Tuscany. Her father was killed, and she and her mother became Henry's prisoners. Had something happened during that time? Released after Henry III's death, she became one of the most implacable enemies of his son Henry IV, sticking at nothing to embarrass him. Aged forty-three she married the seventeen-year-old heir to the south German Welf lands to create a powerful bloc between Pope and Emperor, and she thoroughly enjoyed her part in the humiliation of the Emperor in the snows of Canossa.

Poor Henry IV. Although a brilliantly intelligent man, arguably the founder of the German imperial fortunes, he seems to have had no luck at all in his immediate family. He was betrayed by both his sons, and accused by his second wife, whom he banished for adultery, of forcing his son to commit adultery with his step-mother. 'A flood of filth and calumny beat against the unhappy emperor,' I read in a sympathetic nineteenth-century tome by Bryce. When you throw mud, something sticks. Two Matildas of Qvedlinburg, a princess Matilda dying tragically young and in childbed, an imprisoned Matilda with a mysterious grievance, a scandal with an incestuous flavour: put it all into the great game of Chinese Whispers we call folk memory and somehow out comes a romantic tale with a hint of devilry and plenty of circumstantial evidence. Hundreds of years later, there we were in Goslar, looking at an infuriatingly mute effigy whose story no one can ultimately know.

Andersen had explored the ancient mine-workings in the Rammelsberg, a mountain close to Goslar. Was his trip into it the inspiration for the caverns under the tree in 'The Tinder Box' – filled with copper, silver and gold, and guarded over by the three great dogs, one with eyes like saucers, one with eyes like mill-wheels, and one with eyes the size of the Round Tower of Copenhagen? The mines of the Harz were certainly the source of many of the tales concerning dwarfs collected by the brothers Grimm. Mining is a dwarfish trade, and the hunched, blackened figures and shadowy grey mannikins that flit by on the fringes of so many folktales probably symbolise the miner, removed from the ordinary world by his life underground.

As no children under 12 are allowed into the Rammelsberg mine today, we decided to visit a smaller mine a little west of Goslar at Lauterdal to sniff a little underground atmosphere. Tom took the wheel and for the first time since we left Oxford I sat in the passenger seat. It was a little disquieting. Maybe the hairpin bends of the Harz were not the best place to find out how to handle Bertha, but he learnt fast. There were only two or three avalanches of drawing tools, modelling clay and jampots before he mastered the arts of slowing down several minutes before you think you need to, of inching rather than sweeping round bends, and of changing gear at the very first hint of a gradient. After half an hour I managed to stifle my disloyal lunges for the armrest and relax, enjoying the novel freedom of looking backwards and sideways as well as forwards, reading guidebooks, even popping into the back of the van occasionally. The girls were all beavering away at their maths workbooks for the first time since they left Assen. Having someone take an interest made all the difference. I had to recognise that my forte was the grand design, the sweeping vision. Tom's strength lay in the practical working-out of things.

The woods were lovely, dark and deep, but our actual target for lunch, a large lake called the Innerstetausee, was a disappointment. Most of the tumbling streams and rivers of the Upper Harz have been tamed into these large placid reservoirs, concrete-lined bathtubs that have a hard, organised neatness about them. We bought an over-priced but nicely iced beer in the campsite restaurant at its southern end, inquired fruitlessly after windsurfer hire, and then retreated to find our own picnic spot in the forest. After strawberries for lunch and icy white wine, I put up the camping table and made a gesture towards sorting out the three weeks of post Tom had brought out with him. None of it seemed of the slightest interest at that range, and my concentration was slipping away. Perhaps this would be an appropriate moment for some meditation on the journey as a whole. I spread out a sleeping bag in the hot sunshine and lay back. Dimly in the distance I could hear Tom explaining fractions and long division and something muddling called sets. The rest was silence.

It was nearly four o'clock before we left the woods for the mine-workings in Lauterdal. As we turned in at the gate we saw a huge timber wheel set into the hillside. A small green train was shunting out of the mouth of a roughly hewn rock tunnel. The girls pulled on jerseys and rubber boots and stampeded towards it. I walked over to the kiosk outside the main building. A very pretty girl said a cheerful good afternoon in hesitant English but shook her head sadly. That had been the last train. They only ran when there were enough peoples, or for a group, and it was very quietly at the minute. And the tour was all Deutsch – no English until August.

I countered with smiles and pleas, flourishing a bunch of deutschmarks. Six was almost a group. And the Goslar information bureau had assured us that here we could enter the mountain. We had driven for miles especially to do so – the children would be so disappointed. Tom's German was so good that he could translate all the necessary information. She wavered. We could go into the museum; that she would keep open a little longer. I explained that the children were not really museum types. What they liked were mines and tunnels, dwarfs and silver. I opened up Andersen's *Rambles* and pointed at the relevant passage.

She turned for support to the train-driver, a fair-haired and very undwarf-like miner. The girls looked beseechingly up at him. Victory. He led them over to choose a helmet each and showed us into seats in the heavily armoured little train. We were shut in behind thick mesh gates like chickens in a battery farm, and then with a croaking lurch the train jolted into the mountain. It was pitch dark. The smallest of hands crept into mine, and I heard Susie's voice telling Ellie that it wasn't frightening.

'It's just dark, isn't it, Ellie?'

From the compartment next door where Tom was sitting with Tilly and Daisy came giggles and shrieks and talk of bats.

'Fledermice – flying mice, you see.'

It was a relief when a line of lamps appeared and we could see the tunnel walls. They were slimy, streaked with savage oranges and whites. Underneath each lamp a few frail green seedlings were struggling against impossible odds to flourish in the heavy damp air. Klaus stopped the train and let us out. He showed us the main shaft, a pit dwindling 670 metres down into darkness. An appallingly primitive belt-lift – short shelves to stand on, and nothing to save you if you lost your grip – went vertically down beside it. We climbed up a wooden stair and straggled along the raggedly gouged tunnels to an old working. Here, Klaus explained, silver had been mined. He traced a vein of white quartz with rusty streaks and tiny glimmers. There was nothing worth mining, but there was still a little left. Four pairs of eyes lit up covetously.

Further on we came to a working face. Huge drills were stuck into the rock. Klaus flung a switch and the world vibrated. He beckoned Tilly over to hold on to the shrieking drill. I don't think she would have done it for me, but forward she went and seized it intrepidly. Then Ellie, Daisy and even Susie. Bursting with pride they raced each other back along the passages, while Tom and I proceeded more slowly, trying to get the gist of the geological lecture that Klaus felt was our due. As we passed the old silver seam he stopped, took up a pick, and hacked out a crumb of ore for each of the girls. They were quite overcome. Wealth beyond the dreams of avarice, from a blue-eyed Saxon instead of a round-eyed dog, but real silver all the same.

We spent the night at Altenau, a 'lakeside' campsite highly rated in our camper's guide for its position, but too claustrophobically sunk in the pine trees for my liking. The lake was more of a pond, its banks tidily bound up in wire netting. So far I was a little disappointed in the Harz. All we had seen was a gentle German Lake District, too thickly clad in trees to show the bones of its hills. As it is a popular skiing area in winter, cablelifts scar the hillsides and the prosperous villages, potentially hearty with glühwein and fondue, seemed a little undressed without the snow.

If it hadn't been for the accident that the highest peak of the Harz, the Brocken, lies on the other side of the Iron Curtain, we might have drifted away southwards under the illusion that Andersen's fairytale mountain world had been tidied away for good. But his description of his night on the Brocken, the haunt of witches on Walpurgis night, and the most romantic shrine of every nineteenth-century European in search of the picturesque, was irresistible.

The road began to wind upwards towards the Brocken; the declining sun could not shine in between the thick pines; round about lay the huts of the charcoal burners, enveloped in bluish smoke, so that the whole had a still, strange and romantic character. It was a picture that attuned the soul to sadness . . .

The road went more and more upwards; round about lay enormous masses of rock. The river rushed over large blocks and formed a succession of waterfalls. Sometimes the channel of the river was hemmed in between two narrow cliffs, where the black stream then boiled with a snow-white foam; sometimes it rushed on broad and unchecked between the fallen pines, and carried the large green branches with it . . .

We were now on the top, but everything was in a mist. We stood in a cloud . . . Here stone lies piled on stone, and a strange silence rests over the whole. Not a bird twitters in the low pines; round about are white grave-flowers, growing in the high moss, and stones lie in masses on the side of the mountain top.

When Andersen climbed up, he found about forty other travellers in the hut on the top. Snug behind its five-foot thick walls, he warmed himself in front of a hot stove. 'The mattresses were stuffed with seaweed from Denmark, thus I could rest on Danish ground high above the clouds.' A book was kept there, in which all visitors wrote their names, often adding drawing and verses. Andersen added his, then went outside. 'The wind was driving the clouds over the mountain top as if they were flocks of sheep. Three ladies in large hats ran about and plucked the white Brocken flowers. The clouds touched their legs – it looked like the witches scene in Macbeth.' Some visitors had brought instruments, others seized broomsticks, fireshovels, and whatever they could find to act out a wicked sabbath of their own, and soon Andersen was joining the other travellers in 'a great dance of witches in the declining twilight . . . One took the other by the hand, great and little, stout and thin, all joined in the mad-cap fun and the merry intermezzo began.'

> Dolorem furca pellas ex
> I've sung it in the heather!
> I'm a witch, thou'rt a witch,
> We're witches all together!

By midnight the revels were over, but Andersen stayed awake alone, thinking about Riborg. Perhaps it was that night, with its strange mixture of the real and the fantastical, that inspired him to carry the folktale further than Heine had defined it, to add creativity to the authenticity which obsessed his contemporaries, the Grimms, and to discover his own especial genius: everyday magic.

> The moon began to force her light through the mist, and cast her beams into the long narrow chamber. I could not sleep, and therefore ascended the tower to enjoy the prospect. Whoever has in his dreams soared over the earth, and seen lands, with towns and forests far below him, has a remote idea of this inconceivable magnificence. The pine-covered mountains below me were of a pitchy darkness; white clouds, illumined by the moon, darted like spirits along the mountainside. There was no boundary, the eye lost itself in an infinity; towns with their towers, charcoalburners' huts, with their columns of smoke, all stood forth in the transparent veil of mist, which the moon illumined. It was Fancy's world of dreams that lay before me, full of life.

When dawn broke, he climbed to the witches' altar, drank water from their enchanted spring, and strode down the eastern slopes towards the Ilsenstein with a new perspective on his heartache. 'What cares the world about the longings of a single heart? . . . Mightier passions, the combats and destruction of a whole people, revolutions in nature and the life of man, are its dreams and thoughts.' But he, Andersen, would become the apologist of the single heart; would turn his grief to universal relevance, would make the common loneliness of mankind his theme, love his solution.

From Altenau we wound up steep bends to Torfhaus, an 800-metre hill, crowned with an aggressive tangle of red and white striped radio masts and the gigantic silver saucers of radar receivers. Far in the eastern distance we could see a misty silhouette echoing Torfhaus. It could only be the Brocken, and it too was thick with menacing aerials. Our chances of dancing among the wunderblüme and drinking from the witches' spring began to seem remote. We noticed on our map that the nearby village of Braunlage had a cable-lift to the top of the Wurmberg – the Dragon Mountain – which was as close to the Brocken as we could get this side of the border, and at 971 metres, only two hundred metres lower than our target. It seemed worth taking a ride up there just in case we were unlucky east of the border.

The descent from Torfhaus was rocky and picturesque, with mossy crags jutting out above fast-flowing streams. The smooth back of the great wave of the Harz was beginning to break. We stocked up the van in the well-filled supermarkets of Braunlage in anticipation of the austerity of the next few days, then drove to the cable-lift. The girls disappeared into the station while Tom and I put together a quick picnic. When we joined them in the ticket-hall, they explained that each car held two passengers, that we could have red ones or green ones, closed or open.

'Susie and I want a green closed one,' said Ellie.

'Daisy and I want a red one,' Tilly added. 'And you and Daddy can have a nice romantic ride on your own in an open one.' What a kind thought. We looked out of the station and up at the mountain, where the frail little cabins were swaying up through the pines. Was it foolish to let them ride alone? We decided that the automatic doors would keep them safe enough. So off we went, strung out like beads on a string: first Tilly and Daisy, then us in an open car, then Susie and Ellie. We floated upwards smoothly, jolting slightly every time we passed a support tower, adrift on a great prickly green sea and almost able to touch the clumps of fresh green pine cones on the topmost tips of the pine trees flowing past beneath us.

The summit was over-furnished with cafeterias and gift shops; bulldozed and shaped-up for the benefit of skiers. We walked past the great ski-jump and looked eastwards. Far below us was the high wire fence of the frontier. An army jeep was parked behind the East German conning tower, and through the telescopic lens of my camera I could see an armed guard on top of the tower staring up at me through binoculars. No doubt his lenses were stronger than mine. I waved amicably. The fence wound away into the distance towards another watchtower. Beside it was a broad band of raked sand, the legendary strip that stretches from the Black Sea to the Baltic, carefully raked to reveal any illicit footprints. We looked higher up, further to the north. Over the tallest of the trees we saw a humped summit – one great tower dominating the electronic hardware like a finger raised in warning. The shifting clouds thickened over it; a few minutes later even the silhouette disappeared. The Brocken seemed wilfully elusive.

We ate our picnic in hazy sunshine, a little muted. East-West conflict is a television cliché, the stuff of James Bond films. But those were real soldiers, with real guns. Was it wise to risk getting caught up in it? We looked over at the girls, who had begun one of their intense imaginary games. Daisy was a mischievous princess raiding the royal larder, Ellie a haughty queen tumbling in the juniper bushes.

'Priscilla's going to get a string of race-horses and a care-bear for being so good,' we heard Tilly promising Susie as we lay back with our cans of beer and looked down on the great divide below. Gunfire grumbled in the distance – a NATO exercise, or the Soviet pact in action? The eastern horizon was an ominous deep blue-grey. We were leaving the enchanted garden and heading for the forest.

8
Heart of the Harz

It is not alone the immense masses of rock with their forests, which exceed the range of vision, the tall bushes that bend over the foaming river, nor the dead stone masses of a half-ruined building that makes a country romantic: it is when the place has, by this its particular character, one or other legend connected with it, that the whole gets its perfect magic light.

(Hans Andersen, *Romantic Rambles*)

'What's he looking for?' whispered Tilly as the serious-faced young soldier patiently leafed through the dog-eared Puffin books, smiled approvingly at the massive black volume of Grimms' *Household Tales*, opened lockers full of decaying vegetables and sounded out the drawers for false bottoms.

'Guns, ammunition, subversive books and drugs,' I hissed back, a little pink at his methodical examination of our shiftless mode of vankeeping, and conscious that we had stuffed every spare inch with western luxuries said to be hard to find east of the border – whisky, chocolate, coffee, and the like. The fridge was groaning with succulent meat and exotic fruit. Such indulgence seemed despicable now that we were actually entering this notoriously spartan world.

At last the young soldier uncovered something promising – a carefully wrapped-up parcel hidden deep in the folds of my long-unused wetsuit. He asked if he could open it.

'It's a birthday present for my youngest daughter from a friend,' I explained. Back in Hamelin Jane had tucked it away there for Susie's July birthday. He nodded understandingly and took it over to the privacy of his office to examine, sticking it up again neatly before he returned. Tilly, Daisy and Ellie were most impressed by this tact. Almost friends, we waved him goodbye as we inched to the next halt sign.

The inching was due to Tom's first nervous plunge into the Eastern bloc – he had crashed Bertha's roof into one of the large signs that direct motorists into the right lane at the customs. The mishap had been received in a forgiving spirit by the squad of armed officials who had raced out of their office at the sound of splintering wood, and we had been directed to a broad channel all our own. About every half-hour we moved on fifty yards to be greeted by a new functionary, counted, and offered thin buff forms to fill out and hand in at the next barrier. This was teatime at Teistungen, a tiny frontier post between Duderstadt and Worbis, and life on the whole seemed far from gay. At last we reached the last hurdle, the office that issued us with the currency we had paid for in England. The coins were flimsy, the notes small and severe in design. We tried to use some to buy a detailed map of the Eastern Harz, only to be told that at the frontier they only accepted western deutschmarks.

Feeling slightly insecure, we managed to lose our way almost immediately. I wasn't used to the enormous scale of the new map, and was too interested in my first close look at the terrain around the Brocken to notice Tom missing the left turn made by the main road to Worbis. The bumps as the van hit the cobbled high street of the little town of Berlingerode shook me back to navigating.

We got to the main road an hour later after trekking through a maze of tiny villages that provided a fine set of variations on a Marxist theme. Solitary factories smoked away in the countryside between the villages; proper haystacks stood fatly in the corners of fields where long lines of men and women were hoeing between the young crops. Sovietismus posters urged on the Volk effort by blazoning target achievements on lurid hoardings. A small girl sat on a broad piece of verge with a grazing cow on the end of a long rope. The villagers themselves had evidently not seen anything as sumptuous as our buxom Bertha before: small crowds gathered on the street corners to admire her as we jockeyed slowly over the cobbled streets. Bent old ladies straightened up a little and blew kisses to the girls, children waved their arms like windmills and ran along beside us, everybody stared. Our children grew embarrassed, until we pointed out that the waves and stares seemed to be friendly ones. Then they entered into the spirit of the thing and waved back.

Crowded into the cab beside and behind us, they were pointing out of the windows and asking questions like machine-guns. Why were all the cars the same, and so small and old-fashioned-looking? Why were the roads so bumpy? Why were the houses so rundown – couldn't people afford to paint them? What did those huge posters with the glaring faces say? What was that red sign with the crescent moon and the funny hammer, and why did it hang everywhere?

Soon we were exhausted with explanations, many of them distinctly lame. I realised how little I knew about East-West relations in general, or the true state of affairs on East Germany in particular. Was the superficial poverty deep-rooted, or were they saving up for essentials? Maybe it was better to run those neat little Skoda and Moskvitch cars instead of our degenerately comfortable gas-guzzlers. One of the brightest sights in the landscape was the liveliness of the carefully tended allotments outside each village. They were full of flowers as well as sustaining vegetables. Small sheds and benches made each a tiny Eden, alive with people. In England allotments have an acrid whiff of wartime austerity about them; these had a holiday mood.

The graveyards were another surprise, challenging Chelsea Flower Show for imaginative layout and kaleidoscopic colour. Clearly there is still much interest in the afterlife in old Thuringia. One village we went through had enormous white flags with bold red crosses on them hanging along every street. We stopped the van and Tom asked a passing woman what they were celebrating.

'The bishop has just been visiting,' she explained. 'We are a Catholic town.'

'Gosh,' said Tilly. 'Won't they get done? I thought you weren't allowed to go to church in a communist country.' More adjustments to our ignorant views, but in a sense, as it turned out, she was right. An acquaintance made later on in our visit told us that although Catholicism was officially tolerated, confirmation led to ostracism by universities and made it difficult to get a good job.

By the time we got to our campsite at Neudorf, fifteen miles south of Qvedlinburg, the clouds we had seen from Braunlage had settled over us.

'No wonder the East Germans are so good at sport,' commented Tom after inspecting the Spartan facilities, located five hundred yards away from our allocated position. Several basins, but only cold water. No showers. One special visitors' lavatory, kept locked with a key that hung on a post at the centre of the foreigners' enclosure behind the camp-office. Each morning caravan curtains twitched as the needy estimated their chances of grabbing it before some neighbour made a lightning dash.

I turned for comfort to the kettle. The gas totally failed to respond to my match, and at the same moment the van lights flickered and went out.

'I thought you refilled the gas bottle at Altenau?' asked Tom in a restrained tone.

'I did – unless they handed me back the empty one by mistake. Didn't you switch the battery over to charging off the engine this morning?'

Bad temper spread outwards from us to the girls. Favourite possessions had disappeared under the messy morass that had accumulated over the long drive. Bickering began. Susie sulked in a small sleepy heap, the others snarled over the last crumbs of Fimo. We placated them temporarily with squares of chocolate and squelched over to the camp-office to ask if they had a spare gas bottle. They explained that here in the Democratic Republic they used a different system altogether. I spoke of the meat rotting in our tepid fridge and looked hopefully towards their kitchen, but the hint was either unobserved or not taken.

Back to the squalid twilight of the van. Perhaps what we all needed was a nice bit of fresh air, I announced in a rallying voice, hearing echoes of my mother's voice thirty years before with embarrassment. We took toothbrushes and towels and I frog-marched the four of them down the lane to the washrooms. It did do us good – but I think it was the stiff whisky downed on the return that really concentrated my mind on the problem. Crawling under the table I discovered that a small foot had dislodged a fuse from the front of the battery – one twist and light dawned.

Now for the gas. Squatting under an umbrella Tom and I took out the cylinders and found both sloshing with gas. That meant that there must be something wrong with a connection. By exchanging the valve on the shower-heater bottle for that on the sink-oven bottle we soon had gas too. The ring under the kettle spluttered into action. I cooked – they tidied. Hot soup. Crispy chunks of veal and onion rings, marzipan pastries stuffed with apple. More whisky while we washed up. The rain really didn't seem to matter very much as we played a raucous game of the West German Monopoly

that had somehow passed our young censor's eye. We chased the
girls into bed, and Tom managed to put up our berth without his
usual curses. Leaning back against the pillows we looked smugly
round at an ordered calm – so much better suited to a socialist
democracy than our usual *laissez faire.*

We grew fonder of Neudorf. It was very well-equipped for sport
– three volleyball pitches, two outdoor tabletennis tables, and a
football field. Through the woods was a small lake that would be
fine for bathing later in the year. Most of the other campers were
school parties on summer trips – cheerful kids making a respectable
amount of noise and mischief. The rest were retired folk, privileged
temporary occupants of the permanent chalets which are owned by
firms, and offered to deserving employees for summer holidays.
The rest of the year they were available to senior citizens with the
right connections.

Early the next morning a knock at the door announced the camp
director who had somehow got hold of a spare gas-stove and was
offering to lend it to us. This small kindness made the whole
country seem a brighter place; so did the sunshine. At about eleven
we set off for Qvedlinburg to make our obligatory morning report
to the police-station. Despite the barred windows and padded door
of the waiting room and the formidable female functionaries with
their gilded epaulettes, this was a less alarming procedure than we
had anticipated. The only annoying thing was that they had
understood a visit of three nights to mean a visit of two days,
whereas we had intended to stay for a third day, leaving late in the
evening. There was no possibility of a longer stay – but at least they
let us finesse another visit to the police-station as we had so little
time.

We drove up to the old Abbey, a formidable fortress in its own
right, built up from steeply tilted slabs of rock. On its ramparts, as
far as we and Hans Andersen were concerned, Matilda had once
walked with her faithful dog Qvedl. We looked down. A single
crane on the skyline hinted at the twentieth century – otherwise a
sea of redtiled roofs and spires spread an unspoilt medieval world
around our feet.

Blankenburg was only ten miles away, another elegantly decayed town, softened by time and unspoilt by restoration. On its
northern fringes is the Regenstein, an ancient mountain stronghold
felt by nineteenth-century travellers to embody the essence of the
picturesque. Some freak of geology has left it soaring hundreds of

feet vertically upwards from the plain. Once upon a time it must have been Gormenghast to the life. Now it stands windworn and rainwashed, its rocky summit bare gunnels of stone, riddled with holes like a giant cheese.

'I looked down into the abyss, and shut my eyes when I had done so, to see if I had conceived the whole depth,' wrote Andersen. 'But when I again opened them and looked down, it was far deeper than I had represented to myself; the extent on all sides around was far greater than the moment's memory could embrace.' He was quite right – the downward plunge is unbelievable. One great spur hangs out over the void, with nothing but one slippery metal rail between you and perdition. Inevitably the girls raced over to it, pushing and shoving in their eagerness to lean the furthest out. I saw Tom go seagreen when he caught up with them and looked down. Ravens wheeled in and out of the cliffs. Far below them we could see the scattered ribbons of roads, with ant-like cars crawling along. Villages hidden in the folds of the hills to the west seemed perfect miniatures; tractors and carts toylike in the fields.

The Regenstein was originally built by Emperor Henry I, husband of one of our Matildas, and founder of Qvedlinburg Abbey. Latterly it must have been used as a monastery – the main part of the remaining ruins are a church, hollowed out of the rock itself, and probably converted from the old cellars of the castle. The girls moved to a less dangerous part of the ruins and played hide and seek in and out of the tumbled towers and unexpected underground passages. Tom and I tried to decipher the brief guide we had been given with our tickets, but it gave us rather fewer facts than Andersen had. We went back to the *Romantic Rambles*:

> Hewn out of the rock itself it stands as a gigantic mummy and tells of olden times, although it cannot speak a word . . . With its narrow chambers, its broken walls, and stairs that only lead from the free air up into the same element, it has got its own place in my memory's pantheon. Every such ruin stands bodily as a gigantic epos, that carries us ages back, to other men and other customs; the higher the grass grows in the knights' hall, and the slower the river glides over the fallen columns, so much the greater poetry does the heart find in this stone epos.

We were all but alone on the Regenstein. There were a handful of other sightseers, quietly dressed, and without cameras. No fierce custodians, keep-off signs, or careful reconstructions of how it might once have been to save you the bother of imagining it for yourself.

Just outside was a restaurant with a tasty line in takeaway fried chicken and chips, so we gorged ourselves at big wooden outdoor tables and then boarded Bertha once again. Through Wernigerode, dominated by another enormous castle, and on to Ilseburg. This was the road that Andersen had taken up to the the Brocken, and from which we hoped to scale it unobtrusively. It was not a rapid journey. Held in check when necessary by a man with a red flag, we watched the stately progress of the Wernigerode steam express tacking across the main road five times in all. Horsedrawn carriages laden with farmhands returning to work after lunch ambled along ahead of us; elderly lorries, always with trailers, brought up the rear. But it was an enchanted countryside, rich in blossoming orchards and sedate villages. Their steep roofs and pointed steeples echoed the dramatic edges of the Harz as we turned up into Ilsedal.

The valley is named after the legendary princess Ilse who lost her one true lover in a flood that Andersen identifies with that of Noah.

When the deluge blotted man from earth, the waters of the Baltic also rose high, high up into Germany; the beautiful Ilse then fled, with her bridegroom, from the northern lands here towards the Harz, where the Brocken seemed to offer them a retreat. At length they stood on this enormous rock, which projected far above the swelling sea; the surrounding hills were hidden under the waves; huts, human beings and animals, had disappeared. Alone they stood, arm in arm, looking down on the waves as they broke against the rock. But the waters rose higher; in vain they sought an uncovered ridge of rock where they could ascend the Brocken, that lay like a large island amid the stormy sea. The rock on which they stood trembled beneath them; an immense cleft opened itself there, and threatened to tear them away; still they held each other's hands; the side walls bent forward and backward; they fell together into the rushing flood. From her the river Ilse obtained its name, and she still lives here with her bridegroom in the flinty rock.

Like Andersen's party, we began to wind slowly up the road to the Brocken. The charcoalburners' huts he commented on have disappeared, but the river Ilse is unchanged: at that height a ferociously violent black stream, boiling with white foam and not a place for peaceful dalliance. We passed an extremely grand old house with fretted wooden balconies. Once a hotel, it is now an official holiday camp of some sort. Perhaps deserving party members are sent there to breathe the mountain air. We did see some sober citizens strolling around in a determinedly relaxed way, but none of them seemed interested in the road we took, possibly because it was thick with large red-rimmed signs featuring flashes of lightning and much unintelligible German.

They didn't deter us, as I was driving and I didn't understand what they said. There was a slightly ominous silence from the passenger seat, nothing very positive, a light miasma of disapproval. But this was after all the Brocken at last, and it seemed a pity to let a few forestry notices – probably mere formalities about wildlife – deter us. I pointed out to Tom that the map marked this as a nature reserve, not a military zone, and prattled on to the girls about Walpurgis and broomsticks as Bertha negotiated the ruts and rifts in the track with the caution of an aged mountain goat.

Then our luck ran out. From behind a thick hollybush a soldier jumped out, a machine-gun slung across his back and a large Alsatian chained to his wrist. Tom claimed later that the dog was foaming at the mouth, but I think that was an exaggeration. I stopped Bertha, smiled pleasantly, and pointed to *Romantic Rambles*, which I had open on my knee.

'Is this the way to the Brocken?' I inquired in slow English. 'We're following in Hans Andersen's footsteps. Looking for witches, and so on.'

The soldier, a youngish lad, looked a little bemused. He shot off some rapid sentences and pointed downhill. I shook my head and pointed uphill.

'I'm sure it's this way – look, it says here "The road went more and more upwards; round about lay enormous masses of rock. The river rushed over them and formed a succession of waterfalls." It must be up here.' He shook his head, and pointed downhill again. I made one last effort.

'Brocken. Walpurgis. Witches. What's witches, Tom – I know, Hexen?' The dog yanked hungrily towards Bertha. The soldier grimaced, clearly thinking deeply. Finally he managed to wind his tongue round an unmistakable English word.

'Top Secret. Brocken Top Secret.' The girls were fascinated.

This was just like the cinema. Tom was feeling less secure. He knew that this was no B movie and he hates dogs. I decided we had met our match. Deeper in the woods we could hear the baying of other, possibly wilder, hounds. Discretion was evidently the better part of valour, and all those dogs had probably scared the witches' cats away long ago.

'Right. We understand. Top Secret. Better be off then. Down we go. Thank you very much for your help.' He grinned in relief. I performed a tricky turn among the treestumps and we all gave him a parting wave.

There was still the Ilsenstein to discover. We parked Bertha down by the frilly pleasure palace and walked up a track marked Ilsenstein 2 kilometres. It wound gently to and fro across the flanks of the hill – too gently for the children's taste. They decided to go mountain-climbing, to cut straight up the hillside and meet the track as it doubled back. The first attempt at this was most successful. We left them wriggling through the pine needles, walked the long gradual hairpin ourselves and doubled-back to find ourselves looking down on them as they came puffing and scrambling up. We had some iron rations – more of the dark bitter chocolate we had bought in Braunlage, and then they decided to do it again.

The next slope looked much steeper than the first, and there was a good deal of loose shale about. With some misgivings we realised that the four girls were starting a mini-avalanche of pine cones and pebbles as they went upwards. We waited for a while on the path to protect any passers-by, then set off again to meet them. But this time there was no doubling back of the track – it just went on and on round the hillside. What we had thought was a higher track must have been just some vague levelling. We turned round and started cutting across the hillside ourselves. There was no sign of the girls anywhere. We shouted, and far above heard a muffled reply. One of those unsuccessful parent-child interactions so condemned by transactional analysts followed.

'Where the hell are you? Why didn't you wait for us?'

'Why weren't you there?'

'We said wait and you should have waited.'

'But we didn't know where you were. Or where we were.'

'Where are you?'

Feeling very silly indeed by now, and still kicking down potentially lethal chips of shale on to the unsuspecting heads of the recuperating worthies who had kept to the proper path, we scrambled up to find four very tired children. It was too steep to go down at all easily, so we decided to flog on upwards. Susie was almost carried by Tom, Ellie kept up gamely, jollied along by Tilly. Daisy was rearguard, using a long stick as an iceaxe. But there was none of the lighthearted fantasy we had enjoyed on the conquest of Elbrinxen, no buffalo steaks or grog. In the back of both Tom's and my minds were those red-edged warning signs we must by now be illicitly outflanking. We could certainly hear barking in the distance. The girls and Tom sat down for a little more chocolate, and I went quickly on upwards to where I thought I could see a little light through the trees. I found a little hollow, perhaps once the base of a hut. Then some fresh young larches, a relief after the sombre scratchy pines. At last we found a track. It seemed to be going the wrong way – running north-south instead of westwards into Ilsedal, but at least it was going somewhere. We regrouped and set off southwards a little tentatively. Woodcutters had been at work, and a ladder stood leaning against a tree. Within seconds first Tilly and then Daisy shinned up it and took a view. They sighted a path westwards off the track. When we reached it we found another signpost, not dissimilar to the one far down in the valley beside Bertha: Ilsenstein 2 kilometres. We had gained no ground at all on the Ilsenstein, but we were back on the straight and narrow – and going downhill.

We eventually arrived at the Ilsenstein, a crag which jutted out over the river and offered spectacular views up and down the valley. We held hands and strung ourselves out like mountaineers to get to the famous cross itself. Then we looked hopefully upwards for a glimpse at least of the Brocken. No good. Its cloud cap was firmly in place. It had vanished for good, to remain a mystery for ever.

One final coda. Back in Oxford a few months later, I met a senior British officer stationed in Germany, not far from Hanover. I mentioned our adventures in quest of the Brocken and he told me some interesting things about it. They explained the vagueness with which all East German authorities had avoided direct answers about the Brocken and why there had been absolutely no chance of us getting anywhere near it.

'It's probably the number two target on the Nato alliance hit list. About the most powerful radio interceptor unit that the Eastern bloc possess. They sit up there voiceprinting every officer on the

Allied exercises west of the border. Lorries disguised as freight-liners and stuffed with electronic hi-spy equipment make sorties from it to top secret bases all over Europe. I wish you *had* got up there – I'd have been most interested to hear about it . . .'

We came down the track like good citizens, keeping to the marked paths. Legs buckling under them, the girls climbed into Bertha and flopped on the nearest soft surface that offered itself. It was easily suppertime, but we still had to get back to Neudorf. They woke when we got there, ate, and slept again. Tom and I passed the evening with some neighbours, West Germans on a literary

pilgrimage to Weimar and Dresden, tracking down Goethe and Luther just as we were pursuing Andersen and the rest of our pantheon of children's authors. They told us of their sadness over the contrast between the country as they had known it before the rise of the Third Reich and its present poverty and restrictions. Few people, they said, dared complain for fear of losing what little privileges they possessed. But there was widespread discontent over the concentration on exports, the absence of even such basic goods as cars, televisions and sewing machines.

What we had seen of the shops in these small towns – well off the beaten tourist track – had certainly been depressing. In the Konsums and Lebensmiths, the children screwed up their faces with disgust at the smells of stale grains and second-rate sausage, cheap soap and ersatz coffee. Good bread from the private bakers was sold out early in the morning; queues trailed outside the butchers. We had been hard put to spend the currency we had been required to buy, even though we would not be allowed to sell it back at the frontier.

The next day we drove back into the Harz to visit Rübeland, Robberland, where a bandit's castle high in the cliff had once dominated the road and taken toll from all travellers. We were aiming for Baumann's Cave, following yet another of Andersen's leads. It was named after the unfortunate miner who found the cave but lost himself, wandering around its maze of tunnels, holes and caverns, almost out of his mind with terror and hunger. He did finally crawl out – only to die two days later. Rübeland gained a more legitimate source of income than it had ever had before in mining the semi-precious stones with which the cave walls were once thickly studded.

The cave was well signposted, but not due to open for another half hour. I didn't mind waiting, because the windows of the entrance hall were filled with the best topographical stained glass that I have ever seen – jewel-clear views of Harz mountain beauty spots. I carefully took photographs of all eighteen of them, conscious of silent scepticism from the growing crowd. When I had finished I realised guiltily that the girls were the only people in the room who were talking audibly or moving perceptibly. I tried to hush them down to a suitable volume, and we began to troop with the patient throng through a long passage to the caves themselves. Our leader was a fuzzy-haired matron with sensible shoes and a military bearing, who seemed set on describing in exhaustive detail every inch of progress every stalactite had made in the last million years. I sensed immediately that she and Susie were not going to get on, and we eeled away from her as rapidly as possible. If we could have, we would have exited fast. Although the stalactites of Baumann's Cave do stick tite to the roof, and its stalagmites certainly mite get there some day, they are slimy, whey-complexioned things, lumpy to look at and loathsome to touch. But our progress was strictly regulated. March, pause to regroup, listen; march, pause to regroup, listen. The one thrill was the excellent reconstructed skeleton of an enormous bear cunningly arranged to surprise the unwary explorer. Poor crazed Baumann – I wonder if he heard or saw it? As a grand finale we were lined up rank by rank, smallest at the front, tallest at the back, and told firstly to look at the bear and secondly to watch the birdie. Flash. Preserved for posterity in a mass photograph.

Fortunately this highlight of the tour was also a leavetaking. Rebellion was brewing. The girls had been good for too long. No sooner were we out in the hot bright daylight than Susie declared her intention of blowing the whole of her £5-worth of marks on an absurdly overpriced tawdry plastic doll, tricked out in artificial silk and nylon lace. Ellie and Daisy restarted their running battle over which of the upper three sardines should sleep by the window. Tilly announced firmly that she did not want to drive any further that day because the roads in this country were far too bumpy. They were quite legitimately tired of being stared at, lost in forests, bumped over cobbles and deprived of their usual low but innocent pursuits of windowshopping, buying ice lollies and giggling together under steaming hot showers. They had right on their side, but there was still one sight that I felt was unmissable – the Roßtrapp, according to Andersen 'the wildest, the most romantic point in the whole of the Harz'. We turned Bertha towards Thale.

The gods seemed to disapprove. Perhaps they have an NSPCC in Olympus. I took the wrong road to Thale, reversed into a lumberyard to turn around, and heard a sickening crunch from the back of the van. There had been a large rock just below eye level but nicely placed to twist our exhaust pipe into a passable imitation of the original kirby-grip. Making an atrocious noise, we limped into Thale, and parked the van. Gloom descended. The last thing we had wanted to do was get mixed up with motor repairs east of the border. The AA had given us up as we crossed the frontier. This meant palavers with the police and long delays while the right spare parts were unearthed or even flown out from England.

Tom and I crouched on our haunches behind Bertha and inspected the pipe, doubled up and jammed behind the axle. He was sure the engine would overheat if we left it so pinched together. In desperation I leant underneath and yanked it backwards as hard as I could. It ought to have snapped off, but it didn't. Perhaps a shade narrow now, it was very nearly straight, and had enough of a gap in it to allow a reasonable amount of hot air to escape. Good old Bertha. Even *in extremis* she had not let us down.

We went back inside, made a large pot of coffee and settled back to enjoy a greedy elevenses. The smell of real coffee brought us a lot of wistful glances, but our guilt eased when an elderly man paused, smiled at the children, and asked us about the van in halting English. We invited him to come inside – he hesitated for a moment, then asked if he could come back in a moment with his wife. Soon we were all sitting companionably round in the back of Bertha, having a safely apolitical conversation that centred around her compact and ingenious arrangements.

'In this you could go anywhere,' said our new friend. 'You lack for nothing.'

His wife nodded, sipping her coffee with relish. The girls felt flattered on Bertha's behalf, and relieved that it was probably at her rather than at them that people stared. Quite a different complexion was put on the general interest at the next stop we made, in a small lakeside carpark. Here inquirers asked if we were Russian. A little taken aback, I drew a Union Jack on the back of a postcard and stuck it on the windscreen. There would be no sailing under false colours.

As we wound up the mountains above Thale, I realised that Andersen had not exaggerated. The gorge through which the river Bodo breaks out on to the plain is the most hair-raisingly precipitous I have ever seen. The forest clings at impossible angles to the cliffs, sheer rock curtains fall below it to churning waters and whirlpools. On the eastern side is the strange flat rock formation known as the Hexentanzplatz, the Witches' Dancing Floor; on the west is the Roßtrapp, the Hoofprint itself. We could have visited the Witches' Dancing Floor by cable-car, but we had had enough of witches for the moment. We took the road up the western side of the valley to the Roßtrapp, parked by a largish hotel, one half very grand, one half a cafeteria, and then walked through the oak woods to the edge of the gorge.

Andersen retells his guide's version of the legend – of the giants and wizards who lived in the Harz, tearing up oak trees and using them as clubs to murder women and children, of the Giant Bodo who pursued the beautiful princess Emma with her heavy gold crown and fluttering white dress to the edge of the precipice, of the girl's prayer to the Eternal to save her, of the steed who set his foot so firmly in the rock before taking off that the mark can still be seen today, of her successful leap over the abyss, and of the fall of her golden crown and the giant close behind her into the deep whirling stream.

The place is so extraordinary, the atmosphere so tangibly romantic, that any legend will do. But I found a much more complete version in Cambridge while browsing in Derek Gibbons' Haunted Bookshop, a mecca for all lovers of old children's books. As if patiently waiting for me, there was a handsome green volume – Alfred Fryer's *Fairy Tales from the Harz Mountains*, published in 1908. The very first story made much more sense of the legend, and of its sequel, the hunt for the golden crown.

The princess was not Emma but Brunhilda, and she was in love

with a King of the Harz mountains. Her father, however, preferred the suit of the Giant Bodo because of his great wealth. Brunhilda played it cool, and waited for her moment. The giant had brought her a beautiful white steed, the only match for his own giant charger, and she let him teach her how to ride it. On the very morning of her wedding, in all her finery, she leapt on its back and galloped off as fast as she could to the Harz. When she came to the edge of the precipice that divided her from the King's palace she almost despaired, but with a mighty leap the horse took off and *landed* with its foot in the famous Roßtrapp. Her crown did indeed fall off, and the giant, close on her trail, fell down with it into the deepest chasm in the abyss, the Chrysol whirlpool. He was transformed into a frightful black dog, savage guardian of the crown of his hoped-for bride.

And here was the hoofprint as proof, with a small group of sightseers standing respectfully to one side of it. The legend manages to live on without a Ministry of Works plaque to identify it – as we looked down at the great circular mark in the rock, I heard other parents telling the story to their children, with gestures towards the far-off Dancing Floor and down towards the river below.

I wondered if they were also telling them the sequel. Like Andersen's own stories, few of the Harz legends seem to have happy, straightforwardly moral endings. The Harz King whom Brunhilda loved was away at the wars. She fended off her many suitors by setting them the impossible task of recovering the gold crown. One day, home he came, and they prepared to celebrate. But a murmuring arose among the discarded suitors. What about the golden crown? Like a good sport, the king prepared to do his stuff. The river obligingly froze over to make things easier, but underneath the ice the Chrysol was still a turmoil of evil. Down he dived, and came up – the watchers could see the points of the golden crown above the foaming current. But then a frightful growling was heard – the king and the crown disappeared, and only a spume of blood could be seen. Bodo claimed his own.

'Yuk,' said Daisy. 'How horrible. Let's play touchwood.' Touchwood – a form of kick-the-can, is a good game for woods, not so good close to precipices, so Tom took them back to more level ground. I stayed for a while, looking up the valley to dark wooded ridges dovetailing into each other, regular as a child's drawing of a distant countryside. Far down below was the bridge

Andersen had climbed down and walked across, its span absurdly slender from that height. The river foamed white over the glossy black muscle of the current. There seemed no point in taking a photograph. Nothing could capture it all. 'The wildest, the most romantic point in the whole of the Harz.' Fair enough.

There was little enough of romance in the last few hours of our short eastern excursion. We bumped back along the main road to Worbis, still with money to burn. The shops there were better furnished than the bare-shelved stores we had visited up-country, but as it was past six o'clock they were all shut. The only answer seemed to be a slap-up supper. The Stadt Gasthof was a shock, a fair imitation of a Western restaurant, with dinner-jacketed waiters and a maître d'hotel who bowed and scraped like the best in Soho. I was all for ordering champagne, but Tom, already uneasy about the dinner jackets, thought it would look better to order the best of the Algerian red.

It was not a notable meal. We poked the soggy cauliflower halfheartedly, sipped the Rotgut '85 apprehensively, and wrestled with the pork chops, bending our forks in the process.

'Like the two bad mice in the dolls' house, trying to get the plaster ham off the plate,' said Susie, splattering gravy all over the tablecloth.

By the time we reached the border it was dusk. The western horizon glowed a welcome home beyond the barriers, but first we had to undergo a search much more thorough than the one on our arrival. The children were amazed to see a large mirror on wheels was rolled out and solemnly passed to and fro under the van to see if anything – or anybody – was attached underneath. The bonnet was opened, the engine inspected, all the drawers emptied, the books reshuffled. Nothing could have contrasted more startlingly with the casual waves given at all the other borders we had crossed.

'But if people want to leave the country, why don't they let them?' asked Ellie.

'Not all fairy stories have happy endings,' said Tom.

9

The Fairytale Road?

It seems far from the Castle of Grimm to the Castle of Kakfa; in our world, the hapless dreamer is hunted through all the labyrinths of nightmare by the dogs of war and monster shapes of ideology, and the bristling forest is composed of steel antennae, cyclotrons and radar equipment. But in the skies and in the grass the suns still change partners among the stars, the butterfly threads its ancient round-dance of the grub and the cocoon; and old men still remember the rumour that there is somewhere a Queen who sleeps.

(Arland Ussher and Carl von Metzradt, *Enter these Enchanted Woods*, 1958)

I feel slightly ashamed of the next episode in our journey. Months before we left on our European quest, the German Tourist Office sent me a technicoloured brochure about the Fairytale Road recently established in the heart of the Grimm brothers territory. Inspired by the success of the famous 'Romantische Strasse' or Romantic Road, which carries a million visitors a year between Würzburg on the Main and the Bavarian Alps, they decided in 1981 to transform a hitherto underrated little patch of middle Germany into a folksy wonderland. I was delighted. What could be more useful? So we were lured on to a well-beaten, highly professional tourist trail.

'And if they be not dead, then they live today' was a favourite ending to a Grimm folktale. The Tourist Office decided to provide living, profitable proof of this sanguine hope. 'Germany – a Fairyland', declared their hand-out. 'You meet them everywhere;

the kings, knights and heroes, the giants, dwarfs and sprites, the talking plants and animals, beautiful princesses, wicked step-mothers and good fairies.' From Bremen, with its Four Musicians, down to Schwalmstadt, capital of Little Red Riding Hood Coun-try, no fairytale stone had been left unturned. Rapunzel dangled from a tower at the Bad Trendelburg Hotel, Hansel and Gretel lurked in the woods near Marburg. Our own camera could snap Snow-White cavorting to a dwarf chorus in Bad Karlshafen, or Cinderella rocking and rolling at a Ronnenburg Castle disco. We had already enjoyed Hamelin's reconstructed rat-race. So what went wrong when I unfolded the brochure once again at Dransfeld, a luxurious and popular campers' paradise just west of Göttingen?

Perhaps we approached the super-efficient West Germans' touristification of romance with a jaundiced eye after our experi-ences east of the border. Glad as we were to be safely back in the land of the free, there was something obese and indigestible about the glossy car showrooms that lined the outer avenues of Göttingen. Susie missed 'the dear little East German cars'. Ellie commented on how fat everybody looked. We arrived at Dransfeld shortly before the gates closed for the night, plugged Bertha into the electric system, and slumped down in the bar with ice-cold beers and fresh chips while the children ran riot in the playground. After showers long and hot enough to make up for three days' hygienic default, we went gratefully to bed, except for Susie and Ellie. They decided that tonight was the night to sleep under the stars, and tugged sleeping bags, pillows and an extra blanket firmly outside, much to the admiration of our immediate neighbours, a plump and genial couple, who were watching us from behind the beige bistro frills of their caravan.

Either they had a very soft spot for children, or they thought the spartan Brits needed softening up. In the morning they tapped politely at the door, and offered us a delicious home-made cake for breakfast.

'Danke schön,' I said. 'But not all of it; just a slice each.'

'No, all,' they insisted. 'We have plenty more.' And so they had. They came out a few minutes later and settled down with their own breakfast – a large almond torte, washed down with cream-laden coffee.

The shelves in the campsite supermarket seemed indecently well-stocked. Why on earth does one need forty-four different sorts of biscuit, I wondered, while Tom eyed the delicatessen counter dyspeptically. The sun shone. The children had disappeared into the brilliantly blue swimming-pool. Ample semi-naked bodies ambled past arm-in-arm, gesticulating widely, talking noisily.

All of us were a little discontented, scratchy, ill at ease just when we ought to have been unwinding and enjoying ourselves. The girls snarled at each other over the giant chess pieces in the playground; Tom and I bickered beside the tumble-drier. Supper, a resolutely home-made chicken stew, somehow failed to nourish us, and even a cigar smoked in defiance of government health warnings left the cockles of my heart unwarmed. The night was noisy with weekenders carousing round their barbecues. I dreamed I was Ilse, trapped in the rocky walls of the Ilsenstein, with no gallant prince to come to my aid. Outside the trolls were relentlessly celebrating the death of innocence, but my plight was invisible.

Next morning the charms of the Fairytale Road seemed debatable. I read aloud from the brochure:

'When the hunter took pity on Snow-White and set her free, she was taken in by the seven diligent dwarfs who dwelt in the Solling-Vogler Nature Park.' Frank disbelief was spread on Daisy's face.

'The apple fell out and Snow-White awakened. After that, like a vacationer, she could delight once more at the beautiful panorama views from the Hohe Tafel.' Ellie guffawed.

Tilly was equally unimpressed by the news that Little Red Riding-Hood, the darling of Alsfeld, 'sprang out of the snoring wolf's stomach unscathed' when a passing hunter miraculously opened him up without waking him up. Nothing but anodyne glee is offered to bounty-hunters on the official trail to fairyland. No nasties in the woodshed, no *frisson*, no fears to conquer or problems to solve.

'This sounds good, Mummy,' said Ellie suddenly. She had picked up the map which we had just tossed scornfully aside. ' "Sababurg – Sleeping Beauty's enchanted castle in the Reinhardswald, a partly primeval forest. Historic walled-in wildlife park with aurochs, bison and original wild horses." What's an auroch?' None of us knew. As the crow flew, Sababurg was very close to Dransfeld, even if there was a certain amount of muddle on the map over what the roads did when they got to the Weser, still flowing broad and wide on its way from Hamelin to Hanoversch Munden. We decided to give Sleeping Beauty a try, although as far as I was concerned she ought to wait until we got to France – the Grimm brothers had lifted her neatly from Perrault's tale of the Belle au Bois Dormant. At least we would find out what aurochs were.

Appropriately enough, we managed to get lost on our way. The tiny roads simply petered out as they approached the Weser, and we seemed doomed to a major retreat. Then the little village of Reinhardshagen kindly produced a chain-ferry, and we crossed the river in grand style. As we came closer to Sababurg a forest swelled over the hills, but it was oppressively well-tended. Oak trees grew in geometrically exact rows. Orderly stacks of firebrooms, poker-work directions to ambitious hikers, asphalt roads straight as arrows into its heart: technically it may have been primeval, but no prince worth his salt could possibly get lost in it today.

The sun beating down on Bertha's roof made the setting more akin to Roaring Inferno than misty medieval romance. Then came a road sign which quite changed the atmosphere. We had become used to warnings of deer – stately plodding stags in Denmark, light-footed gazelles on Lüneburg Heath. But this was something else. Snarling jaws in a long hairy snout; forefeet braced, tail rampant.

'Wild boars!' shouted Tilly. The forest thickened overhead, darkening from translucent beeches into ancient pines. The under-growth became impenetrably thick with brambles and ivy. We saw no limp bodies of failed suitors gripped by the thorns, but I expect the aurochs had eaten them all. Just as we were wondering if Bertha could possibly bulldoze her way through to the palace the illusion vanished. The forest ended abruptly. Sababurg, its plump domes gently shrouded by a pretty wood of oak and ash, was surrounded by nothing more menacing than vast fields of oilseed rape. Broad roads approached it from three different directions, and a huge coachpark warned of hordes of visitors.

Worse was to come. Today the old fourteenth-century hunting palace of the archbishops of Mainz is a hotel. Gigantic umbrellas over the café tables gave it a carnival air, echoed by the crude chevron stripes of the wooden shutters. In a glass-fronted booth an amiable matron offered Sleeping Beauty stickers, snowstorms, plastic prismatic rulers, postcards. No poisoned spindles.

'How do you know that this was Sleeping Beauty's Castle?' I asked her as the girls frittered away a few deutschmarks.

'It says so in all the stories,' she answered shamelessly. I wondered whether to take issue with her. The only geographical reference I had discovered in the three or four best-known versions of Sleeping Beauty was to the home territory of the good fairy, 'the kingdom of Matakin, twelve thousand leagues away' mentioned by Perrault. Otherwise all authorities remain studiously vague. Time and place are awkwardly limiting frames for legends which have universal human significance, and Dornröschen, Briar Rose, is one of the most ancient of stories.

What the castle did have was exactly the right sort of tower, complete with spiral stair up which an inquisitive nubile princess could climb to meet her destiny. As we mounted higher, I could hear a father ahead of us telling the ancient story to his daughter.

'At last the handsome prince came to the tower, and opened the door into the little room where Briar-rose was sleeping. He stooped down and gave her a kiss – she opened her eyes and looked up at him sweetly. Then everyone else in the palace woke up too, yawning and stretching. The prince and princess were married straight away, of course, and lived happily ever after.'

So the popular version runs, a perfect Mills and Boon synopsis: passive maid wins love of rich and vigorous man. There used to be much more to the story. Perrault lifted his tale from a seventeenth-century Italian collection of stories by Basile, the *Pentamerone*, Basile in turn was indebted to the famous fourteenth-century prose romance *Perceforest*, an ambitious work which links Alexander the Great with King Arthur. All three have a significant variation from the Grimms' tale. Considerably more ardour than a kiss was shown by the king or prince who finds Sleeping Beauty. In fact, she gives birth to twins nine months later – still asleep. Only when one of the twins nuzzles out the poisoned splinter in her finger does she wake. But her troubles are still not over. Perrault makes his prince's mother a childeating ogre; Basile, with more convincing logic, gives a cannibal bent to his king's first wife. Happily the hero arrives in the nick of time to save Sleeping Beauty from either death at the stake or simmering in a cauldron of vipers.

Peter and Iona Opie point to the similarities between the legend and the Volsunga Saga, in which Brynhilda is touched with the thorn of sleep by Odin, and placed in a castle behind a wall of flame to ensure that she does not marry a coward. Arland Ussher and Carl von Metzradt offer a more fantastical analysis in their interpretation of the Grimms' stories, *Enter These Enchanted Woods*. They see the chamber where the old woman sat spinning as 'that Tower of confusion which is the human head and sensual body'; the spinner herself as 'one of the Fates of ancient sagas', the winding stair 'the Serpent's coil around the Tree of Life'.

These meaty elaborations give psychologist Bruno Bettelheim much food for thought, but his conclusions are slightly more down to earth. 'The message is similar to that of "Snow White": what may seem like a period of deathlike passivity at the end of childhood is nothing but a time of quiet growth and preparation, from which the person will awaken mature, ready for sexual union.' The pricking of Beauty's finger neatly symbolises menstruation. Beauty's father is over-protective – perhaps himself a trifle incestuously inclined. But he can only postpone his daughter's sexual awakening. The princes who perish in the thorns are precocious suitors – 'a warning to child and parents that sexual arousal before mind and body are ready for it is very destructive.' Once the princess has gained the physical and emotional maturity necessary for love, and with it sex and marriage, the walls of thorns turn to big beautiful flowers, and the prince can enter. 'The implied message is the same as in many other fairytales: don't worry and don't try to hurry things – when the time is ripe the impossible problem will be solved, as if by itself.' Although the German version drops the earlier specifics, its title, Dornröschen, emphasises both thorns and, by the use of the diminutive röschen, the girl's immaturity.

Should I interrupt, I wondered, and tell the little girl plodding up the stairs above me the unexpurgated truth about what life held for her? No – 'it destroys the value of a fairy tale for a child if someone details its meaning for him,' Bettelheim had written. 'All good fairy tales have meaning on many levels; only the child can know which meanings are of significance to him at the moment.'

We circled the walls towards the ruined towers and courtyard which mere tourists are allowed to ramble over while the honeymoon couples munch croissants in the Briar Rose Diner. At one point a uniquely horrible smell – decayed cabbage combined with bad eggs came to mind – rose from below the curtain wall. Three or four hairy beasts were snuffling into a large stone trough. Aurochs? Certainly wild boar, but were aurochs and boars one and the same? To be honest, we were all a little disappointed in the wild boar. They looked utterly revolting, and not all that wild. Almost complacent, in fact, as they gorged themselves on the leavings of the hotel guests.

It was only ten o'clock in the morning, but it was Sunday and sunny into the bargain. A huge American Mercury slewed up the hotel drive, some latterday prince or errant king, no doubt. Three gleaming armchair-filled highway liners, air-conditioned, and with self-contained boozing and lavatory facilities were disgorging matching sets of rubbernecks, one of golden American oldies, one of serious young Japanese, one of gum-chewing Swedes. The children were much more taken by an English doubledecker bus that had parked beside Bertha. Top Deck Travel was emblazoned on its sides. When we got back to the coachpark we looked at it more closely. We could see bunks in neat ranks upstairs, a fitted kitchen below, figures lounging on the long bench seats with cups of coffee, a shower sneaked into the conductor's cubbyhole. Our hitherto steadfast loyalty to Bertha, unshaken by the sleek recreational vehicles and elaborate Winnebagos that lorded it in the travelwagon hierarchy, wavered for the first time.

'Couldn't we buy a doubledecker bus next time, and do it up like that?' begged Tilly. 'With curtains and everything.'

'Then we could all bring a friend,' said Daisy. 'There'd be lots of room.'

'Can I bring Eleanor?' pleaded Ellie.

'I'll ask Alice Marsh,' announced Susie.

'We could go to Greece,' said Tilly. 'I wanted to go to Greece this time but you said it was too far. In a bus like this it would be brilliant.'

When we turned away from the doubledecker ('we could call ours Bertie, like in Tank-engine Thomas' said Daisy, a faraway look in her eye) we saw Bertha sitting forlornly behind us. For the first time we noticed how much grime she had accumulated over three thousand miles. An average morning mess of nighties, odd socks, papers, pens and biscuit crumbs added to the sordid *déshabillé* of her interior. We looked back longingly to the splendours of Top Deck Travel.

'Glorious, stirring sight!' murmured Toad . . . 'The poetry of motion! The real way to travel! The only way to travel! Here today – in the next week tomorrow! Villages skipped, towns and cities jumped – always somebody else's horizon! O bliss! O poop-poop! O my! O my! . . . Oh what a flowery track lies spread before me henceforth! What dust-clouds shall spring up behind me as I speed on my reckless way! What carts I shall fling carelessly into the ditch in the wake of my magnificent onset! Horrid little carts – common carts – canary-coloured carts!'

With a sudden access of remorse we rushed aboard Bertha and

began a frenzied clear-up. Windows were polished, drawers sorted out, the fridge washed down. It took us a mere half-hour, and there was only the occasional glance towards our seductive neighbour. The finishing touch was a large glittery Briar-rose sticker which Susie bought Bertha with her own money. Enough of infidelity: it was time to return to our quest, to make for Kassel, the base from which the brothers Grimm, court librarians, used to sally forth to record the tales they eventually published as their *Kinder und Haus Märchen*.

These *Household Stories* were not just for children. They used to be told to while away the hours of darkness when artificial lights

were a luxury, or for the entertainment of workers at home – spinners, weavers, and the like. Like Bettelheim, the brothers Grimm were attuned to the inwardness of the stories. In them, wrote Wilhelm Grimm, were 'fragments of belief dating back to most ancient times, in which spiritual things are expressed in a figurative manner'. There was a 'mythic element' in them, he felt, resembling 'small pieces of a shattered jewel which are lying on the ground all overgrown with grass and flowers, and can only be discovered by the most far-seeing eye.' Although their 'significa-tion has long been lost', it was still felt, and 'imparts a value to the story'.

Perhaps today some of them read as strong meat for tiny palates, but perhaps we are too protective in our modern separation of nursery life from the real world. Learning the facts of life from myths and legends is one of the oldest and most international of educations. Plato suggested the citizens of his ideal republic start their literary education with legends rather than mere facts or rational teachings. Bowdlerising the legends does us no service; it makes them empty echoes of themselves. Forewarned, they say, is forearmed. Explaining that there can be bad feelings between members of a family was a major function of folktales, and to deny the possibility of such a thing is a mystification which may cause children serious trauma.

The Grimm family had been settled in Hesse for centuries. Jacob and Wilhelm's parents married in 1783, and lived first at Hanau, then Steinau, both smallish provincial towns in the shadow of Frankfurt. Originally, it appeared, there were six little brothers Grimm and one sister, Charlotte, always called 'die liebe Lotte', and who only cried 'when too many people wanted to kiss her at the same time'. In the mornings and evenings the boys wore smocks, Jacob remembered,' tied at the back, wide shirt collars turned out, the smocks made of brown and grey floral cotton. During the day, shorter or longer jackets, made of purple linen. In winter, coats of heavy grey cloth, with white buttons.' Life at Steinau was, according to biographer Ruth Michaelis-Jena, an idyll.

They settled happily into their new home: Philipp Wilhelm, a loving father, busy, well-respected, and aware of his new and more important position, Dorothea, now thirty-five, filling the house with cheerful bustle, supervising the maids, looking after the house and garden, baking bread, making preserves, adoring her husband, and caring affectionately for her five boys . . .

The year fell into seasons naturally, a time for sowing and for reaping, and a time for gathering in the lamplit room where the linen was spun. In the spinning rooms of Steinau, perhaps, but certainly from the lips of their mother, Jacob and Wihelm heard the first Hessian tales. The countryside was full of old traditions. White ladies, fairies, elves and witches were real, and the Grimms' very home was haunted by a former town justiciary. It was a world, too, in which animals held a part quite as sensible and ordained as humans. Every spring the swallows returned, and the Grimm family almost had a private pair of storks which nested year after year on the tower outside the house. In the evening the cows came back on their own from the common grazing, while the goosegirl brought her flock home from the green.

I get a little fidgety reading this sort of account of people's childhood. Can it all have been so perfect? It seems so much more likely that an exhausted nine-times pregnant mother would snap 'Get lost' to her kids, or that the goosegirl's intentions on their father would be far from honourable. More convincing was Jacob's recollection of the weekly 'headache soup' – so-called because only a headache saved them from having to eat it – the pedantic old tutor so strict and demanding that even such a diligent little boy as Wilhelm watched the clock all through his lessons, the tension between their mother Dorothea and her widowed sister-in-law, Aunt Schlemmer.

Idyll or not, it was broken abruptly by the death of Philipp Grimm in 1796. Two years later, Jacob and Wilhelm left home to live in lodgings in Kassel and attend the High School there – they were twelve and thirteen years old. Later they went on to Marburg University, and Jacob found work as a war office clerk. But in 1808, just as the broken family was getting together again in Cassel, Dorothea herself died, leaving the twenty-three-year-old Jacob as the head of the family. Apparently the rest of their lives were devoted to recreating a family atmosphere as similar as possible to the one they so suddenly and tragically lost. What could have been more appropriate a tribute to that childhood than the creation of the *Household Tales*?

But there was more to their assiduous dredging of folk memory than nostalgia. Although they ducked their heads down behind their books as much as they possibly could during the Napoleonic wars, the Grimm brothers were both acutely politically aware. One response of German intellectuals to the pressure of Napoleon's Imperialism was to reassert the medieval vision of German wholeness – the Holy Roman Empire, the glorious days of Goslar and Henry IV. As students the brothers became 'intoxicated by joy and delight' on reading collections of ballads by the old German troubadours, the Minnesingers, and they decided to devote every moment that they could to unearthing a medieval heritage that might inspire the present. At Marburg, Wilhelm wrote in his autobiography,

the ardour with which the studies of old Germany were pursued helped to overcome the spiritual depression of those days. Without doubt, world events and the need to retire into the peace of research contributed to the re-discovery of this long-forgotten literature; but not only did we seek some consolation in the past, it was natural too for us to hope that the course we were taking would add something towards the return of better days.

That sense of purpose is an important matter to grasp, otherwise there are some strange contradictions between the legendary commitment of the Grimm brothers to authenticity and the actual elaborations and amendments they made to the tales in their collections. As John Ellis has recently pointed out in his *One Fairy Story Too Many*, not only do the stories become considerably longer over the six editions of the *Household Tales* he has examined, they are also amended quite profoundly both in meaning and content. Cinderella's sisters, he points out, did not originally come to a ghastly end dancing on redhot coals – they are generously forgiven. It was Snow-White's mother, not her stepmother, who could not face demotion to the world's second most beautiful woman. It was the father, not the devil, who cut off his daughter's hands because she would not marry him, and set her adrift in the world.

The Grimm brothers, he argues, systematically purged the stories they examined of successful crime, sex, suicide, illegitimate births, and wanton violence within the sacred circle of the family. Instead they introduced what they saw as more desirable social characteristics – respect for order and authority, veneration of courage and the military spirit, fear and hatred of outsiders, and a virulent anti-semitism. This often meant introducing more violence where they felt like driving home a moral message – hence the awful fate of Cinderella's sisters.

Which brings us to an interesting point. Ellis accuses the Grimms of deliberate falsification. After reading their own account of their methods, and considering the immense volume of scholarly achievement which their *Dictionary of the German Language*, their *DeutscheSagen* and the *KunstMärchen* represent, I don't think this can be accepted. But we may well ask ourselves why Wilhelm chose one version of a tale rather than another for publication, why he played down some elements, and emphasised others. At any one time, people will be drawn to the stories which express the mood of that time the best. What Wilhelm chose to dwell on undoubtedly reflected on his own very happy childhood, his later experience of war and uncertainty, and his consequent concern for order and authority.

144

Today we are becoming more open to our weaknesses, franker about the workings of the psyche, less afraid of ourselves. There is a new quest in progress, a desire to start again with the crude and simple truths or archetypes, to tell the stories anew. That retelling in the terms of our own times must always be the essence of the storyteller's duty. To me that was Hans Andersen's major contribution to literature. He gave the old patterns a distinctively modern slant, and the messages he conveyed in them are still relevant and meaningful to us today – if we have ears to hear them. The most

striking of all of his tales is 'The Shadow', the story of how a man's shadow escapes from him and outdoes him in worldly terms, finally enslaving the man himself as its servant. A more powerful indictment of materialism, of the divorce between the heart and the head, feeling and reason, has yet to be written.

Bruno Bettelheim has complained that some of Andersen's tales are not 'true fairy stories' because they do not offer happy endings. He defines the function of fairytales as enlightening the child about himself, fostering his personality development, offering him consolation and hope for the future. But Andersen never limited his purpose to educating children: his tales were intended to mirror every stage of a person's life, from birth to death. Psychoanalyst Stephen Wilson has seen in 'The Nightingale' a useful illustration of the struggle within an individual – in this case the Emperor – towards healthy relations with the outside world. The nightingale's simplicity and honesty contrasts with the brittle quality of the porcelain palace and the sycophantic courtiers who conceal reality from their Lord. When the Nightingale sings Death and the Emperor's fears of his misdeeds away, and then stays 'to sing of the good and evil that are lurking about you' it is a metaphor for the movement from the paranoid-schizoid personality to the more desirable and integrated depressive position – a stage not generally reached until an individual is mature. Seen in this light, 'The Nightingale' is an adult parable rather than a child's comfort.

In a sense a modern writer like Roald Dahl is doing for us today what his fellow Scandinavian Hans Andersen did for his contemporaries a century or so ago. Both appeared to be writing for children, both have adults as their final target. Both convey a forceful sense of morality, of right and wrong, behind their fantastical humour and nonsense. But they are also realists. The children in their stories are not always pretty or good; sometimes they come to terrible ends – sometimes they win through, despite hideous witchlike parents and grandparents. Parents today feel as uneasy reading Roald Dahl as they once did reading Andersen – but it is far healthier for them to do so, and to accept the limits of the protection they can offer their children, than to try and preserve a perfectly innocent world all round them – a glass bubble which, once shattered, leaves the child defenceless. A Mills and Boon Sleeping Beauty is an anachronism now, but the original parable about maturity has a value that will outlast the brittle fantasy of romance.

10

Castles in the Air

Maps are not reality at all – they can be tyrants. I know people who are so immersed in road maps that they never see the countryside they pass through, and others who, having traced a route, are held to it as though held by flanged wheels to rails.

(John Steinbeck, *Travels with Charley*)

As we drove out of Kassel we found ourselves aimed down a great boulevard straight at an incredibly sited palace. It stood halfway up a hill, in a massed treescape that Capability Brown couldn't have bettered. Above it, formal gardens led up to a gigantic statue of Hercules, built on a scale to make it a fair match for the Trafalgar Square Lord Nelson. The trouble with great tourist attractions is that they can be irresistibly attractive. I leafed through the green Michelin Guide. This was clearly Wilhelmshöhe, the German Versailles. And Hercules actually outdid Horatio – 71 metres to the British hero's paltry 52. The huge castle park was laid out for the Landgrave of Hesse in 1701, and rapidly became a standard Grand Tour attraction because of its astoundingly ambitious cascades.

'The best time for a walk', Michelin informed us temptingly, as if it knew it was noon on a Sunday, 'is when the fountains are playing, at 2.30 p.m. on Wednesdays, Sundays and holidays. Go up to Neptune's Basin at the foot of the great cascade; wait until the first falls are in full flow, then follow the water down to see the various features at their best: the Steinhofer Wasserfal rocks, the Devil's Bridge, the ruins of the Roman Aqueduct and finally the Great Plume of the castle's major pool.' This unforgettable experience would take us an hour. We needed somewhere to picnic – what could be better? There were certainly crowds of people waiting to

147

be astounded by the waterworks, but Wilhelmshöhe is on such a gigantic scale that they made about as much impact as a colony of ants on Silbury Hill. Antlike ourselves, we toiled up the steep hillside past the palace and found an artfully natural cascade to pose on for lunch. Beer and fizzy lemonade flowed freely; spirits were high, feet wet. There seemed to be plenty of time before the 2.30 deluge to visit the palace, which a collection of Rembrandts, Titians and Breughels made a three-star attraction.

Normally our progress through picture galleries and museums is indecently rapid, but today was different. We bought the girls each four postcards in the entrance hall, and then set them the challenge of finding the originals. Since the gallery is spread over three enormous floors of the palace, linked with slick steel lifts, Tom and I very soon lost sight of all four of them, and enjoyed a restful halfhour guessing painters wrongly. I was unmoved by the grinning Jan Steens and the florid Franz Hals. What captivated me were the early Renaissance Italian masters. I'd spent three months in the little Tuscan hilltown of Perugia before going to university, and suddenly I was back in my teens, wandering happily around Assisi and Siena. Germany palled. Like Hans Andersen I felt the pull of the South. He had visited Wilhelmshöhe himself on the way to Italy, but had been more moved by the sight of the name of Napoleon, his father's superhero, painted over but still visible on a wall in Kassel than by the artificial wonders of the park.

Occasionally we glimpsed the children passing to and fro at different levels, pressing lift buttons, flourishing their cards importantly. After half an hour or so every keeper in the place seemed to be helping them to search. Some of the pictures were in reserve collections, others were in special galleries opened only between two and four in the afternoon. At last we were led up and down and round about to each set of paintings, by now regarded as personal possessions.

Time had passed fast. Through the windows of the gallery we could see an army of waterwatchers marching up towards the fountains. It was nearly 2.30. There was no hope of getting to Hercules' feet before the waterfalls began, so we settled for a halfway position close by the Devil's Bridge, in the company of a Dutch TV team. The coming of the waters was heralded by the descending crowds, scampering to position themselves at snapshot distance from the bridge. Then came the climax as the water first trickled, then surged, down the fifty-foot ivy-hung cliff under the bridge. The TV camera was spattered with spray, and Flemish curses punctuated the oohs and aahs of more cautious spectators. Caught in a flood of people heading for Pluto's Grotto, we had to race downhill for the next miracle plunge. It wasn't long before being washed along by a living river of lemmings in relentless sunshine lost its attraction. We deserted, skipping downhill through kneehigh grass thick with wild flowers to the carpark ice-lolly stall, never to experience the final wonder of the Great Plume.

Close to Kassel is Frankfurt, where in the small backstreet of Schubertstrasse a museum is devoted to Heinrich Hoffman, author of what has been seen as the most bizarre of all children's books – *Struwwelpeter*. Children are fascinated by it, but adults have their doubts. Even Freud declared himself foxed. Donald Brinkmann's theory that 'a certain formal relationship exists between the Indian God Shiva the Destroyer and the defiant hero of Hoffman's book' seems a shade strained, despite Hoffmann's known involvement with a group of intellectuals interested in Indian mythology. Jungian seekers after symbols of the collective unconscious are interested in the similarities between the shaggy-haired, talon-fingered image of Peter and the masks worn by Balinese dancers. In 1954 a detailed analysis of its hidden meaning was attempted by a Freudian with none of Freud's uncertainties. Rudolph Friedmann spotted the message from the instant he saw the teapot – 'of course, the missing penis' – tumbling from Santa Claus' sack towards the little girl on the first page of the book. Struwwelpeter – shock-headed Peter – 'really is a shock'.

He is a castrated child, grown fat as a result of glandular disturbance caused by the castration. His hair is a luminous halo of uncombed black and yellow out of which a frightened feminine face tries to gaze with schizoid severity and direction to compensate for the lost and holy genital eye . . .

To make up for the genital loss his outstretched hands possess five fingernails uncut and grown into five long sadistic claws sharp like erect tails. And yet the claws are no longer really cruel, there is only a façade of cruelty. The whole growing pyknic obesity of the figure gives the nails a self-crucifying and drooping look; just as the hair at its ends curls again inwards and downwards onto the breast of introversion. There are no life-lines or heart-lines on these outstretched hands, openly stigmata forming little folds of death. The whole figure, dating from 1845, as one is moved by its mute message to unveil it, is a tragic commentary on the impending fate of the German Nation.

When I got to the moment in Friedmann's commentary when the Inky Boys are tossed by Agrippa, 'the punishing father and still living German super-ego', back into 'the black well of their mother's womb to be reminded of their origin' I thought I could probably stop reading. Why did things have to be so complicated? To my mind, the inkwell punishment of the three little racist pigs was well-earned, Cruel Frederick got no more than his just deserts for whipping the faithful dog Tray, and Harriet, the pyromaniac fool, should jolly well have done what she was told.

But after all, Hoffman was a psychiatric surgeon, founder of the Frankfurt State Asylum, and particularly interested in mentally disturbed children. His *Observations and Experiences on Mental Disturbances in connection with Epilepsy* was published in 1859, and for thirty-eight years, much respected for his understanding and humanity, he was the house surgeon at the Asylum. In his introduction to later editions of the book, Hoffman explained that *Struwwelpeter* was written and drawn as a Christmas present for his three-year-old son because he could find nothing in the shops but 'long tales, stupid collections of pictures, moralising stories, beginning and ending with admonitions like "The good child must be truthful".' This he thought a waste of time, as 'a child does not reason abstractly'. One tale or fable would 'impress him more than hundreds of general warnings'. Hoffman came home, took an exercise book, and started to compose a picture-book himself. He had already published a small book of verses privately, and habitually put his small patients at their ease by drawing them comic figures as he took down their case histories. The book – originally called 'Merry Stories and Funny Pictures' – delighted not only his son but his own friends, who eventually persuaded him to allow it publication. It was an immediate success – selling out its first edition in four weeks, and running into its hundredth on the 31st anniversary of its invention.

The attraction of *Struwwelpeter* was not limited to German readers. One of the most remarkable aspects of the Frankfurt museum's collection is the range of its foreign language editions – from the interestingly early Russian edition of 1857, to the interestingly late Japanese *Bobo Atama* of 1936, and the Hebrew *Jiftach Hamelukhlakh* of 1970. *La Struvelpetro* was made available in Esperanto in 1921. Mark Twain translated it as *Slovenly Peter* for the benefit of his own children, W. H. D. Rouse made *Petrulus Hirrutus* the plaything of the classical sixth in 1934. Finally, in 1985 a polyglot *Struwwelpeter* was published, in the original German and in new, specially commissioned English, French, Spanish, Italian and Latin translations, to warn children of the perils of thumbsucking in six different languages. There are a few losses in the scrupulously accurate new English translation. Harriet is more rightly called Pauline and originally had no Nursy, only her mother, to advise her against lighting matches; Faithful Tray was merely a 'large dog' that happened to be passing. Still, to compensate, the horrid Agrippa is revealed as not Agrippa or a 'punishing father-figure' at all, but St Nicolas, Father Christmas himself.

What the polyglot translation does show very well is the light-heartedness of the original German. The commonest vices of child-hood are pilloried in a totally absurd manner – the book is not an attempt to moralise but a parody of a cautionary tale. It is actually making fun of parents' attempts to discipline their children – Harvey Darton described the collection as 'the Awful Warning carried to the point where Awe topples over into helpless laughter'. The only flaw in it is the Scissorman; absurd as the idea of cutting off a child's thumbs is, Hoffman's image of it is too vivid to be easily forgotten.

Or was it Hoffmann's image? I looked again at the original lithographs, which Hoffman took great care to have copied accurately 'to make sure my amateurish style was not artificially improved or idealized', and then at the much better-known illustrations redrawn for the wood engraving process in 1868. Hoffman's Peter is a mucky little beast, with hair straggling over his shoulders and longish fingernails, but with none of the 'schizoid severity' or 'frightened femininity' seen by Friedmann. And the unpleasant face (to Friedmann the punishing parent) which grins above the stricken thumbless figure after the visit of the Scissorman simply does not exist in Hoffman's version – nor do the gory drips of blood from the hands. It appears that the person responsible for the savager aspects of *Struwwelpeter*, the anonymous wood-engraver who made the illustrations now generally accepted as authentic, was not Hoffman at all.

Undeniably there are dark ambiguities behind the crude images of *Struwwelpeter*, but in its original intent, I believe the book's nonsense was in the same essentially innocent class as that of Edward Lear – although maybe somebody somewhere has all sorts of theories about the Blue Baboon from the Land of Tute. It has suffered, like many of the best children's stories, from a certain squeamishness among adults: an unwillingness to let children in on the unpleasantness of the world which lies ahead of them. If we hide away *Struwwelpeter*, along with the gorier of the fairytales, Roald Dahl's grubby Twits and Raymond Briggs' revolting *Fungus the Bogeyman*, we risk creating bored, vulnerable children with no idea what a messy world they are growing up into.

As I muddled myself thoroughly over meaning and deeper meaning, Tom gave Bertha her head down the autobahn. We had a wild urge to move really fast across the map of Europe. The children were established at the table, happily creating their own versions of the *Struwwelpeter* saga. We had discovered that they preferred a long, uninterrupted drive to one major objective rather than a day punctuated by short halts, and the space and facilities of the camper made possible far more progress than we could have made in the cramped quarters of an ordinary car. Bertha swept along the motorway, making a steady 60 or 65 miles an hour across the huge central German plateau. By six o'clock we were bypassing Würzburg, having achieved a dramatic five-inch drop southwards. We stopped only once, to buy petrol and a map of Italy. Tilly made an odd discovery on the garage's sweet counter: a packet of good old English Love-hearts, made in Stockport, Cheshire, but with German mottoes. It was heartening to feel that British enterprise was not yet quite dead.

Our plan was to dart off the motorway at Rothenburg-ob-Tauber, a walled medieval hill-town that Jane had recommended very highly. Unfortunately I misread the motorway signs and set off inexorably eastwards to Nürnburg instead of southwards to Rothenburg. Hungry, hot, tired, accelerator-foot aching, I was close to tears as we took the next exit, and hacked across country on mystifying backroads that seemed to take a malicious pleasure in tapering into cul-de-sacs or doubling back on idiosyncratic diversions. An Inn sign promised rural comforts, fine prospects, local specialities, so we wound up a little lane for a much-needed rest. There was an ominous scattering of Mercedes, two Volvos and a Porsche in the carpark, and the restaurant door was papered with credit card stickers. I looked at the menu. One main dish cost

Sieh einmal, hier steht er,
pfui, der Struwwelpeter!
An den Händen beiden
ließ er sich nicht schneiden
seine Nägel fast ein Jahr;
kämmen ließ er nicht sein Haar.
Pfui, ruft da ein jeder:
Garstger Struwwelpeter!

roughly what we reckoned to spend on a meal for the whole family. Wearily we retreated. I gave up the wheel to Tom and sulked.

Fate suddenly relented. We found ourselves in Ochsenfurt, an appropriate home from home for an Oxenford family. Some towns have instant appeal, and Ochsenfurt's unpretentious air of solid comfort was just what we needed. We parked the car underneath a tower that Ellie plausibly identified as Rapunzel's and wandered off to find a restaurant. We were not by then particularly fussy about either food or price, but were lucky enough to find somewhere that suited both purse and palate perfectly. The Golden Lion Gast Haus was heavy with woodcarvings, thick with pipe-smoke and noisy

with juke-box and one-armed bandit. A motherly waitress putt frothing biersteins in front of Tom and me, iced orange juice in front of the children. After wienerschnitzels all round – kinderschnitzels for the girls – served with crisp fresh chips and a salad of pickled vegetables, we were in a state to become expansive, even witty.

'Wouldn't do to look a gast haus in the mouth,' Tom offered. I didn't even wince. The girls fell about. More and more excruciating puns were supplied. Weak with laughing, comfortably full, we wandered back to the van. Somewhere a brass band was playing waltzes, the sun was setting, a road sign frankly admitted the whereabouts of Rothenburg, and we set off with new energy. Eating out was not something we reckoned to do very often – I felt it reflected badly on the commissariat not to cook in the van. But on occasions like this, when we were all too tired to be civilised, we felt we needed a little cherishing.

Because of these human frailties, we didn't reach Rothenburg until around eight o'clock in the evening. Still, we quickly discovered that this was probably the best time for a large family of limited means to visit the star attraction of the Romantische Strasse. Every other house appeared to be a hotel or restaurant, every shop full of covetable goodies. We pressed our noses to the window panes of the Christmas shop, which was offering a passable pageant of Hoffmann's King Nutcracker, the story of how all the Christmas toys unite to give poor sick Reinhold a merry Christmas. Splendid wooden King Nutcrackers glared back at us, dressed in every military uniform under the sun, and ranging from a giant bigger than Tom to a thumbsize dwarf. A glittering Christmas tree, surreal on a hot midsummer night, displayed mouthwatering marzipan decorations; angel chimes swung round slowly in the warmth of the spotlights.

'What a pity it's closed,' said Tilly.

'Yes, isn't it?' I replied disingenuously.

Dusk was falling as we walked through the symmetrically curved streets, thick with carved gables and geranium-filled window boxes. Pointed turrets, round bottle-glass panes blinking in overhanging bay windows, half-timbered balconies topped with faded red tiles, graceful wrought-iron signs silhouetted against the sunset: On the façade of one particularly fine building we saw statues of the seven virtues and seven vices, alternately male and female, good and bad. Compassion flanked Gluttony, Motherly Love jostled Treachery. Family life in a stony nutshell. Rothenburg is almost absurdly picturesque, a perfect setting for fairytales.

We walked through an intricate triple gateway into the Castle Gardens, built out on a spur of the city walls. By now it was completely dark, and we could look back to the lights and imagine ourselves back in the Middle Ages. Walled towns had a special attraction for the children. Perhaps it was the security of their stone embrace, perhaps the ease with which the shape of the city could be seen from the vantage point of the ramparts. They raced around the dark gardens, discovering grottoes and low box-hedged mazes, and leaning over the outer walls in defiance of gravity to admire the multicoloured searchlights trained on the city's towers.

Then, quite suddenly, they tired. So did Tom and I. Surfeited with showpiece cuteness, we limped back across the town to the van. The illusion was fading. Rubbish bins were overflowing with fastfood debris, cans and bottles. Cars were perched on every scrap of kerb. Why on earth not make the city a pedestrian precinct like Hamelin? Even the appearance of two drummers and a piper beating the curfew in seventeenth-century costume failed to delight us. We tucked the children into bed and headed south again. The plan was to drive until we dropped but it didn't take long to admit defeat. Oncoming lights seemed more dazzling than usual, cars behind us more aggressive. That night's campsite was rock-bottom – just a shallow lay-by on the road – but none of us flickered an eyelid all night.

The next day was Whit Monday. We woke around five, made some tea, and drove on without waking the children. Dawn is easily the best time to cover long distances in Bertha, and the Romantische Strasse lived up to its name: hills wreathed in mist, a red orb of a rising sun, a flight of grey doves against the bright pastels of Nordlingen's houses, and not another soul stirring. Three hours later we were nearing the Austrian Alps and the tourist's Holy Grail, the fantastical castles of Mad King Ludwig. Our timing was perfect. We would be among the first rubbernecks to arrive, able to leave before the doubledecker fleets caught up with us. But once again the siren song of the guide book drew us astray.

Wies church, an amazing realization of Bavarian Rococo art, stands amid forests, peatbogs and meadows that characterize the last slopes of the Ammergau Alps . . .
　　The lower parts – the walls and paired pillars defining the ambulatory – are deliberately sparsely decorated, for in the mind of the decorator they symbolise the Earth, while the upper parts, symbolising the heavens, are thick with paintings, stuccoes and gilded work. The immense fresco on the dome shows Christ returned, the Gate to Paradise and the Last Judgement before the Judge has arrived.
　　The choir has an unparalleled decoration: columns, balustrades, statues, gilded stuccoes and frescoes make up an extraordinary symphony of colour.
　　The organ and its loft and pulpit mark the height of Rococo art in Southern Germany by the delicacy and richness of their carvings.

I vaguely felt that we had been a little remiss on visiting churches so far. At least one set of the children's twenty-four godparents reckoned to take in dozens of churches on any European tour worthy of the name; reproaches could follow. And some out-rageous rococo excesses would be a good contrast to the Lutheran restraint of Haarlem, Ærøskøbing, and Lübeck. At ten to eight we drew up outside the little rural paradise of Wies to the sound of a tolling bell. Velvety-skinned dun cows wading through fields of buttercups echoed it with their own dull chimes. Dark-timbered barns on the fringes of the fir-trees, snow-capped mountains on the skyline – our first sight of the Alps. And a church unlike anything we had ever seen, ochre and white under a red-tiled roof. It was simple and restrained enough from the outside, but something about the flaring curves of the windows hinted at the riot of colour inside. The local residents were strolling up the path to the church in Tyrolean Sunday best: lederhosen, rakish feathered hats, black velvet bodices and bright print skirts. I was puzzled for a moment, and then light dawned. *Whit* Monday. Masses every hour.

Should we turn round and forget it, or hang about until the service was over, then creep in briefly before the next one began? A friendly smile from a waitress in the little guest house close beside the open door of the church decided us. The girls and I rummaged in our lockers for skirts and respectable shoes; hats we couldn't manage. Tom unwillingly forced his feet into heavy leather lace-ups. In full fig we sat down at a table outside the guest house and ordered a Bavarian breakfast: thick trenchers of bread, butter and jam, frothing hot chocolate and strong black coffee, pretty blue and white china.

It was not a restful meal. The long day before cooped up in the van had left the girls with lots of frustrated energy, but since we could hear the chanting congregation, they could no doubt hear us. Tom and I shushed ineffectually. Before long a plate had smashed to the ground with a crash worthy of the last trump, and the waitress's smile began to evaporate. The size of the bill made me realise ruefully that we could have made a passable Bavarian breakfast and as much noise as we liked in the van at a fraction of the cost to pocket and peace of mind. Still, the organ was thundering dismissive chords, and the children were temporarily silenced by the fine display of traditional costumes exiting from the church.

We lurked in the shadows until the last of the devotees had left, then made for the entrance. I had deliberately kept the girls away from the souvenir stall so that the full impact of the 'extraordinary symphony of colour' could be made.

'Close your eyes, everyone,' I carolled, Joyce Grenfell to the life, and led them into the church. Then I was struck dumb. Not by the 'unparalleled decoration' but by the thick shrouds of sacking, the towers of scaffolding, and the general dinginess that decorators bring with them. We had hit Wies at an all-time low – it was in process of restoration. The spectacular surprise was ruined – I felt as disappointed as a small child who happens on Father Christmas having a quick fag in the kitchen. The girls did their best, running from saccharine madonnas to bedizened saints with enthusiasm.

'We do like it – very much,' Daisy assured me.

'The ceiling's really beautiful,' said Tilly.

Grubby putti simpered from the intricate pulpit; St Peter beamed down from his veiled sentry box. We went outside and bought postcards of Wies as it wasn't.

Tom spun Bertha's wheels towards Fussen and the Chitty-chitty Bang-bang castle of Neuschwanstein. We would be arriving there at about ten o'clock, not late but not early either. A deep loathing of guidebooks began to grow inside me. What tyrants they are, telling travellers what they ought to see, instead of leaving them to explore for themselves. By offering so many attractions they give their readers a constant sense of opportunities missed, luring them off their chosen trails, and complicating sensibly simple ambitions. Worst of all they destroy the magic of the very places they elect as magical.

Nowhere is this more true than at Neuschwanstein. When King Ludwig wrote to Richard Wagner in 1868 that he planned 'to re-build the ancient castle ruins of Hohenschwangau near the Poellat Gorge in the true style of the ancient German knights' castles', he did not foresee the 30-acre coachparks, the interminable queues of tourists doubling back and forth like cattle between rails in the courtyard, the desolate unlived-in fate of his dream palace. Getting to Neuschwanstein, the New Castle of the Swans, had been a much anticipated treat. Back at home we had all gloated over pictures of its tapering white towers, its green turrets, its incredible setting among lakes and mountain peaks.

The first glimpse of it from the road into Fussen was spectacular enough. The truly romantic traveller should stop right there, get out his telescopic lens, take some photographs at dawn or dusk, through fresh spring fronds, autumn colours or amid the winter's snow. Then he must about face and retreat, leaving his illusions unshattered. But nobody will take that advice. Like us, they will follow the broad highway to the Hohenschwangau carparks, debate whether to walk the steep mile to Neuschwanstein on foot or ride up, for a stiffish price, in a horsedrawn wagon. They may or may not disagree as we did, but perhaps the information that it is actually quicker to walk than to ride will settle a few family disputes.

The feelings of unreality grew as we followed the herd upwards. At closer quarters the castle seemed to have been put together with breezeblocks; it was grey rather than white. Unweathered, perfectly false, Legoland in Brobdingnag. It was almost a relief to turn to the souvenir stalls, festooned with the famous image against clouds, snow, autumn russets, or spring flowers, and applied indiscriminately to dishcloths, table mats, and ashtrays. When we finally walked through the gateway into the inner courtyard it was with a sense of anticlimax. We joined a throng of sightseers milling rebelliously around the entrance. No one looked entranced. Bossy couriers increased the bad feeling by jostling their flocks imperiously past the independent tourists. I was determined to stay patient. After all, there weren't that many people in front of us, and from the postcards on sale it looked as if the interior was fabulously exotic. A famous place like this was bound to be crowded. And of course the tickets would be expensive – I didn't even bother to translate deutschmark to sterling. There was no going back at this point. We shunted past the ticket office at last, then up a broad spiral stair, enjoying the great vistas framed in its narrow windows. But then came another halt, in a long corridor with iron barred gates at the far end. It appeared that we would have to wait again, this time for a tour in our own language. Tom, not the most patient of men at the best of times, began to champ a little. A French tour was announced, and a large squad of Parisians began to press their way forward. We glanced at each other, grabbed the children's hands and followed on. The courier barred our way.

'Mais vous comprenez français?'

'Bien sûr!' I exclaimed firmly. 'Ça va très bien'. The girls' jaws dropped, but they followed.

'I didn't know Mummy could speak French like that,' said Ellie. 'It sounded really French.' I felt my stock had risen, but the triumph was a brief one. Although we could understand the guide's slow French, the girls were bored by it. Translating took time, and they didn't like the way everybody else's interest turned away just as theirs focused. By now Tom was being openly subversive, suggesting that we lag behind or race ahead of the tour and try to get the feel of the castle itself. Unfortunately tour followed tour so quickly that either ploy led us into collision with another group. We gave up, and trailed along obediently. The rooms were gloomier, darker, and smaller than they look in photographs and playing 'spot the swan' soon lost its charm. Even Ludwig's famous bedroom, with the heavy wooden tracery that took fourteen sculptors four and a half years to complete, was ultimately absurd. Who in their senses

could sleep easy when wherever they looked they saw Tristan panting after Isolde, or Isolde panting after Tristan? I wasn't at all surprised to learn that Ludwig had never been married and had spent fewer than a hundred days actually living in the palace.

We were too weary of official organisation to look over the neighbouring castle, Hohenschwangau. In 1854, before Neuschwanstein was thought of, Hans Andersen had sipped tea there with Maximilian II, and chatted to his nine-year-old son Ludwig, an eccentric small boy who already had a passion for swans. Andersen sympathised, himself a swan-lover. The swan motif decorated Hohenschwangau because this was the country of the legendary Lohengrin, son of Parsifal, who was led by a swan to rescue the Princess Elsa. A few weeks before, Andersen had visited Maximilian and his queen at their hunting lodge on Lake Starnberg.

When they sailed on the lake, Maximilian asked Andersen to read some stories to him. Andersen chose, as he often did, the 'Ugly Duckling'. Thirty-four years later Ludwig, by then a living legend in eccentricity, drowned himself and his doctor on the same lake a few days after he had been declared insane.

The children were overdue for a decent break. We had promised them three or four days beside the sea near Venice; no driving, just swimming, sunning and busboats into Venice itself, and a pretty summer outfit from the Italian chainstore, Standa. So we belted on again – through a narrow strip of Alpine Austria, nodding at the suburbs of Innsbruck, admiring the formidable engineering of the Brenner Pass, spending a night on the fjordlike shores of Lake Garda, a windsurfer's mecca, and finally crossing the vast flat valley of the Po to arrive at Punta Sabbione, the tip of the arm of Venice's great lagoon. Italy at last.

11

Harlekins and Gondolas

'Is it so nice as all that?' asked the Mole shyly, though he was quite prepared to believe it as he leant back in his seat and surveyed the cushions, the oars, the rowlocks, and all the fascinating fittings, and felt the boat sway lightly underneath him.

'Nice? It's the *only* thing, said the Water Rat, solemnly, as he leant forward for his stroke. 'Believe me, my young friend, there is nothing – absolutely nothing – half so much worth doing as simply messing about in boats . . .'

(Kenneth Grahame, *The Wind in the Willows*, 1908)

Well, it looked like Italy. The countryside was picturesque enough. Sad cypresses flanked robber strongholds in the Dolomite gorges. The immaculate wooden chalets of the Austrian Alps had changed to dilapidated farmhouses with crumbling terracotta roofs and peeling plaster walls. Olive groves and vineyards replaced the flowery alpine pastures.

'It's funny,' said Tilly. 'The houses here are shabby again, like they were in East Germany, but it doesn't look as if the Italians mind, somehow. It looked as if the East Germans couldn't afford to do anything up. But it looks as if the Italians can't be bothered.'

Perhaps one of the reasons for their inertia was the steady roar of German engines heading down to the coast. Roadsigns were in German as well as Italian, garages were little meccas of souvenirs calculated to attract the Teuton en fête, and every other car sported a large D or A.

When we finally negotiated the long flat road that winds through the delta of the Po to its farthest tip, Punta Sabbione, and collapsed into a chintz-shaded restaurant for our first Italian meal, the waitress greeted us with a 'Guten Tag' and handed us a menu in German. I countered with a torrent of inaccurate Italian enthusiasm. It was a little rusty after twenty years' neglect of those Perugian grammar books, but she took it kindly. A pair of Austrian honeymooners were lingering over their capuccino at a neighbouring table. As our zuppa di pesce, tagliatelle al burro, gnocchi and vitello tonnato were delivered, a lowslung white Mercedes convertible roared up, and a lowslung tanned Wunderjugend swaggered up to order ein bier. We began to understand why the waitress found it impossible not to lapse into German.

The story was the same at the enormous campsite that we trundled into late in the afternoon, Marina di Venezia. Marina di Munich would have been an apter name. Lacking a natural Brighton to Bournemouth leisure strand, the Germans and Austrians have adopted the Tyrrhenian gulf as a south coast of their own. Although the supermarket tannoy was bravely broadcasting *Rigoletto*, its meat counter was thick with wurst and its wine shelves loaded with Liebfraumilch. We needn't have bothered to change our deutschmarks to lira at the frontier; they were being accepted at the checkouts here as unquestioningly as if they were local currency.

Not that this worried us very much at the time. The real Italy could wait. We were looking for a limbo and we had found one. The whole 600-metre square campsite is dedicated to providing well-regulated ease for its several hundred guests. Far more completely than in any campsite we had yet been to, each little unit had created a never-never-land world of wendy house chic. Shops in the campcity centre encouraged the completion of these flimsy domestic dreams in miniature by offering the tinny gadgetry at 'affordable prices': campari-people parasols with matching white fringed folding chairs, barbecues fired by Calorgas pokers, insulated bags to keep things cold, battery-heated casseroles to keep things hot. Everything could be done on site, from carwash to coiffure, from developing photographs to disco-dancing. There was even a church.

Siesta time was taken seriously. Punctually at 12.30 every day the loudspeaker network announced the closure of the gates from 1.00 to 3.00 and a prohibition on radios and loud noises of any kind. Relaxation was taken like medicine by the obedient family groups, slumped on airbeds, swooning in hammocks, snoring in recliners. Even the weather was regulated: a fresh, sharp dawn, a sweltering calm at midday, a light evening breeze, a midnight shower. Nothing was allowed to impede the slow systematic roasting of worthy citizens. A few teenagers were defiantly debauching themselves in tents pitched pioneer-style around central hearths of charred sticks and empty bottles, but even they were subdued by the bourgeois complacency all around.

We were happy enough, with Bertha parked as close to the beach as we could get her. More than slightly anaesthetised to new impressions by the litre – can it have been a litre? – of Po valley white we'd downed quite effortlessly over our belated lunch, Tom and I watched the children drag out their swimsuits, towels, buckets and spades and disappear towards the promised sand. By the time we followed them, they knew everything there was to know, and rained the information on to our torpid minds. The ice-lollies in the beach café were much too expensive. It was better to buy them in the supermarket. I would be able to windsurf tomorrow when the head of the school came back from buying new boards in Munich. The water was really warm, and the sand ideal for building castles.

I was struck by how intrepid and enterprising they had become. I thought back to the first cold clammy morning at Hook of Holland, the tense moments in the pool at Duinrel, the many greater or lesser panics we had negotiated since then, the different languages they had grappled with, the strange foods and unpredictable encounters. And here they were, irrepressibly high-spirited, racing across the beach into brand-new waters with no hesitation at all.

That night we feasted on kebabs and cherries, and, elated by the holiday atmosphere, planned a midnight swim. That is, five of us did. I am ashamed to say that I sank into so deep a state of stupor after supper that I completely failed to go for a bathe myself, but Tom told me in the morning that it had been wonderful, incredibly warm, phosphorescent, and all the things a midnight swim should be. Next day was for 'la dolce far niente'; making and mending, lying in the sun, gliding across glassy waters on a battered Hi-Fly in a force 2 breeze. Tom and the girls took their maths books down to the beach, a small but dynamic thinktank among the lotus-eaters on their lilos, while I studied the guidebooks to Venice.

Clearly, there were far too many unmissable sights. Even the most halfhearted attempt to do the city justice would leave us footsore and frustrated. There would be time enough for them to 'do' Venice when they were older. In fact it would be altogether healthier for them to see it in their own right rather than trailing in our wake. We just wanted to give them a few glimpses of its unique character – a city of dreams floating on a fairytale lagoon. So we could ignore the Accademia and its masterpieces, the endless staircases and corridors of the Ducal palace, the gloomy splendours of the Tintorettos in the Scuola San Rocca. We would approach by water to preserve the island illusion and limit their picture of Venice to a city of carnival and craftsmen, of boats and waterways.

'Can we go in a gondola?' asked Tilly. Tom and I looked at each other. On our own in Venice two years before, we had turned up our noses at the gondoliers who had importuned us at every canal-bridge. With the children, true romantics, things seemed different. Maybe this was the time to try one.

'All right. If they aren't too expensive.'

Since we planned to laze at Marina di Venezia for three or four nights, we reckoned we could make about three early evening sorties into the city. Boats left on the hour, and took three-quarters of an hour to get to the Grand Canal. Bertha was cooped up by the afternoon moratorium on activity, so we set off on the afternoon of our second day in plenty of time to walk the two kilometres to the 'bus-stop' – the boat station on the lagoon side of Punta Sabbione. I stopped off at the camp office to collect our passports – we only had enough money for a oneway ticket into Venice and the campsite bank was having its siesta. Catastrophe. Our passports were locked up in the bank's safe. I tore my hair in fine Italian style, and a lugubrious girl ambled off to see if she could rouse somebody. Tom and the girls set off for the boat while I waited for her return. Miraculously she did find Tom's passport at least, and I set off at a jog trot in the sun to catch up the rest of the family.

They were far ahead on the long dusty road, heads skewing round anxiously to see if I was following. Bless their loving hearts. To my despair, when they did see me, they started running back to join me. What had been good time to catch the boat was fast evaporating. Puffing and panting we finally got to the boat station with ten minutes to spare. The best-laid plans . . . Originally we'd planned to camp at the very nearest site to the boat station, Miramare, but since it was just inside the lagoon itself, it had no beach, and the promise of a swimming pool seemed no substitute for proper sea and sand.

The boat arrived; the girls wriggled ahead to get seats up on the top deck, then changed their minds and explored the saloon, then reversed yet again to find their original choices filled by suburban Venetians, who were eyeing them with detached amusement. After some courteous reshufflings by sympathetic neighbours, we were all seated together. The ship's siren barked a farewell, and we moved off across the glassy surface of the lagoon. Near and far islands floated, their reflections gently blurred by the rhythmic wake from the steamer. Fishermen inspected their nets, great spider's webs hung out to dry on the shores. A speedboat careered past, its bows raked high out of the water, its steersman lying sideways across the stern gazing up at the sky. Hazy in the distance the turrets and domes of the Venetian skyline shimmered like a mirage.

'There was a lagoon in Peter Pan, wasn't there?' said Daisy. 'John's dreamworld was a lagoon with flamingoes flying over it, and Michael's was flamingoes with lagoons flying over.'

'Do you think there are any crocodiles?' said Ellie. Susie looked nervously over the rail.

'No,' I said firmly. 'It isn't that sort of lagoon.'

We were approaching the Lido, once a melancholy and romantic wasteland on which Byron asked to be buried, now the most famous and fashionable beach in Europe. More interesting to the girls was the news that for many years the body of Father Christmas, or Saint Nicholas of Myra as he is officially known in the canon, patron saint of a motley collection of second-class citizens – pawnbrokers, slaves, virgins, sailors, robbers, prisoners and of course children – was supposed to lie in San Nicoló di Lido. I read them Jan Morris's account of how the Venetians, jealous of the eleventh-century trading boom in nearby Bari, claimed that they had raided its most notable shrine, and stolen the famous corpse. In fact, they announced, his uncle, yet another St Nicolas, was buried there too. 'The uncle, indeed, may really be there,' Morris comments drily:

> but Bari has long re-established itself as the undoubted resting-place of Santa Claus, for the silver reliquary of St Nicholas there is one of the principal miracle shrines of Italy, and has for nine centuries consistently exuded a liquid Holy Manna of such purity as to be indistinguishable from the clearest spring water. San Nicoló di Lido thus has an abashed, hang-dog air to it, and the more house-proud of the guide-books prudently circumvent its history, and linger with unbalanced emphasis among its fine carved choir-stalls.

We didn't linger at the Lido at all, as the steamer was under way in a matter of minutes for Venice itself. But the seeds of another adventure were hatching. To Spain for St Nicholas' childhood, Bari for his grave, Holland and Germany briefly for his legendary flowering. Then to his eternal home in the far North, chasing trolls and reindeer through Norway to Lapland and the Pole itself. Not in homely Bertha or ample Bertie but in a ship . . .

As casually as a London 2B bus draws up outside the National Gallery, our vaporetto made a U-turn across the Grand Canal and came alongside the Palazzo Ducale. The conductor wrapped a hawser deftly round a bollard, pulled it tight, slid back the rail and stepped back to let an eager flood of passengers off and another wearier wave on. The girls had wormed their way to the front of the crowd waiting to disembark, and jumped off well ahead of us. They followed the zigzag white marble slabs laid in the pink-grey pavement round a corner into the Piazza d'Imbroglio, classic home of conspiracy. Its modern lords and ladies are the fourteen licensed postcard sellers and the hawkers of pigeon food, plotting to divest the 6,000 visitors who will mill through Venice every day of the summer season of as much money as possible. They smiled civilly on us, and Tom spent the last of our lire on bags of maize. The girls set to stuffing crops with great gusto, and I left to find a bank.

When I did, its elegant steel doors were firmly closed. I realised

that the one flaw of our carefully timed late arrival was that all
financial services closed at five. Happily the San Marco branch of
Thomas Cook, founded in the infancy of the daring Mr Cook's
Tours, could oblige instead. I dipped into my copy of Morris's
Venice in the queue. Had Henry James and Marcel Proust, Whistler
and Kokoschka, Freya Stark and Rose Macaulay also lined up at
these respectable wooden counters for pocket money or tickets
home? I wondered. Probably not, but they might well have waited
anxiously for letters from home at my next port of call, the palatial
post office in the Fondaco dei Tedeschi, once the prestigious centre
for visiting German merchants.

Caught in a pedestrian time warp by the accident of its
geography, Venice must be the most unchanged of all cities, the
perfect place for following in distinguished footsteps. I wandered
dreamily among the warren of alleys musing on Mahler, seeing
with Corot's eyes, towards, as I thought, my rendezvous with
Tom and the girls at Standa. I wasn't really concentrating, just
relishing being alone for a change. Turning into a new and
unfamiliar piazza instead of the Campo San Luca that I had
expected, I was finally forced to admit that my single week in
Venice was not enough to save me from the inevitable fate of the
inexperienced visitor. It is easy enough to follow the tide to and
from Rialto and San Marco, or even make a diversion to the
Accademia – yellow metal arrows point at every turning. Everywhere else requires a good map or an excellent sense of direction.
Abandoning my knowing swagger, I bought a map and arrived
shamefacedly half an hour late to find the girls halfway through
their second icecream and gazing impatiently into Standa's windows. Tom tactfully bit back the reproaches natural to the
situation, walked over to the icecream stall and came back with a
large lemon cornet.

Next came the flustered undressings and dressings of the
outfitting, an intricate exercise in girl-management and diplomacy.
They left Standa in singing greens, blues and pinks. It had taken
time – nearly an hour and a half, to Tom's disbelief – and a fair
amount of money despite the bargain basement prices, but as we
watched them racing happily ahead of us along the sides of the
canals and up and over the stepped bridges like a flight of butterflies,
it seemed worth every minute and every penny.

The vaporetti are cheap fun on the water, so we boarded one for a
few stops along the Grand Canal to the Accademia, walked to the

Campo San Stefano, and sat down for beers and spremute di limone in the café which had been our breakfast haunt two years before. Then we ambled through the narrow lanes, window shopping among boutiques full of marbled papers and flouncy glass, browsing in an unhurried, academic bookshop, where I found a real Italian version of *Pinocchio*.

In a quiet corner, we came upon a small workshop devoted to the manufacture of carnival masks. Sunrays and spectres, blackamoors and butterflies, every fantasy could be fulfilled with the flick of a gilt-laden paintbrush, the flourish of an ostrich feather. We watched through the window as an intent young man painted pear-shaped tears below the vacant eyes of the mask of sorrow he held. A girl in the shop saw us, and beckoned us in. I hesitated. Thoughts of bulls and china shops flashed across the anxious parental brainpan. But it seemed too good a chance to miss. We walked round slowly, admiring the sharp sickle moon, the two-faced Janus.

Wearing masks has an ancient history in the theatre, but the function of the carnival mask is traditionally more than dramatic. Hidden behind a mask we can pretend to be totally other than our real selves. Paradoxically, it is while wearing a mask that we dare to reveal the most disturbing and profound aspects of our personalities. 'Everything that is deep loves the mask,' wrote Nietzsche. It is a way of escaping from the conventions, the social structures that normally hedge in the wild man. It has been likened to a safety valve, an annual licence to excess which makes conformity for the rest of the year more bearable.

Carnival – literally a leavetaking of meat – is followed by the heightened restrictions of Lent, when people take off their masks, return to their senses and their proper place. In the eighteenth century, the height of the carnival, the Venetians were living on borrowed time. Once America rather than the Orient was the significant target for traders, and the Turks captured the vital Venetian outpost of Crete, Venice lost her strategic importance. She turned from trading to tourism, from merchandise to melancholy. The palazzos rotted away on their insecure foundations. But what signalled decline then is big business today. The carnival is now grander and glossier then it has ever been, but it is no longer authentic – an old story certainly, but embellished beyond recognition. What are the real Venetians up to while the foreigners caper about in their natural theatre provided by those smooth inscrutable façades?

I liked the traditional idea of carnival, but I didn't regret missing the modern version. It felt cold-blooded and artificial, somehow. But these masks were undeniably splendid. One fascinated me more than the rest – the devilish black features of Harlequin. He is one of the traditional characters of the Commedia del'Arte, Harlequin and Columbine, Pantaloon and Pulcinella. All have their accepted personality – Harlequin the mischiefmaker, Columbine, pretty and quick-witted, the shrill unpredictable Pulcinello and the miserly merchant Pantaloon. But Harlequin is the wildest, the most ancient of them all. Harlequin is an elf.

As Arlecchino, he certainly came from Italy to France in Renaissance times and to England in the eighteenth century, but he derived from France in the first place, from the harlekin folk mentioned by Ordericus Vitalis at the end of the eleventh century: damned souls, ragamuffin mischiefmakers. According to the thirteenth-century playwright Adam de la Halle, harlekins were used as intermediaries by a prince of Fairyland, King Hellekin, when he courted Morgan le Fay. As spirits of the air, harlekins could become invisible at will, and this attribute is still preserved when in pantomime Harlequin carries a sword like a bat, with which, himself invisible, he works wonders. The first Italian reference to an 'alichino', a devil from hell, was in canto xxi of Dante's *Inferno*. Gradually his ancestry was lost and a much more clownish nature succeeded the devil in him.

From the fifteenth century onwards, Harlequin, Columbine, Pantaloon, and their associates were the backbone of the immensely successful Italian comedy teams that toured all Europe. They were still popular in the late nineteenth century, and their final debased legacy is in the Punch and Judy shows that still entertain sandy sunblistered infants on the beaches of Bognor and Blackpool.

We had missed the only surviving regular performance of the classic Harlequin mime in Tivoli Gardens by a mere twenty minutes. Venice didn't seem to be offering any pantomime just then, nor could we afford to buy one of the exquisitely painted masks. But outside the shop hung thick bunches of the little china harlequin dolls. With their dead white faces, sooty masks, and diamond-chequered suits, they are a favoured Venetian souvenir because of their association with the carnival. We picked out the harlequin with the saddest eyes and sweetest smile we could find, and our new friend wrapped him up tenderly. He could join the Dutch tiles, our Andersen silhouettes from Odense, Susie's Harz princess, and our other storybook relics.

It was nearly eight o'clock. We walked to the covered market near the Rialto bridge to find some food for a picnic supper. Apart from a basket of nectarines captured from a fast-closing fruit stall, we failed completely. Still, in those backstreets fresh pizza was cheap, and by now we needed the facilities of a café. So we sat down facing an unfashionable part of the Grand Canal, and gorged ourselves on hot light dough, laden with tomatoes and mushrooms. Real Italy at last. And that was it for the day – a pathetic achievement in comparison with the ambitions of the itineraries, but enough for us. The children had got the feel of Venice, felt pretty and cosseted, had learnt something of the magic of carnival. We made for San Marco and the boat home. The two smaller girls slumped along the benches, heads in my lap; Tom, Tilly and Daisy stayed up on the upper deck to watch the lagoon at night. The worst part of the day was the long walk home – two kilometres of unlit road, alternately dazzled by oncoming head-lights and chased into the ditch by cars zooming up behind us. There was no talk of a midnight swim that night.

Next afternoon, after a lazy morning preserving our energies, we set off with new cunning. This time we moved Bertha outside the gates just before they shut. After a leisurely lunch we drove to the boat, leaving her on the free verge just beyond the beseeching touts outside the expensive carparks. Carrying a simple picnic of bread, wine, ham, chocolate and apples we headed straight for the sheltered seats at the very front of the boat. On arrival at San Marco – we were already beginning to feel blasé – we stepped out in tight formation over the heaps of exhausted tourists and dipped briefly into the cathedral to admire the gloomy gold mosaics and the infinite variety of its marbled paving. Unashamedly holding the map in front of us, we made for the Carpaccio paintings in the Scuola San Georgio.

We crossed Campo San Maria Formosa, pausing to buy a bag of crimson cherries, eat them, and wash purpled mouths and fingers under an old iron pump. Then we wound along the waterways to the little Scuola modestly tucked away in the shadow of San Giovanni. Its one dark cool room provided the girls with immedi-ate relief from the heat outside, and a single set of fine, related, paintings was plenty for them to take in and enjoy. They each chose a postcard of the detail that had appealed to them most – for Ellie and Tilly it was Jerome's fluffy little dog, for Daisy the monks in startled flight, and for Susie the adoring lion. Pre-empting weariness, we suggested an icecream in the nearest café, and sat down with sweet black expresso coffees to write postcards home while the girls explained in their now fluent cornetto dialect which flavours they would each like.

Nearly an hour later we rose refreshed and virtuous to find a postbox. After a while the girls stopped in front of the window of one of the little glassware shops that are two a penny in Venice.

'There's a man actually making things in there,' said Daisy. 'Can we go inside and watch him doing it?' I had thought that all the glass was made on Murano, where the glass factory is, but Daisy was quite right.

'Yes.' I said, 'if you promise not to wriggle an eyebrow.'

I took Susie firmly by the hand as we went inside. It was a terrifyingly fragile interior, a real glass menagerie with whole orchestras of inch-long frogs, ballrooms full of butterflies, crystal circuses complete to the sleek shiny black of the ringmaster's hat. Their creator, a silent silver-haired man in dark glasses, was sitting at his workbench putting the last touches to the arched neck of a tiny giraffe. Solid straws of different coloured glass stood in a pot in front of him, others lay in a rack, their ends kept white-hot by blazing gas burners. He smiled a welcome, more secure than I was about the gentle manners of our children, and went on with his work. We watched a giraffe being created from horn to hoof while he talked a little about technique, colours, the Murano methods he'd learnt and improved on.

But words were unnecessary. What mesmerised the girls were the dexterous twists and turns of the molten rods, the making of something so beautiful from nothing but sand, air and fire. I've never been a great one for glass animals, but here, in their own world, they had a kind of fascination. It was hard to remember that our cluttered noisy house was very different from this hushed showroom. The giraffe wasn't cheap, but having seen it born we could hardly refuse to adopt it. Two months later, when I wandered over to the shelf of treasures from the trip hoarded in the relative security of my room I saw that it had been decapitated. I daren't tell the girls. One of them obviously doesn't dare tell me.

Tilly and Ellie still had enough money to debate which of the minute hedgehogs had the most winsome tilt to its snout, which duck most deserved to quit its pond for an Oxford mantelpiece. Three carefully padded parcels were constructed, and handed to

Tom, who clearly looked the most capable of getting them back to home in one piece.

'Tutte la sua famiglia?' asked the patron.

'Si, tutte,' I answered. 'Quattri figlie.'

'Bellissime,' he relied courteously. 'Que marito.' He rattled on a little, and I looked at Tom with new respect.

'What's he saying?' said Ellie.

'He says that in Italy they have a saying, it takes a man to make a daughter. What sort of man does it take to make four daughters?'

'I like the Italians,' said Tom.

It was time for the high point of the day – the promised gondola ride. We had investigated the gondola hire situation a little the day before, and the standard rate appeared to be £25 whether hired from the Rialto bridge, the Piazzale or one of the lesser pitches on the inner canals. I thought the best of the gondoliers we had seen was a slim chestnut-eyed youth on the Riva degli Schiavoni, Harlekin to the life. He had had the nous to concentrate his charm on the children, and on the trip home the night before they had all voted to take his boat and only his the next day. Unhappily for my sense of the aesthetic, children are prepared to give up any uncertain future for a solid present, and just then a very solid present offered itself in the shape of Gian Carlo, a portly veteran of the waterways.

'Gondola! gondola!' he yodelled after us from the recesses of the café next door to the glassworker. The girls' heads whipped round eagerly. Sensing the ripeness of the moment, he sprang out of his chair and on to the little bridge over the canal. Pointing down to what was certainly a beautifully maintained craft, he put his arm round Susie ('Que Biondina!'), took Ellie's hand ('Bellissima!'), and started down the steps. Tom shrugged. He had no strong feelings on gondoliers. Chestnut-eyes was forgotten, although I did try to draw Tilly aside and mutter a reminder in her ear. I comforted myself with the thought that Gian Carlo's barrel chest would probably project a more powerful baritone than the lissom stripling could offer. He might look like the larger of the two Ronnies masquerading in matelot shirt and straw boater but he'd be standing behind us. I nodded graciously and waved Daisy and Tilly towards the gondola.

He arranged us to his liking: papa and mama at the back with la piccola bambina between; the two signorine upright as convent girls on black and gold laquered chairs amidships, Ellie lounging in the prow beneath a plastic bunch of roses in a brass vase. Then, adjusting his hornrimmed spectacles and straightening his hat, he poled the gondola away as smoothly as if she was sliding on butter.

'Hoia, hoia!' he bellowed in warning as we swept out of the narrow side canal into a broader thoroughfare. A motoscafo swerved to avoid us, and was snarled at for its pains. Several close shaves and as many impassioned wrangles later we realised that we had probably lit on the most outrageously badtempered of all Venice's gondoliers, a real Growltiger of a man.

A wrinkled nut-brown drunk sitting in another gondola began an erratic rendering of O Sole Mio. He gave me an idea. Perhaps Gian Carlo could be distracted from his vendetta by an appeal to his musical sensibilities. The children knew all about serenades from the current advertisement for Italian icecream.

'What about a song?' I said.

'No,' he replied shortly.

'But I thought all gondoliers were wonderful singers.'

Gian Carlo's lip curled. I gave up. He relented a little, and began an intermittent staccato of information: 'Palazzo Sambucci . . . Palazzo Pelegrino, *very* beautiful . . . Marco Polo's 'ouse . . . Rialto Bridge.' The slanging matches had been a good deal livelier.

Still, here we were swanning along the Grand Canal like grandees, the brass seahorses at each side of the boat glinting in the setting sun, the great black-toothed prow silhouetted against the crumbling pink façades, our reflection distorted and unreal in the convex mirrors set on blind canal corners. What struck us more than anything was the timelessness of it all. In these watery backstreets with their balcony gardens, we could be back in the Renaissance heyday when Venice ruled the Mediterranean and the Doge bowed to no one.

As we continued our progress my heart warmed a little to Gian Carlo. Curmudgeon, yes, but how skilfully he swept round those blind corners, shaving intrusive motoscafoes by centimetres, deriding the attempts of barges to block his way, cutting up the less experienced of his rivals with suave insolence. I forgave him his pot-belly, his refusal to sing, and admired instead his superb timing and finger-tip sensitivity to the curved steering oar. The girls loved every minute of it – restful action, a winning combination. Tom dozed off, at last in the hands of a superefficient navigator. There was no denying that there is *nothing* – absolutely nothing – half so much worth doing in Venice as simply messing about in gondolas.

12
Pinocchio and Pisa

The wood out of which Pinocchio is carved is our very own humanity.

(Bernadetto Croce, *La Letteratura della Nuova Italia*, 1939)

Of all the books we looked at over our journey, *Pinocchio* was the most full of surprises. All I remembered about it from my childhood was a nose that grew when the puppet told a lie, and a talking cricket that got squashed against the wall because Pinocchio didn't like its preachy ways. I had no idea of the richness of the original or of its dual nature – part political tract, part classic quest story.

Its author, Carlo Lorenzini, was born in Florence in 1826, the oldest of nine children. His father was cook to the wealthy Garzoni family, his mother – 'a cultured woman of rich sensibilities' – seamstress and chambermaid in the same household. The marchese paid for Carlo's education at a Catholic seminary, but instead of becoming a priest he turned to journalism and politics. He fought with his fellow Tuscans against the Austrians in 1848, and became secretary of the Tuscan Senate. He was also editor of the *Private Eye* of his day, the influential satirical journal *Il Lampione*. When Austrian rule was restored, he lay low, editing a theatrical review called *La Scaramuccia*, but after the campaigns of the 1850s he returned to politics, this time as secretary of the Prefecture of Florence, and reopened *Il Lampione*. He first used the pseudonym Collodi, the name of the village in which his mother had been born and the country seat of the Garzoni family, in 1860, when he wrote a short book justifying the unification of Italy.

Lorenzini was notoriously lazy in putting pen to paper, and it was apparently gambling debts that finally pushed him into writing for children. He contracted to translate a selection of French fairy stories from Perrault and Madame d'Aulnoy and this collection appeared in 1875 as *I Racconti delle Fate*. The following year he updated a children's reader, and called it *Giannettino*, Little Johnny. This was the first of an extremely successful series of Giannettino books, on history, geography, grammar and arithmetic. He had the rare knack of mixing fun and information successfully.

Pinocchio was the fruit of his retirement from political life. In 1881 a friend started a magazine for children called *Giornale per i Bambini* which rapidly became a best-seller, with a circulation of 25,000. Lorenzini was one of the first people he asked to contribute to it, but only shortage of money and the enthusiasm of the editor finally induced him to write something. A large envelope arrived in the editorial office one morning. It contained a manuscript called *La storia di un burattino* – the story of a puppet – and a message. 'I am sending you this childishness to do with as you see fit. But if you print it, pay me well, so that I have a good reason to continue it.' It took a great deal of persuasion from the editor and demands from children who had enjoyed the first few instalments to get him to do so, but at last *Pinocchio* was completed. Two years later, it appeared in book form and was a sell-out – within a few years its sales had soared to a million in Italy alone.

Why? Historically it was the right moment for a national children's classic. The language, impeccably Tuscan and vivid, was exactly what the newly unified country admired. One eminent Italian scholar, Glauco Cambon, has likened its impact on the Italian people to that of Dante's *Divine Comedy* and Manzoni's *I Promessi Sposi* because of its rich idiomatic legacy. Everybody in Italy will understand you straight away if you refer to a pair of unsavoury schemers with the Collodian label, 'the Cat and the Fox'. Moreover, however casual the birth of *Pinocchio* appeared to be from the circumstances it was written under, there was no concealing Lorenzini's political commitment to a united Italy in its message: it was a call for Italians to give up the irresponsible opportunism of their old hero, Harlequin, and unite the good points of his character with the backbone of Italy's old strength, commitment to the family. Symbolically Pinocchio meets Harlequin, they greet each other as 'brother' and both are prepared to die in the flames of the Puppet-master's fire to save the other. But

Pinocchio graduates from being a mere puppet to becoming a boy who acknowledges his responsibilities to society.

Pinocchio's importance to other countries than Italy lies in its nature as a classic folktale, in the sense defined by Italo Calvino in the introductory essay to his *Italian Folk Tales*.

> These folk tales are a catalogue of the potential destinies of men and women, especially for that stage in life when destiny is formed, that is, youth, beginning with birth, which itself often foreshadows the future; then the departure from home, and finally, through the trials of growing up, the attainment of maturity and the proof of one's humanity.

Like many fairytales, Collodi's story is a classic quest, a search for maturity. Pinocchio wants to be a real boy so that he can grow into a man; as a puppet he will always stay the same. But to become a boy he has to master his selfish impulses, a challenge he finds almost impossible to meet. Wild and wilful, Pinocchio commits the greatest crime in the canon of Italian family law before he is even completely carved: he shows 'want of respect' to his father. Although he adores the bizarre blue-haired fairy whom he adopts as mother, he repeatedly disappoints her.

He tries – and fails – to grow up the way his 'parents' recommend: not lying, being obedient, working hard at school, and deciding on a useful trade. Interestingly, when he does achieve maturity, it is through his good heart and on his own terms, much more adult ones than Geppetto and the fairy envisage. His compassion for his poor broken father makes him turn willingly to real work; he sacrifices the new coat he planned to buy with his hard-earned savings when he hears that his fairy mother needs expensive medicine. The wheel comes full circle – the coat that Geppetto sold to buy his naughty puppet son a spelling book is balanced by the one that Pinocchio forgoes to save the life of his ailing fairy mother. But before this happy resolution, the puppet encounters as extraordinary a galaxy of monstrous characters as Ulysses ever did: a gorilla judge who wears spectacles with no glass in, and sends Pinocchio, the victim, to prison instead of the wily Fox and Cat who rob him, a great Serpent who lures him by a deadly inactivity, then bursts a blood vessel laughing at its own cleverness, a grotesque grass-haired green fisherman 'like a lizard on end', who offers the puppet a choice of being fried or stewed in tomato sauce 'in token of his friendship and particular regard', and above all the sea-monster which swallows Pinocchio just as Jonah was swallowed.

'Well done, Pinocchio!' says the fairy to him in his final dream. 'To reward you for your good heart I will forgive you for all that is past. Boys who minister tenderly to their parents, and assist them in their misery and infirmities, are deserving of great praise and affection, even if they cannot be cited as examples of obedience and good behaviour.' Pinocchio does not win a princess – his blue-haired fairy becomes first his sister, then his mother. Family rules O.K.

'They are very nice to us children in Italy, aren't they?' said Daisy. 'That man in the glass shop in Venice was really interested in our family. And the people here seemed really pleased to see us when we came in.'

We were sitting in a small restaurant in backstreet Ferrara, face-deep in pasta, half watching a spaghetti western, half talking of the infamous Duchess of Ferrara, Lucrezia Borgia. Tom was trying to persuade the proprietress, a charming but formidably deter- mined opponent, that the lady, one of his heroines, was much maligned – more sinned against than sinning, the tool of her family.

'That's as maybe,' she said, or words to that effect. 'Ma' no lo credo. I casi son tanti.' She was unwilling to allow Lucrezia to lose any of her villainous lustre. 'Anyway – what you do for your family is done with honour.'

Her daughter brought over our next course.

'Che bellissima!' she murmured, and stroked Susie's fair hair. Susie simpered – she was beginning to trade on the Italian weakness for blondes. The other three scowled. Fortunately for our own family politics, a handsome young man, obviously an accepted sweetheart, swaggered in, and from then on the waitress concen- trated her efforts on him. Susie tried to catch her attention again, but it was no use. The sharp-eyed signora chuckled, and invited all four of them over to the counter to help themselves to icecream. They wandered outside to leapfrog along the pavement bollards, and I asked her about our next story.

'What about Pinocchio?' I asked. 'Is he still read here in Italy?'

'Very much – every child knows it well. So much fun, not all nonsense, either. You must go to Collodi,' she added. 'Parco di Pinocchio. The children will enjoy themselves there. It's built for them especially.'

We hadn't been to a purpose-built pleasure park since Tivoli, I

realised. There had been a point earlier in the journey when I had
wondered if we were ever going to get away from deliberately
created fantasies and find enchanted places of our own. Holland had
been too tidy, and Denmark was a place for romantics to take off
from rather than dwell in, although its long windswept beaches and
scattered islands still haunted me. In the Eastern Harz we had found
plenty of undisturbed magic, but Western Germany had been
charming rather than enchanted. Still, we had been busy enough
with our quest not to need any of its many funfairs. Was it worth
going to one now? Our original plan was to head for Florence,
where I knew there was a house dedicated to Lorenzini. No doubt it
would be full of early editions of *Pinocchio*, portraits, letters . . . I
looked at the children hopping about outside and thought about hot
pavements and dry-as-dust museums.

'Very good for children,' the signora said again. 'Parco di
Pinocchio, just west of Pistoia.'

We tucked the girls up in their beds and drove on, falling asleep
around midnight in an Apennine lay-by near Pistoia and waking at
five to see mist in the acacias and a carpet of delicate wildflowers.
While the children snored contentedly, Tom and I had a rare
opportunity alone to unwind, sip tea, let our thoughts meander in
and out of each other's minds without interruption. One of the
stresses of the trip was the absence of such sessions. We didn't
realise how much we needed them until too late, nor could they
easily be prearranged. I tended to fall asleep instantly every night,
and normally in the mornings one person rising woke everybody
else. I think on reflection we were often too cautious about letting
the children off the leash, and so finding ourselves some solitude.
But that was partly because of the change of crews. Just as I
overcame my early nervousness and was encouraging the girls to
run off a bit, Tom arrived with a fresh instalment of my old fears.
By the time we were breezing back through France, both of us had
much more confidence in the children's basic good sense.

We picked up some fresh rolls in Pescia, and finally reached the
tiny Tuscan village of Collodi at around eight o'clock. At first sight
it didn't seem to be profiting much from its famous namesake. The
sign to the Parco di Pinocchio was badly in need of repainting, the
wooden puppet arrows that directed us through the shabby streets
had a hangdog air. The carpark was empty except for a grizzled
Nero lookalike who was methodically setting out souvenirs on a
stall near the entrance gate. While the children ate their breakfast

and got dressed, I went to reconnoitre. The standard souvenir, a wooden Pinocchio, attracted me at once. Bold as brass, with rolling black eye, scarlet shirt, neat green shorts, and a nose as long and pointed as his conical red hat, it had the same classic quality as the wooden Nutcracker Kings we had coveted in Rothenberg. Nero bowed a grave welcome, sensing a sucker.

'This one has a removable nose. You can screw in a longer one.'

I examined the solid little doll, felt its smoothly turned limbs, admired the wooden screw. I bought four in the end: the grand two-noser for my own collection, a smaller stouter one for the children, and two tiny three-inch lads on elastic that could be hung from the driving mirror in vulgar Italian fashion. I also fell for a Pinocchio card game, which seemed a short cut to reminding the children of the plot of the story. I rejected a plastic and blue tinsel fairy, a fur-fabric talking cricket pyjama case and a three-foot high inflatable Disney-style Pinocchio. But Nero was more than satisfied. He threw in a small plastic Pinocchio keyring for nothing.

By this time the girls were dressed and ready to sally forth into the park itself. It could easily have been an anticlimax. Collodi only got round to a material recognition of its most famous son in the 1950s, when the then mayor of Pescia, Rolando Anzilotti, suggested creating the park. Designed by architects Baldi and Luigi, it opened in 1956. We rounded the corner of a hideous pink building (later to be revealed as the Inn of the Red Crayfish, nest of the villainous Fox and Cat) and were brought up short by an absolutely brilliant piece of sculpture, a light, dancing impression of Pinocchio and his fairy mother, set against a startlingly beautiful backdrop: the baroque Villa Garzoni.

As Tom and I stared up at the statue, the girls were quick to spot its purpose. They climbed into it and up through the intricate base, until perched like a small flock of starlings they were waving at us from all sides of it. Schooled in the English keep-off tradition, we shouted at them to get down, but then realised there was no need. The dull bronze was worn shiny in patches, a comfortable legacy of thirty years of active children. Climbing up the statue was exactly what was intended. Here was a monumental park with a difference, calculated by a genius well in touch with what children find fun.

Through high bay hedges we wound our way from surprise to surprise, recognising in each the elements of the zany story we had been reading at bedtime over the past few days. There was the policeman barring the way to us as he had to Pinocchio, there was the Serpent, the Snail, the fairy's house. We could make the Crab soak unwary passers-by ourselves by stepping on a water button. We climbed right into the mouth of the Giant Dogfish and saw Geppetto in the heart of darkness, then went up a spiral stair to the top of its head and filled the whole of the pool around us with a mighty waterspout.

Finally, when Pinocchio, a real growing boy at last, waved us a cheery farewell, we got thoroughly lost in a little labyrinth. At this point Susie decided she needed a lavatory, and everyone else suddenly felt the same. In some disorder, we managed – at least, they all managed – to find their way out. I caught them up fifteen minutes later, thanks to the kindness of a small boy who had obviously been in the labyrinth before, and we triumphantly sat down for real refreshments in the Inn of the Red Crayfish. Although the park had been very empty while we explored it, I had been vaguely conscious of a low buzzing behind us, which had by now become a hubbub. When we came out of the gate the early morning calm had disappeared. A throng of Italian families was struggling to push through the turnstile as one huomo. Souvenir stalls had mushroomed everywhere. Battalions of wooden Pinocchios, many of them taller than Ellie, glared at us, legions of jiminy crickets leered, plump sorbo-rubber fairies smirked. We decided to dispense with a visit to the Villa, in whose kitchens, the guide unreliably informed us, Lorenzini had worked as a boy. Instead we fled past the ranks of coaches, the rows of ricketty Fiats and sleek Alfa Romeos and headed for the hills.

High above Collodi we parked Bertha on the edge of an olive grove. There were two or three houses close by, and I wandered over to the nearest to ask permission to picnic. A stout signora waddled out on to her geranium-bordered patio, and we exchanged courtesies.

'Four girls! It takes a man . . .' I nodded. She, it emerged, had had three boys. 'Meno facile', less easy, she remarked, eyeing her swollen ankles in resignation.

Suddenly the peace of our tiny Eden was shattered by a small international incident. We realised later that it was just one of hundreds that had occurred that particular week, but to us it was a startling reminder of how out of touch with reality we had got, how far into our fairytale world. It was around five o'clock in the afternoon by then. Good progress had been made with projects and diaries and it was too hot to sit out in the sun any longer, so we made a cup of tea, and were drinking it inside the van. I had Susie on my knee, reading her the garishly illustrated modern Italian *Pinocchio* bought in Venice. Several cars had driven past us, full of football fans in scarves and T-shirts. We guessed they must be returning from some local match – Pistoia versus Pisa perhaps, or Lucca United against the Apuan Allstars.

One little white saloon stopped behind the van. It drove on, paused, reversed, and stopped again. Three young Italians swaggered towards us. I recalled dozens of similar friendly encounters in Perugia – conversations in cafés, siestas by swimming pools, village hops. How nice of them to stop and pass the time of day. I wasn't at all ready for the torrent of abuse that hit us. Susie listened, and cuddled closer, sensing rather than understanding the menace.

'What are they talking about?' said Daisy.

'I don't know,' I said. 'I think there's been some football disaster.'

I explained to the angry young men that we didn't know what had happened. They told me. Liverpool. Juventus. Brussels. Many dead. The English brutes, stupid wicked brutes. I shook my head. I didn't know about football. They probably were bruti (this was no time for patriotism). I had heard that football fans were often very very stupido. I said I was sorry. That the children didn't understand. That we didn't live anywhere near Liverpool. That we had been to see the Pinocchio park. I held out the four wooden pinocchios as peace offerings. Would they like some tea?

They hesitated, looking regretfully at Tom. If he hadn't been so hemmed around by his young family, I think he might have been yanked out for an impromptu game of football. Then with a final violent blow on poor Bertha's bodywork, they lurched off, luckily only a little drunk, certainly very angry indeed. I realised then that I hadn't seen an English paper since we left home four weeks before.

Much sobered, we drove down the hillside and faced weekend traffic coming back from Via Reggia, the Blackpool of the Tyrrhenian Sea. Horns hooted, clenched fists waved from car windows. Something had clearly gone very wrong indeed with Anglo-Italian relations. But when we left the main road from the coast and drove through broad tree-lined ramparts into the deep cool streets of Lucca all was calm. I had a moment of panic as the ancient lanes – Lucca's original Roman plan is still preserved – got narrower and narrower and Bertha, in my imagination at least, swelled. A lucky turn brought us into the cathedral piazza. A fountain plashed. The girls are complete suckers for plashing fountains, and they insisted that we stop Bertha there and stay the night. It wasn't such a bad idea. The road to the Pisan coast was roofrack deep in aggressive traffic, and Lucca felt like a well-fortified oasis. I looked up at the riot of animal and vegetable life cavorting in lacy frivolity across the front of the cathedral, and saw that across the square a Swiss Dormobile had raised its concertina roof and was primly drawing its frilly curtains. Not at all a bad idea. We drove into the discreet corner made where the nave crossed the north transept, and let Bertha nestle like a large cuckoo under the duomo's sheltering wing.

We made a little formal effort that evening. Lucca is an elegant city as well as a businesslike one, and we were after all in a fairly public place. A vase of the wild flowers we had picked early that morning, a bunch of grissini breadsticks, a bottle of wine and the only remaining glass. Tagliatelli, a rich tomato sauce, a melon. The girls dressed for dinner – all their shorts were clean, Susie put on a hairband. Passing heads looked in approvingly; we felt we conveyed a suitably sophisticated mood. I lit a cigar and put a cello suite into the tape-recorder. Bertha, tidy for once, felt wonderfully snug.

Next day was an unexpected gift. We hadn't meant to come to Lucca at all, let alone stay there for a night and a day, but we did. We ate a leisurely breakfast in another little square, climbed the bizarre treetopped Guinigi tower, admired the old Roman amphitheatre, and walked halfway round the shady city walls back to Bertha. Inside the cathedral Tilly found an early Renaissance effigy of silky marble, the young wife of Paolo Guinigi lying in state. It was far more beautiful than the crude sandstone figure of our unhappy German Matilda, but at her feet was a small dog that had exactly the same bereaved sadness as little Qvedl. We all loved Lucca, both for its beauty and for its down-to-earth quality. It was a good solid reminder of everyday reality.

The prospect of Pisa excited the children enormously. Like the Little Mermaid, Neuschwanstein, the Eiffel Tower, and Legoland, it was something they knew of as legendary, and they reckoned a visit to it scored them several useful points on the classroom argonaut scale. Although neither of us had ever been there, Tom and I were less enthusiastic. We could already imagine the charabancs and crowds, the snapping cameras and whiffs of hotdogs. We even suggested giving it a miss, but the girls were having none of that.

'Don't you realise it's *leaning*, Mummy?' said Ellie scathingly. 'Any day now it could fall down, and we would miss it. You took us to Venice because it was sinking, and Holland because it was nearly flooded. We *must* go to Pisa.' I rather liked this Near Disaster Tour theme. How close to death had Ellie felt we'd been? And how often? Had she taken the 'Danger – Wild Boar' signs seriously at Sababurg? What had she thought about that Alsatian on the Brocken? I asked her.

'Oh, that was fine,' she said reassuringly. 'He was on a lead.'

'Why is it leaning?' asked Tilly. I looked at Tom hopefully. He looked back.

'Well, there are lots of theories. Some people think it happened halfway up, when it was being built. Sort of slipped, you know. But they decided to go on just the same. Some people think it happened after it was finished – subsidence. Those people are still waiting for it to go on slipping. Then some people say that it was a challenge – to actually build a leaning tower from scratch – an interesting exercise.'

'But why is it leaning?'

I gave up. 'I don't know. Nobody knows.'

We decided to outflank the crowds, go for a late afternoon swim, find a campsite, and then get up at dawn's crack to get to the tower as soon as it opened. So at first we bypassed Pisa, heading down an unusually quiet, straight and smooth road to a little place called Gombo. This turned out not to be little at all, but extremely grand: Italy's Sandringham, the holiday home of the President of the Republic and strictly not approachable by touring grockles like us.

'No wonder the road was so flat and straight,' said Tom drily as we swung back on to the usual pockmarked highway with its manic drivers. The east-coast beaches were very different from the wide open spaces of Punta Sabbione. Every inch was allocated, patrolled and governed by potbellied mussolinis in yachting caps. When we finally settled on the smartly blue and white painted sand city of Il Paradiso, we were firmly ushered to a pair of chairs as far away as possible from the sea. Since all the other deckchairs were empty, this seemed rather unnecessary, but there was no arguing. We stared over the backs of them at the distant sea as if we were in the back row of a cinema showing an extremely boring film. I felt distinctly unblessed, deprived of the usual warm welcome the Italians offer their admirers, but the girls dived into the water with their usual zest. Once we'd joined them, the heat and bustle of the traffic and the towns was quickly washed away. The café jukebox wailed of the taste of salt and sea, the pungent scent of Ambre Solaire recalled innumerable other beaches and long-lost lives. In and out of the water, dip and dry and doze and dip. On the beach sensations are everything. The mind dissolves into miasma.

That night we camped at the spanking new campsite we'd seen advertised on every lamp-post in Marina di Pisa – the girls insisted that such a thorough effort should be rewarded; besides, it was called St Michael, a sure sign of quality. In fact its tacky new technology was already breaking down; we all washed together in the Damen as the Herren was not functional. German, it appeared, was still the beach lingua franca. But none of that mattered in the least. St Michael turned out to be the best campsite of the trip as far as the children were concerned because it gave them friends. Three slim, fair-haired girls were hovering around the gate as we drove in. They turned out to be English, from Kenilworth, on a three-week holiday in Italy during termtime because their father, an engineer, was mixing business with pleasure, taking his family with him on a trouble-shooting trip for his firm. One disadvantage to taking time off during school term was that we met very few other children on our trip and our girls are a gregarious bunch. It did improve family relations for the girls not to have friends as allies against sisters, and I think that all four now get on better after their enforced imprisonment together. But just then they thoroughly enjoyed the release that outsiders provided.

Tom used the campsite hose to scrub down Bertha ready for Switzerland. She had acquired an impressive range of stickers. The best of them, a silhouetted Pied Piper from Hamelin, seemed very appropriate as Abbie, Lucy and Hannah Barnacle, equally pleased to have company, raced around the campsite with our four girls. I hung up a long line of washing, feeling a little like the old woman who lived in a shoe when I noticed four neighbouring motorcyclists counting the fair heads and looking at me with disbelief. Later on Tom and I shared the last of David's Grolsch with their parents, Liz and Bruce, and heard, for the first time, the full story of the Brussels football disaster. Bruce told us of cars overturned at Turin, of tourists being attacked much more ferociously than we had been. A shadow fell over the rest of our stay in Italy. We found it much more difficult to approach the Italians we met, shuffled silently through supermarkets, and even considered removing the GB sticker from the back of the van.

At seven next morning we rumbled out of the campsite and into the tourist attack. Luckily the guide book was wrong about the opening hours of the leaning tower. It, like the cathedral, was open at quarter to eight, and we were very nearly the first to climb its uncanny stairs that morning. It reminded me immediately of one of the oddest films I've ever seen, the 1920s expressionist masterpiece, *The Cabinet of Dr Caligari*. Every set is built distorted, since the world is seen through the eyes of a madman. Climbing Pisa's tower gives exactly the same powerful sensation of wrongness. None of the stairs were quite where we expected them to be. Our sense of balance was put off key, out of time. Ellie clung to my hand, Susie to Tom's. Daisy gripped the walls of the stair. Only Tilly was unperturbed, but then her favourite sport is tree-climbing. As we got to the level of the great bells, an unintelligible message came over the loudspeaker. Panic-stricken, I looked at my watch. Just on eight o'clock. I remembered the bells of Notre Dame that made poor Quasimodo deaf to all sounds but theirs. Maybe this was why we were the only people up the tower.

'Quick, Ellie, sit down here beside me, and put your hands over your ears,' I said. We huddled together and waited, Ellie resigned to yet another peril. Reality was far gentler than imagination. Pisa's peals are pretty carillons, not the crashing brazen throats of Paris. When the others joined us, we laughed about it, peered over the well-railed edge, tried out the phone-guides (three out of four were broken) and compared notes on our vertigo. Then we sensed another presence. Looking up at the highest rim of the tower we saw a young Japanese woman nonchalantly leaning over a very flimsy looking rail. How had she got there? At first we could see no steps at all, but she waved her hand to one side of the tower. Tilly and I walked outside the arches and saw a tiny staircase in their thickness. In single file we all followed her up and walked round the crazily tilted tip, our hands glued to the rail and each other.

'I want to go down,' said Daisy. 'I feel funny.'

'So do I,' said Ellie. Susie and Tom had already started a cautious crabwise descent. Tilly and I decided to walk all round the outside at the highest level of open arches. With wild disregard for human life, the cultural powers-that-be have not thrown the usual cordon of safety rails around their famous tower, except at the level of the bells. Presumably they are prepared to risk the odd casualty rather than spoil its imperfect symmetry. So one can walk all around it at any level, peering over a sheer drop to see where Galileo dropped his marbles. There are even rain gunnels so we could roll our own over the edge, calling out 'gardez-marbles' first, preferably. Given that even if you don't lose your sense of balance, you could easily trip over one of these shallow channels in the paving slabs, a tour round the outside of the tower requires considerable concentration. Tom and I agreed once we were safely at the bottom that it was both an unmissable experience and the most dangerous place that we had ever paid to get into. Tilly thought it was great.

The next hour was a failure. Succumbing to the fatal temptation to 'do the place properly once we're here', we set off on a tour of cathedral, baptistry, and cloisters. I won't dwell on Susie's dragging steps up and down the gloomy aisles of the cathedral, Ellie's mutinous circuit round the baptistry, my sulks at their philistine disregard for the beauty all around us. What we should have done was to send them all off for an icecream while we enjoyed Pisano's masterpieces. There was just one exception to the general unconcern. On the lowest bronze panel of the great west door there is a domestic scene: a fourteenth-century lying-in. The mother sits in a fourposter bed in the background while her brand-new baby is being admired in the foreground. The deep green of the old bronze had been highlighted to gold by generations of tiny caresses in three places – the baby itself, a little petdog at one side, and a tiny lizard lurking in the foliage of the border. Somehow that brought the whole place to life in a fresh and human way.

'Forget the cloisters,' said Tom. 'Let's go to the beach and have a last swim with that English family.' As we turned for a last look at the tower, we saw an energetic American grandmother signalling to several generations of her family who were ranging themselves on all the different levels of the tower for the family photograph to beat all family photographs. A twinge of regret that we hadn't thought of doing it passed through me, quickly followwed by an acute sense of relief.

Later that afternoon, driving northwards along the coastal motorway, the girls came hustling up to the back of the cab.

'Look up there – snowy mountains! Let's go and camp up there.'

'But there can't be snow this far south,' said Tom. 'Unless the Apennines are much higher than I thought they were.'

I looked at the map. Carrara. What looked like snow-capped peaks were the famous marble mountains, glaciers of white dust trailing down their sharp edges, rose-tinted by the setting sun. It looked too romantic to miss – we decided to forgo the comforts of a campsite and find somewhere among them to stay the night.

Long boulevards lined with marble-working factories led us into the tangled old city centre of Carrara. Although rich in finely chiselled street signs and profligate with chipped marble brick walls, it seemed low on civic pride. But with a constant veil of dust over everything, with even the rivers running white with the spoil from the hills, what chance had even the most well-intentioned of housekeepers? Once we'd grasped that Cave meant quarries, the route to the marble mountains was not hard to find. The two most famous are Colonnata and Fantiscritti, and we chose the road up to Colonnata. Bumpy and occasionally very narrow, it wound up the mountainside in a series of hairpin bends We passed a skinny shabby village, built on a knife edge of rock, and saw the open face of the quarry high behind. Although it was early evening, they were still blasting, and the occasional explosions and attendant rumblings added to the excitement of pathfinding into the unknown. We came to a smallish working where there was a house, a shack selling 'souvenirs di marmo' and a sandy lay-by edged with shady sweet chestnut trees. A scarlet Citroën 2CV was parked there. As we paused by the roadside its owners, who were playing boules in the sand, beckoned us hospitably in. A little vinehung terrace offered a perfect view of the quarries up and down hill. The boules-players, three students from Lake Constance, explained that all we needed to do was to ask permission of the stall owner, so we walked over to the house to find her. She was a stout Mrs Tiggywinkle of a character, with a beaming grin, full of stories of other stranieri who had camped there. There was one especially attractive signora who had washed her baby in the fontane of her casa. Perhaps I would like to freshen up my bambini there too? The girls were delighted, and grabbed their towels. If they were surprised to discover that the promised fountain was merely a stout water pipe with a tap on the end, dribbling icy spring water into a large stone trough, they hid their feelings well.

Scrubbed pink after their icy wash, it was they who discovered the quality of her stall. Tom and I had automatically veered away from it, much more interested in setting up a couple of chairs for ourselves and a table for a large bottle of Carrara Red, but the children rushed inside with the gullibility of very young oysters. Or so we thought. In fact, when they returned, carrying some exquisite small treasures – tiny classically proportioned vases, smooth marble eggs and cubes veined black and white, we couldn't resist going over ourselves. We came away with a bowl and a cakestand of natural Travertine, a stone which looks like petrified cork, and with a magnificent green and white alabaster chess set for Daisy's September birthday – all absurdly cheap.

Then we had a feast: thin slivers of turkey fried up quickly with mushrooms and peppers, with sour cream stirred in stroganoff style at the last minute. Long thin fagioli, a bowl of rice, then huge peaches and bitter black chocolate washed down with icy cold water from the fontane. As we sat there, looking up and down at the vast manmade chasm, the mountain thundered again and we heard the crash of the great blocks of marble, sawn through by steel cables oiled with water and sand. Behind the signora's house we could study the method of cutting close up. First the cut is made with a wire, then it is jacked open, and boulders hammered down to force the block to fall away from the rock-face. A cushion of debris is arranged to break its fall – but even so it may crumble into thousands of useless fragments if some internal flaw exists. The girls were fascinated by the carpet of marble chips large and small; and decided to arrange a stall of their own from what they could find. Tom and I wandered off through the chestnut woods to get a better look up at the unnaturally jagged peaks and the hair-raisingly narrow roads winding far up towards them.

Later that evening I turned back to Andersen. His story 'The Shadow' opens in Italy: 'a learned man from the cold countries – a young man and a clever one' is sitting on his balcony when he sees a mysterious lady on the balcony opposite. She disappears, and he longs to know what is in her room. Then he realises that his shadow has somehow made the leap to the other side and is hesitating at the door. 'Go in,' he tells it, half joking. To his surprise it does – but it doesn't return. Unlike an earlier tale of a lost Shadow, Chamisso's *Peter Schlemehl*, the young man grows a new shadow – but one day, years later, an extraordinarily thin man comes to his apartment . . . The bizarre tale of how the shadow leeches off his master is a profoundly disturbing one, but the lady on the balcony was undoubtedly a symbol of Poetry, the key as Andersen saw it to genius. And it was in Italy that he felt her influence most deeply.

By coincidence Andersen came into contact with another of our quarries, Robert Browning, in Rome in 1861. The Brownings had set up home there, partly for the sake of Elizabeth's health – she was seriously ill by then with consumption – and partly to get away from her intensely jealous father. Elizabeth described the visit in a letter to Thackeray: 'Hans Andersen is here, charming to us all, and not least to the children.'

Together they celebrated the birthday of the son of a friend, the American sculptor William Wetmore Storey, with a reading by Hans Andersen of his 'Ugly Duckling' story, and another by Robert Browning of 'The Pied Piper' – accompanied by William Storey on a flute. The Browning's twelve-year-old son Pendennis seems to have taken Andersen's measure brilliantly – in a later letter Elizabeth wrote: 'Andersen the Dane came to visit me yesterday – kissed my hand and seemed in a general *verve* for embracing. He is very earnest, very simple, very childlike. I like him. Pen says of him, "He is not really pretty. He is rather like his own ugly duck, but his mind has developed into a swan." That wasn't bad of Pen, was it?'

Elizabeth had admired Andersen's long autobiographical novel about Italy, *L'Improvisatore*, written after his visit to the country in 1833. The last poem she ever wrote was for him, a tribute to the skill with which she felt he conveyed the magic of Italy. It ended:

'Yet, O for the skies that are softer and higher,'
Sighed the North to the South;
'For the flowers that blaze and the trees that aspire,
And the insects that make of a song or a fire!'
Sighed the North to the South.

'And O, for a seer to discern the same!'
Sighed the South to the North;
'For a poet's tongue of baptismal flame
To call the tree or the flower by its name!'
Sighed the South to the North.

The North sent therefore a man of men
As a grace to the South;
And thus to Rome came Andersen:
'Alas! but must you take him again?'
Said the South to the North.

That hillside high above Carrara was the best of all our unofficial campsites, even though we woke around five-thirty to the sound of huge lorries grinding up the hill empty, then inching down again loaded with gigantic blocks of stone that threatened to unbalance them at every bend. I quailed at the thought of either meeting one coming up or having one on our tail going down. So we ate a hasty breakfast, said goodbye to our kind hostess (she didn't seem to have heard of football at all) and started down the road heart in mouth, Tom at the wheel. Fortunately we found ourselves following rather than leading a marble lorry, and soon realised that there was in fact a semi-official one-way system up and down the hill. At one bend there was a sculpture garden – half workshop, half open-air gallery. Weird animals and enormous stylised figures stood frozen in the grass like pillars of salt. Carrara was man-made magic, but it had far more of enchantment than the deliberately created fantasies of the Fairytale Road.

13
Heidi's Alp

I saw also in my Dream, that when the Shepherds perceived
they were wayfaring men, they also put questions to them,
for but few of them that begin to come hither do shew their
face on these Mountains. But when the Shepherds heard their
answers, being pleased therewith, they looked very lovingly
upon them, and said, Welcome to the Delectable Mountains.

(John Bunyan, *The Pilgrim's Progress*, 1678)

The rest of the day was one long slog. Although the Apennines are
beautiful, driving nonstop through them made them seem unreal,
as if we were seeing them on a cinema screen. At one tiny village,
through which the motorway had sliced like a hatchet in wood,
people were standing at the roadside waving white flags to
announce not a truce but fresh goat's cheese and plate-size
mushrooms for sale. As soon as we passed them I wished we'd
stopped to buy some, but that awful compulsion to arrive had
seized us. I had begun to hate our engine. If we'd really been in a
canary-coloured cart, drawn by a patient plodding horse, we'd
have paused, passed the time of day, learnt of the ways of the
mountains, communicated something of ourselves. Instead we
swept by with the vague impersonal gape of the motorist, seeing
only his own image, touching nothing.

Originally we planned to cross into Switzerland by the Great St
Bernard Pass, getting lost in the snow on the top in order to check
that the famous shaggy dogs were still doing their stuff. Now it
seemed wise to give Turin, bereaved and angry, a wide berth. So
we had skirted Parma and Milan, lunched by the lakeside at
Lugano, and then started the switchback up to San Bernardino.

'There's a St Bernard.'

'No it isn't. It's too small.'

'Perhaps it's a Little St Bernard. This is the Little St Bernard Pass, after all.'

'Two out of ten, Daddy.'

Jokes in our family are graded on a nought to ten basis, but I thought two was pretty mean for something as snappy as that. I didn't protest because I had retired in dudgeon to the back of the van, and was lounging on a pile of cushions with a carafe of chianti, carousing to the beat of the Rolling Stones 'running for the shelter/Of mother's little helper'. Ellie and Susie, always on for a spot of bopping or a rough and tumble, were joining in. I had been in a thoroughly bad mood ever since Tom had criticised me earlier in the morning for (a) always knowing best and (b) complaining because no one made any decisions but me. This was true enough and unreasonable enough, but I wasn't going to admit it just then.

Tom wisely ignored my debauchery, and concentrated on talking dogs to Tilly who was sitting companionably beside him in the passenger seat and producing a passable imitation of me in didactic mode. She discovered a handout from the Swiss Tourist Office on St Bernards and filled the others in on them, just in case we spotted a puppy.

'The monks say that the dogs become restless as much as an hour before the beginning of a storm, and try to get out into the open just in case. They never lose their way, even in the thickest fog or most blinding snow, sense the presence of a buried avalanche victim from as far away as three hundred yards, and lead rescuers to exactly the right spot for digging them out. The most famous of all St Bernards was the legendary Barry, who lived from 1800 to 1814, and saved the lives of forty travellers.'

'I wish we had a St Bernard,' said Ellie.

'We could have one each,' Susie added.

'And they could pull Bertha when the engine broke down.'

'And we could ride on their backs.'

'Or they could pull a sledge, if we did go to the North Pole.'

'Why not?' I said benignly. Reality seemed comfortably removed. I was determined not to offer advice of any sort for the rest of the day, and found to my surprise that I was rather enjoying irresponsibility. I lay low as Tilly directed Tom northwards through Splugen and Thusis, and stayed silent while Daisy struggled to interpret the symbols in our international camping guidebook. I didn't utter a word of criticism when she triumphantly came up with a campsite on the upper reaches of the Rhine at Chur, although it was some twenty miles short of the place I really wanted to get to, Maienfeld, heart of Heidiland. Bossy, was I? I'd show them. As we groped our way through an industrial estate on the outskirts of Chur to park Bertha in a midgeridden wood, cut off from the river by an impenetrable barbed wire fence and echoing to a regular fusillade from the nearby army rifle-range, I felt a moment's ignoble glee.

But it soon passed. In fact, once the army stopped their daily target practice, it turned out to be a very fine campsite indeed. Switzerland lived up to its reputation for cleanliness and efficiency; the showers were hard and hot, the kitchen beautifully laid out, the shop imaginatively provisioned. Hygiene had sunk to a low ebb in Italy, where very little in the way of plumbing seemed to work for long. Like housework, washing is more fun when things are really grubby, and by the time we had all emerged soaped, showered and reconditioned from the shower block and bought some expensive fast food, good tempers were restored all round.

We sat in the dusk watching fit Swiss jog past the perimeter fence. Two little doughnut Dutch children, fresh and bright as Gouda cheeses, sat beside their tanned and athletic parents outside a neighbouring caravan and eyed our girls hopefully. A few minutes later Tilly and Daisy took a ball off to the playground with elaborate casualness and soon the doughnuts wandered over to join them. Children were an international fraternity, it seemed. An even more battered GB campervan than ours was parked close by, but its adult occupants didn't want to acknowledge fellow countrymen. Tom and I grinned wryly at each other across the table, tacitly signalling a truce.

'What's the plan tomorrow?' he asked innocently. I threw a handy teddybear at him.

'Heidi's Alp. I'll drive.'

I don't know if *Heidi* has ever been officially canonised by the woman's movement but it is no bad reader for today's feminist young idea. Joanna Spyri was on holiday in Maienfeld when the idea for the book occurred to her, but she actually lived in or around the city of Zürich all her life. As part of a circle of liberated Zürich intellectuals, she was interested in improving the infant mind without talking down to it. But in *Heidi* she succeeded in doing much more. Her heroine is a robust, clear-sighted little girl, totally uninterested in the pursuit of traditional feminine accomplishments, and with no time for the frills and furbelows of polite society. She pulls off her clothes as she climbs the Alm and announces unrepentantly that she'd rather be dressed like the goats. She equals or outdoes Peter in management of the village herd, and is quite unconcerned with the impression she makes on the sternly conventional housekeeper of the Sesemann's Frankfurt household. Interestingly, nobody except the housekeeper seems particularly bothered about her unconventionality – she is generally respected as an individual, and considerable pains are taken, once her homesick distress has been recognised, to get her back to the mountains she loves. Clara is symbolically liberated from conventional restraints by learning to walk when she is in the mountains visiting Heidi and the Alm Uncle.

Perhaps the failure to recognise this aspect of *Heidi* has been due to the shadow cast by such sequels as *Heidi Grows Up, Heidi's Children*, and the many others which mercilessly toss her back on to the domestic treadmill that captures even such exceptional little girls. The sequels were not written by Joanna Spyri, who would certainly have been no party to Heidi marrying the gormless Peter, but by Charles Tritten.

We would find out more about Joanna Spyri herself when we reached her home village of Hirzel, just south of Zürich. For the moment we were going to take Heidi literally. The opening paragraph of the book itself seemed as good a guide to the finding of Heidi's alp as we could wish:

> From the old and pleasantly situated town of Maienfeld a path leads through green, shady meadows to the foot of the mountains which look down from their majestic heights upon the valley below. As the footpath begins to slope gently upwards, the fragrance of the nearby heath, with its short grass and vigorous mountain plants, fills the air; then the way becomes more rugged and the path rises steeply towards the Alps.

Dete and Heidi climb through 'the hamlet called Dorfli' to 'the little brown alm hut which was situated in a sheltered spot some yards off the path . . . more than halfway up the Alm from the village' where Peter and his grandmother live. Three quarters of an hour later they reach 'the top of the Alm where the uncle's cottage stood on a ledge of the mountain.'

Along the side of the cottage facing the valley, the uncle had made himself a bench, and here he now sat puffing his pipe, both hands on his knees, calmly watching the children, the goats and aunt Dete as they climbed. Heidi arrived first. She went straight up to the old man, stretched her hand towards him and said, 'Good evening, Grandfather!'

Good on you, lass. No maidenly blushes, no hanging back. Just a straightforward handshake, person to person. Their relationship continues as an essentially comradely one, with none of the condescension which some adults feel is appropriate to relations with children. This respect for children's competence seems an element common to all the best-loved stories. The Steadfast Tin Soldier and the Little Mermaid never falter in the face of danger, Hans Brinker and Pinocchio take adult responsibility, even Peter Pan plays the man when he stands up to Captain Hook. The art of writing for children centres round the ability to believe that children are not some separate and lesser species but capable personalities in their own right. I thought about our own family. Certainly we got the best out of the girls when we allowed them to share in the planning of the day, a say in the direction we took, and an opinion about its merits. With four of them, though, that was easier to do in theory than in practice. I knew I resorted too often to the steamroller tactics which Tom had protested about as we left Italy.

So that day I was full of good resolutions to let them make decisions. Truly democratic action was temporarily postponed because we left Chur at seven o'clock in the morning. The girls were still fast asleep while we drove along the quite old road that runs along the Rhine towards Lichtenstein. Maienfeld itself was closed and sleepy that Sunday except, fortunately, for a bakery where we bought soft, deliciously sweet white rolls, just the sort that Heidi hoarded to bring back to Peter's grandmother. The baker spoke excellent English, and when I told her about our quest she disappeared into the back of the shop to dig out a glossy carrier bag, with a colour photograph of the Maienfeld monument to Heidi, a charming little statue of Heidi bending over a stone water trough. We never saw it in reality: we took the wrong road out of Maienfeld and bypassed Dorfli altogether, but as it turned out we couldn't have made a better mistake.

We drove through the town, an elegant rural backwater little

197

changed, it seemed, from Spyri's day, and up towards the mountains. But instead of arriving at Dorfli we found ourselves at the Heidihof Hotel. We parked Bertha in a discreet corner of the carpark, put on the kettle for coffee and opened our glossy bakery bag. The children sniffed appreciatively as the rich scent of warm dough filled the van, wriggled out of their sleeping bags without protest, and groped for their clothes.

The gods were with us that day. The first thing we saw when we looked out of the van was a peacock, displaying in fine style to a dun-coloured peahen. His efforts were wasted. She turned away indifferently, and he strutted away disconsolately, tail between his legs. Then we noticed a little flock of sheep, settled in biblical ease under the shade of an oak tree, while a small boy in lederhosen held out a bottle of milk to one of the lambs.

'Peter to the life!' I trilled. Tilly looked up from her book and curled a lip. She seemed to have given up on the set texts of the voyage and was deep in one of the Agatha Christies she and Daisy had surreptitiously slipped in among the secondhand paperbacks. Perhaps she was too old for this pursuit of the real Heidi – and too young to find the prospect nostalgic. Unusually subdued, I agreed with Tom's suggestion that we treat ourselves to hot chocolate in the hotel.

As we sat in its ostentatiously rustic interior, a baby goat, a small bell chinking at its throat, started nibbling at the roses just outside the window. I took Susie over to admire it and its three larger relations, but we were interrupted by the sudden appearance of a very sleepy, very angry fat man who chased the goats off down the garden path, yelling imprecations and yanking a pair of badly fitting shorts up his plump white legs as he ran. The hotel owner? Peter in mid-life? I resisted suggesting this to the girls, just as I was keeping quiet about my theory that the waiter had just the right proud profile and pale falcon-lidded eyes for William Tell. He had realised the girls' disappointment at the disappearance of the goats, and he gave them each a handful of sugar lumps, pointing to the pasture at the end of the garden. Much satisfactory nuzzling of small fingers followed.

Meanwhile Tom had packed up a picnic between the four fjällräven knapsacks. The early mist had cleared, the sun was shining on the green meadows; high above we could see the twin peaks of Falknis. Susie looked doubtfully upwards. Presumably from her height the alp looked just about twice as high as it did to us. The baby goats and the hotel playground seemed much more attractive. She walked halfheartedly behind us for a few yards, then stopped. I spoke cajolingly of wild strawberries and edelweiss. She sat down, unmoved. Tom snapped a parental summons. She lay down. I ranted impatiently, all grand democratic resolutions abandoned. Then Tilly had a brainwave.

'Come on Susie – you be the Scout and tell us what's ahead.' We watched in disbelief as Susie not only stood up but ran ahead of us through the woods and up the hill.

'There's a signpost up here,' she called back importantly. Small, yellow and discreet, two wooden arrows pointed upwards to Heidialp, straight onwards to Dorfli. Triumph. All had been guesswork so far, simply following the facts given in Joanna Spyri's book, although the account of Maienfeld and Dorfli that I'd found in a 1927 centenary edition of the book had given me some reason to hope that Heidi country might still be much as it had been when Spyri described it in 1880.

Marguerite Davis, the American artist commissioned to produce the centennial illustrations, took her responsibility seriously enough to cross the Atlantic and visit Maienfeld for herself. There she found a latterday Peter called Bernard, 'taking his way through the town, blowing his horn to call the goats from stable to shed, and to the accompaniment of the merry tinkle-tinkle of their little bells, trudging the steep path to the upland pastures'. She followed his route up to the rocky cliffs and 'the upland pastures, the true "alps", soft green slopes which give their name to the mountains themselves.' Her illustrations reflect her passion for accuracy; her description of her journey, included as a postcript in that 1927 edition, reveal her to be a true romantic.

Let us shoulder our knapsacks some early dawn, even before the stars have faded, and make the long ascent to the Maienfeld Alp. The zigzag trail leads up through pleasant woods and through open spaces that permit glimpses of the spreading valley, past nodding clusters of bluebells, foxglove, gentians, cyclamen, bright clinging stone cresses, and, higher still, the scarlet alpenrose. Above, against the skyline, on Vilan, we make out the moving forms of sheep and cows, and perhaps the gleam of a new roof. Another hour, and we have left this alp far below. Up and over a shoulder of Furniss, with the lofty pinnacles of Falknis facing us and snow-capped Scesaplana in the distance, we come at last upon two huts nestling in a sheltered fold of the wide barren landscape. Two shepherds, leaning on their staffs, stand outlined on the ridge against the sky. Silent, wind-swept figures, their heavy hooded cloaks about them, they watch over their flocks and herds.

All sorts of modern interference could have spoilt that picture in the last fifty years – coach parks, tarmac roads, cable-cars, son et lumière. To find the mountain unspoilt, its footpaths barely visible in the long grass, was an enormous relief.

We trekked up and across the first alp in single file, found another little signpost pointing into the depths of a steep beech wood, and began a demanding trudge up a dank streambed. The woods petered out after half a mile into a hayfield. Swathes of flower-filled grass were toppling like discarded bouquets behind a large motor-mower, guided expertly along the steep gradient by a sun-tanned farmer. Near the pine woods that reached up the mountain above the meadow were two old timber huts; further away was a newer farmhouse. We had reached the right level for Peter's house, where his grandmother shivered in the dark and draughts until Heidi came to lighten her life, bringing the Alm Uncle with her to patch up the old walls. These were the cheese huts, just as Marguerite Davis had described them. It was too early in the season for us to meet the 'two brawny sons of the soil' she saw making great round Swiss cheeses, but we had elevenses in the freshly cut hay with our own cheese, squirted out of bright blue tubes, but Swiss-made nonetheless.

At this height the view across the valley to the snowcapped mountains on the other side was vast and uninterrupted. But there was still a long way to go. We set off again, losing the lightly marked path within minutes and finding ourselves scrabbling blindly upwards through a pinewood in a manner unpleasantly reminiscent of the Brocken. Even with stout staves and generously distributed iron rations it was hard going, and Ellie and Susie began to flag badly. Then we hit a forestry track, which provided easier, if less picturesque, progress. We'd been walking for nearly four hours, off and on, and muttered remarks about obscure forms of child abuse were being exchanged between Tilly and Daisy.

'What does walking people's feet off mean?' asked Ellie. 'And how long does it take?'

'About three hours, I should think,' answered Daisy heartlessly. 'I should think yours will drop off any minute. They look pretty loose.'

But what was that? Bells. Hope leapt abundant. Goats? Little Bear? Little Swan? Goldfinch? We raced up the rocky track to a gate which led into an even higher pasture. The goats turned out to be enormous soft-eyed cows. There wasn't a hut of any sort in sight. Discouraged we sat down and considered.

'Why don't we camp here? said Tilly, inspired by the sight of a pile of burnt sticks where somebody had made a fire. Just then a lanky young man swung up the track, driving two more cows up to the pasture.

'Let's ask him if it would be all right.'

Tom approached him. The cowherd explained that the pasture belonged to a man who lived about a kilometre further on. We could ask, he said.

The prospect lent wings to our heels, for a few yards at least. Then the steepness of the hill took its toll on the shorter legs again. Vast cowpats buzzing with fat orange flies had to be negotiated with fascinated fastidiousness. Progress grew slower and slower. When we rounded the next bend of the hill and found that there was still no sign of a house, Susie declared UDI. Definitely time for lunch. Tom and the girls slumped down in the grass, cropped short up here by the cows, but still full of flowers, and began to unpack the picnic. I couldn't resist going on a little further.

'I'll just take a quick look over the next rise,' I called to them. But before I reached it, after only a couple of dozen steps, I saw the tip of a wooden roof very close by, just a little further round the hill. I ran back with the good news, and we hastily repacked the knapsack. Exhaustion forgotten, the girls raced ahead of us. They found a small wooden chalet, slightly shabby, and halfheartedly rendered against the weather. In front of it was a bench, arranged to give the best possible view across the valley. Nailed into the lintel was the whitened antler of a deer, carved on the doorframe was a single magic word: Heidialp. 1119m. Tom looked at Susie in awe.

'Susie! You've just climbed Helvellyn.' Susie was more interested in getting inside.

'Knock at the door. Let's see if anyone is in.' A little nervously, I knocked. There was no sound from inside. I knocked again. Then a scraping noise from above the door made us all look up. Out of the tiny square window an old man with a long silvery beard was leaning, puffing at a fine old pipe, fixing us with very bright blue eyes.

'The Alm Uncle!' shouted Tilly, Daisy, Ellie and Susie as one

girl. The situation was the more unreal in that Tom and I had been
cracking jokes on the way up the mountain about the good living
some senior citizen could make by living in a hut there, greeting
passing visitors with a regal wave. There was only one possible
question.

'Is Heidi there too?'

He chuckled and shook his head, then disappeared. A few
moments later he opened the front door, and nodded courteously.
He wore a blue peasant smock with a red embroidered collar, thick
corduroy trousers and no shoes. A toe peered inquiringly out of one
sock. Tom asked him whether we could camp in one corner of his
field, but his academic German was far removed from the Alm
Uncle's dialect. At first there was nothing but head shaking. Then a
slow nod. I pulled a bottle of Tuscan red out of my knapsack, and
suggested in my best sign language that we take a glass together to
celebrate. He chuckled again, and to Susie's joy – she'd been itching
to explore – invited us to come inside.

It was a very small room, wood-lined, a little gloomy, with a
brown-tiled woodstove and a low dresser at the back of the room.
A ladderlike stair led up to the loft above; a velvet-smooth pine
table stood in one corner with a highbacked settle curving round
two sides of it. On the walls were pictures of animals cut out of
some glossy calendar, and brass holders for candles. Leaning
against the wall near the stove was a large milkcan with carrying
straps like a knapsack and a pair of stout hobnailed boots. The Alm
Uncle disappeared into a small scullery and emerged with a huge
white jug and four paper cups, incongruously gaudy with orange
marigolds.

'Would the children like some milk?'

Tilly scowled a negative at me as she hates both milk and butter,
but this was too good to miss.

'Ja, Ja, danke schön!' I answered enthusiastically, signalling to
Tilly that I would drink hers. We seemed to be literally reliving
Heidi's first meal in the grandfather's hut:

> Heidi lifted her little bowl and drank without stopping.
> 'Do you like the milk?' the grandfather asked.
> 'It's the best milk I have ever tasted!' replied Heidi.
> 'You can have more,' said the grandfather, filling the little
> bowl again and putting it before her.

Well, not quite. By the time I had gulped down three out of the four beakers of milk while the Alm Uncle was putting the jug back into the cool of the scullery, there was no demand for refills.

'Best milk I've ever tasted!' said Susie loyally. So it was; thick and creamy and quite unlike the average pasteurised pinta.

The halting conversation between Tom and the Alm Uncle was flowing more easily, as each got used to the other's accent. It began to take an interesting turn. Clearly, from his gestures to the sky, he was uneasy about us sleeping in the field because it was going to rain that night. The sky looked so faultlessly blue that I could hardly believe this, but when the old man pointed up the stair, I wondered whether this was all some fevered wishfulfilling dream.

'Where shall I sleep, Grandfather?'
'Wherever you want to.'
This seemed to please the child and she began to inspect every corner. By the grandfather's bed, wooden steps went up, and when the child climbed the little ladder she found herself in the hay-loft. A bale of hay, fresh and sweet-smelling, lay on the floor, and from a little window in the roof she could see far down into the valley.

'Oh this is where I want to sleep!' she cried joyfully. 'It is lovely! Come and see how lovely it is, Grandfather!'
'I have seen it before!' came from below.

But it was true. He was suggesting that we have a look upstairs and see if we could all fit in. The children raced up the stair like monkeys. Tom and I climbed up more soberly but equally elated. The attic was no longer a hay loft. In the front part were two highsided wooden beds, each topped with a red and white checked duvet. Looking out of the little window through which we had first seen the Alm Uncle, we gazed down the valley. We saw, just as Heidi had, a limitless view down the valley, the Rhine winding away, snowcapped peaks opposite. There was no thought of damp corners of fields any more – this was where we wanted to sleep.

At the back of the attic was a large clear space, with a pile of neatly folded cream wool blankets and some thin mattresses. Andreas, as we had by now discovered this particular Alm Uncle was called, pointed first to them, and then to one of the beds. He explained his wife was away at the moment – she didn't spend much time up on the mountain, but had a market gardening job in a nearby village. Two of the girls could have her bed, and the rest of us could make something of the mattresses. Perhaps we had sleeping bags?

We looked at each other. To have come all these hundreds of miles with only the vaguest of directions, and find ourselves sleeping in a Heidialpine attic seemed too good to be true. But the gods, as I said, were with us that day. Tom nobly volunteered to walk back to the van, drive it as far up the forestry track as he could, and then hump the sleeping bags and anything else he could carry up the hillside. We waved the Alm Uncle goodbye for the moment and set off to find a good place for our long delayed lunch.

We found a fine grassy hump in the middle of the meadow, pulled off shoes, socks and as much clothing as we could decently remove and set to. Food, in Lucy-Ann's memorable words, always tastes better out of doors, and that day it was eaten with an appetite that only climbing a decent-sized alp can provide. Then Tom disappeared down the hill, and the girls and I headed up towards the pine woods to explore. They seemed to have multiplied rather since Heidi's time.

'What about the glacier?' said Tilly. 'And the wild strawberries; Peter and Heidi found lots of wild strawberries, didn't they? Can we climb higher up and look for them when Daddy comes back?' How I had underestimated her. As she talked knowledgeably of how steep and rocky the precipice must have been where Goldfinch nearly fell, I realised that her grasp of Heidi geography was rather more complete than my own. One never knew with Tilly. One day she would be reading an old-fashioned classic like *What Katy Did*, the next it would be Judy Blume or esoteric pop magazines devoted to Wham. Fortunately for me, just then she was all for Heidi and her early morning superciliousness had vanished. I suggested that the two of us went on an exploratory climb to the top of the mountain when Tom came back. There was no question of Susie and Ellie going further that day, and even Daisy's stronger legs had had enough mountaineering.

We didn't get far into the woods – the thistles and pine needles were too much for our tender townee feet – but we settled down on an ancient tree stump to play one of the girls' favourite games, one of the few that for some reason they play without conflict of any sort. They describe, according to strict rules of precedence, what sort of houses and gardens they'll have when they grow up. No plagiarism is allowed, although a polite request to include a similar feature is treated on its merits. First the outside appearance of the house is drawn by each of them in turn. Then the garden. Then each room inside.

As I dozed off to this gentle litany, I recalled a very similar game I used to play walking to school with my best friend. When we walked past the burnt-out ruin of a Victorian villa in the Hampton Road, it started automatically: systematic rebuilding and restoration by mutual agreement. I'd never told the girls about that, yet here they were rehearsing their domestic futures in exactly the same way. Their imaginations had obviously been well-fuelled by their recent experiences. Ellie included a giant water-chute; Tilly wanted a carved Tyrolean balcony edged with red geraniums. One of the most unexpected of my experiences as I watch my children grow up has been the slow, intermittent recollection of my own childhood, as if I was watching the patchy fragments of an old and long misunderstood film, its sound distorted and interrupted, its meaning occasionally devastatingly clear. I suppose all parents go through it. It ought to be a salutary experience – natural psychotherapy. Just then it seemed like a predetermined tyranny.

After an hour or so, we wandered out of the woods and down across the meadow to a steep cliff. Beech trees were clinging to the edge with gravity-defying tenacity, their roots gripping the crumbling rock-face like long desperate fingers. In the hollows between them, the girls, still doggedly domestic, began to make tiny log-cabins out of twigs, rooms furnished with moss and flowers. Tilly stitched together beech leaves with pine needles for a quilt, stuffed a leaf pillow with thistledown. Daisy arranged a banquet along a board of bark: starry white flowers as plates, acorn goblets, leafy napkins. The world shrunk around us as they laboured, giants intent on creating a world in miniature.

The afternoon passed unnoticed. It had been three hours since Tom started down the hill. We decided to send scouts to look out for him at intervals. Third time lucky – we saw a weary figure collapsed beside an enormous pile of sleeping bags halfway up the final steep slope. Recklessly losing height, we raced down to form a baggage train back up again. Bertha had made easy work of the forestry track until the very top, where Tom had backed her into a clearing to turn round. The gradient was deceptive – too steep for such a portly old lady. Only by patiently revving her up and bursting forward a little before she stalled had he managed to inch her back onto the track. Still, here he was and there she was, close enough for me to go down later on and bring up some supper.

The pasture which Peter usually chose and where he spent the

205

day was situated at the foot of the high rocks. Bushes and fir trees covered the lower parts but nearer the summit the rocks rose bare and rugged towards the sky. On one side of the mountain jagged clefts stretched far down, and the grand-father had been right to warn Peter of the danger.

Tom had earned a rest, and Daisy, Ellie and Susie were all for continuing their elf village, so Tilly and I set off alone to find our way to the mountain top. There was no need for coaxing, no pausing for unenthusiastic feet to catch up. Gloriously un-hampered, we climbed rapidly up through the pine woods. The path got steeper and steeper, then petered out altogether into brush and broken rock. Sticks helped a bit, then it became a matter of hands and knees. But the top was in sight – or so we thought. We hauled ourselves up to find that we had only got to the lowest tip of a long narrow ridge. It was about two metres wide, with a grassy rabbit track running along it. On the other side was a true precipice, a vertical drop downwards where 'a heedless little goat might easily tumble down and break his legs'. We decided this could well be the setting of the dramatic scene of the saving of Goldfinch.

Peter arrived just in time, for the little goat was just about to jump towards the edge of the precipice. Peter, lunging towards the goat fell down and only managed to seize one of its legs as he fell. Goldfinch gave an angry cry at finding herself caught, and tried desperately to free herself. Peter could not get up, and shouted for Heidi to help because he was afraid that Goldfinch might wrench her leg. Heidi was already there and at once saw the danger. She quickly gathered some sweet smelling plants from the ground and held them towards Goldfinch, saying coaxingly, 'Come along, Goldfinch, and be good! Look! You might fall down and hurt yourself.'

What about the wild strawberries? We looked carefully around, and found a few leaves, but no berries at all. Tilly's face fell. She had a vision of filling her white sunhat with them and carrying them down the mountain in triumph. Perhaps it was too early in the year – perhaps this ridge was too shady – perhaps higher up it would be hotter. The flowers up here – exquisitely small yellow pansies, a lacy purple vetch with bright turquoise buds, tiny violets hiding their heads beneath thick dark leaves – were quite different from the plump luscious blooms in the meadowgrass. It was time for a rest. I pulled out some thick dark Perugia chocolate. Tilly produced a couple of apples.

Refreshed, we climbed on, clinging on to anything that looked strong enough – tree roots, rocks, fallen branches. Two more illusory summits later I looked up to yet another apparent peak, steeper and crumblier than anything we'd scaled so far, and suddenly felt very small and a long way from home. The sun had disappeared into some dark grey banks of cloud; I wasn't sure whether going down would be any faster than climbing up. We retreated – still without either strawberries or the glimpse of a glacier. But on the way down we looked right across the precipice to the east and saw a great double-peaked mountain soaring up on the other side of the chasm. It was topped with snow even then, in early June, and its sides were laced with waterfalls. Falknis, without a shadow of doubt. Then we saw something even more exciting. Unbelievably high up on its steep sides was a wooden house, bulwarked from the gorge below by a stone wall. It looked well kept – we could see splashes of red geraniums at the windows, a wood pile stacked against one side. There was absolutely no visible way of getting to it. Landslips of rock flanked it, and below the woods looked if anything steeper than the ones beneath us. I strained my eyes for the frail thread of a cable-car, but I could see nothing but a narrow road winding deep into the head of the valley and showing no signs of turning towards the house. Was that the true Alm Uncle's house? Was there an approach to it from the other side of the ridge we were exploring? Or had Joanna Spyri climbed this far as we had, seen it there, and spun her story around its inaccessibility? Certainly only the most misanthropic of men could live there – it was a true eyrie.

'Grandfather, why did the eagle screech so?' Heidi asked.
'He screams in mockery of the people in the villages down in the valley where they sit gossiping together. He wants to say "If you would all mind your own business or climb up into the heights like me you would be much happier."'

We half walked, half slid back down to the meadow. Tilly ran to join the housebuilders, and Tom and I walked together down to Bertha's cosy domestic comforts. Feeling very middle-aged and distinctly weak in the knees, I heard myself saying 'What about a nice cup of tea?' as I crept inside. How feeble, to revel in these bourgeois comforts with all that splendid nature outside. I should be sitting magnificently out there somewhere, a crust of bread, a hunk of cheese and a beaker of milk beside me, scanning the splendid view with eager eyes. Instead, I fossicked about happily with onions and rice, cooking up all our left overs in a big black pot, listening to an inane country and western tape, and drinking large quantities of very strong tea. I often used to stress the value of Bertha as security for the children. I knew by now that she was just as necessary a nest for us as well.

Tom went back up the hill with two more sleeping bags. Half an hour later, the cooking completed, I followed him. The perfect weather of the morning had vanished. It was raining as I toiled up the hill, a bulky knapsack full of children's necessities on my back, the iron pot of risotto in my hands. Heavy going. But once near the hut, seeing the girls wrapped up under the trees listening to Tom telling stories·from the *Odyssey*, the excitement returned. It was nearly six. Time to find the grandfather.

Loaded with the baggage, we returned to the little wooden house and knocked at the door. No answer. A tremor of uncertainty. Had we misunderstood? Was it all some sort of joke? Had he been merely showing us round? At last the door swung open, and a sleepy Alm Uncle in his braces greeted us with a grin. He showed us in, and we sat around the table once more, stricken with sudden shyness. Then he pulled on his boots, swung the curved milkcan with its leather straps on to his back, and made a sign towards the girls and the cows. They got the message, leapt up in excitement, and disappeared after him to witness the evening milking. The rain – only a passing shower – had stopped. Tom went too, while I arranged the black pot on the stove at the back of the room, scraped some raw carrots, and laid the table, using my initiative to find plates, forks and spoons, just as Heidi had.

Then I sat outside on the bench with a glass of wine in my hand, watching the sun hit the tops of the peaks, reminded of my own father's little wooden house high on Norway's mountain spine. His roof was thick turf, bright green in spring, like long blonde hair waving in the wind at the end of the summer. There was the same smell of woodsmoke as you went in, the same soft golden pinewood, the same sensation of sitting somewhere near the roof of the world. I watched Andreas trudging back up the hill with the full milkcan on his back, talking to Tom; the girls skipping and laughing behind them, stopping to splash each other from the stone trough that held a pool of clear icy water from a little mountain spring. I think that moment was the high spot of the whole journey.

Daisy got to me first, bursting with excitement.

'He pulls the cow's udders, Mummy, and the milk comes out hiss hiss!'

'How many did he milk?' I asked.

'Just one – he says the other are mädchens. That means they're too young, Daddy says.'

Andreas swung the can off his back, strained some milk into a jug, and poured out four beakers for the girls. Ellie took a mouthful and pulled a face.

'Urghh. It's warm!' Then she tried again. 'But I do quite like it.'

Hungry from their exertions, Daisy and Susie managed to drink a beaker each, but Tilly, too shy to refuse, again looked desperately at me. I discreetly intercepted hers and swigged it swiftly when Andreas disappeared into the scullery.

Supper was a great success. Andreas and Tom had got used to each other's German, and we learnt that he did get quite a few visitors in the summer – mainly Japanese. This struck me as incongruous until I remembered the thorough throngs of oriental tourists at Neuschwanstein, the early eastern bird perched on the top of Pisa's leaning tower, the young Japanese couple I'd talked to in a campsite laundry who had explained that since they, and most Japanese, only got two weeks holiday, they were determined to see everything possible when they came over to Europe, even if that meant beating pavements from dawn to dusk. It takes some determination to climb Heidi's alp – clearly the Japanese are tourists with true grit.

'But not many stay the night,' he said with a twinkle, as he laced our coffee with some lethal home-made schnapps. A rosy glow pervaded the evening, not entirely due to the sunset, good as that was against the mountains. We looked down on the great clouds racing along the valley floor below us. The peaks opposite were disappearing. Andreas gave the children a pair of binoculars to look at them.

'There's rain on the way again. The field would not have been much fun,' he said, lighting a candle. The children were eager to go to bed, and I was quite happy to keep them company. Tom and Andreas sat up a while longer, then came up the ladder too. The night was punctuated by gentle, very contented snores.

I heard Andreas creaking downstairs at five thirty. Dressing quickly, I followed him, and enjoyed a cup of coffee in companionable silence, watching the dawn come up, tipping the peaks with a softer, pearlier pink and gold. Tom got up soon, and went for a walk across the hillside. But the clear skies didn't last. By the time the girls had clambered sleepily down at seven o'clock, the clouds had massed again. Not wanting to outstay our welcome, we decided that we had better hurry back to the van for breakfast. Goodbyes were said, hands shaken all round. Finally the Alm Uncle put his hand in his pocket and took out a great silver watch. It was beautifully engraved with mountain emblems, and apparently belonged to his own grandfather. He handed it to the girls, and they each admired it in turn. It felt like a ritual of some sort, a promise of a return in the future. As we swung back down the hill to Bertha, I hoped that it had been.

14

An Arrow Escape

To travel hopefully is a better thing than to arrive, and the
true success is to labour.

(Robert Louis Stevenson, *Virginibus Puerisque*, 1881)

We were just in time. The heaviest deluge since Ærøskøbing hailed
down on Bertha's roof as we majestically negotiated the bends of
the forestry track. And we had nearly reached the decency of the
public highway when a forester in a khaki jeep approached us and
told us in no uncertain terms that heavy fines, if not prison
sentences, were incurred by members of the public who invaded
forestry territory. If he had found us parked for the night at the top
of the forest we would probably all be mouldering in an immaculate
Swiss jail. This was not the last time we were to find ourselves on
the wrong side of the Helvetian authorities. Whether it was due to
their unnatural strictness or our absence of luck, I don't know.
Perhaps that chance remark by our talkative neighbour – Swiss
disapproval of large families – had sunk in too deeply. Perhaps we
already had an exaggerated respect for Swiss *moeurs*. Whatever it
was, it made for a tense week for us, and a positively punishing one
for Bertha. When we finally rolled over the French border, I swear
that she gave an audible sigh of relief.

Not that we didn't have good times as well as bad. We drove
from Maienfeld towards Zürich, and even in the pouring rain there
were fine views along Walensee and Zürichsee, the long lakes
beside which the motorway runs – ranks of mountains flanking us
to the south, lakes edged with picturesque stone towns to the north.
It was as yet all a little ordinary: only marginally Swiss and certainly

not alpine. Just after Wadensil, about 22 kilometres before Zürich itself, we turned southwards off the main road and drove up a steep and winding road to the little town of Hirzel. Here, in Joanna Spyri's actual birthplace, I knew there was a small museum devoted to her and her works and I was hoping that it would tell me a little more about her.

Marguerite Davis, illustrator of *Heidi*, explored Hirzel as well as Maienfeld and it has hardly changed from her description of it.

There are flowers everywhere. In the village the houses are neat and tidy, with vegetable gardens, and of course, flowers. Everything looks orderly, clean and comfortable. Just outside the village, and still higher up the mountain, is the white house that belonged to Joanna's parents. From the house, if you look down over the tops of the fir trees into the valley, you can see the great lake of Zürich, with snow-covered mountains behind it.

We asked a breezy girl in a butcher's shop the way to the Spyri Museum. She seized a carton of locally packaged milk. It had a view of Hirzel printed round it.

'That's the church, you see,' she explained in fluent and precise English and tracing a route with her finger. 'You turn down here, past two or three old houses, and you will see it on your left.' We thanked her, and bought the carton of milk, the most wholesome guide one could imagine. But then Switzerland is wholesome, relentlessly wholesome.

Despite the assurances given to me by the Tourist Office I had talked to in Lucerne, the Spyri Museum was closed. It was still pouring with rain, and the only passer-by we could see was scuttling towards her car with excusable haste. Tom managed to collar her just as she was closing the door, and she suggested we ask at the school, just up the road, as Herr Winkler, the museum curator, taught there. We walked to the school, a modern building, much more sophisticated than the little room off the church where Joanna Spyri had learnt with her alphabet. A bell sounded the lesson changeover, and Tom tapped at a door marked J. Winkler. He disappeared inside for what seemed an endless time. We sat in the hall, suntanned gipsies, strangers from another planet in the eyes of the orderly troops of young Maienfelders who were hurrying to and fro. At last the door of the classroom opened. Tom and Herr Winkler came out with a short, neat boy who was holding a key with a large label on it. This was Peter, Herr Winkler explained. He would lead us to the museum and show us round.

The house was a black and white timbered building with a steep red-tiled roof, lapped round by an old-fashioned herbaceous border. Peter unlocked the door carefully and let us in. With the competent wave of an experienced showman he indicated a large model of the Alm Uncle's hut.

Ellie looked at it critically.

'It isn't very like our Alm-Uncle's hut. I don't suppose they've really been there and climbed the alp like we did.'

'The goats look a bit moth-eaten,' said Daisy.

'And Heidi shouldn't have fair hair. She had short dark curly hair.'

More acceptable was the next exhibit, a wheelchair of the type pushed over the precipice by goat-Peter. The girls each sat in it in turn, and gave each other a short Clara experience, while Tom and I admired the old views of Maienfeld and Hirzel on the walls. Then scholar-Peter showed us upstairs and led us carefully through literary relics, letters and mementoes, editions of *Heidi* in all sorts of unlikely languages, and portraits and photographs of Joanna Spyri herself. Bright-eyed, with thick dark hair, she smiled contentedly out of an oval gilt frame: uncannily like her own description of Heidi. Was the book a self-portrait? Who exactly was Joanna Spyri? There is still no English-language biography of her – possibly because her life seems to have been as unexceptionally virtuous and dull as that of our American friend in Holland, the worthy Mabel Mapes Dodge.

She lived in Hirzel from her birth in 1827 until the time of her marriage in 1852 to a friend of her brother, the Zürich lawyer Bernhard Spyri. How much of Heidi came from her own experiences? Joanna too was a late reader. Bored by the village school, she needed the special interest that a new pastor took in her to get going with her books. And her relationship with her grandmother was an extremely close one. The two grandmothers in *Heidi*, Peter's and Clara's, were certainly a tribute to the deep affection she felt for her own mother's mother.

Heidi's singleton position might have been a case of wish-fulfilment. Joanna herself was the fourth daughter in a family of six children: two boys and four girls. Moreover, two aunts, two girl cousins, and the much beloved grandmother all came to live at the large rambling family house high on the hill in Hirzel. Her father was the village doctor, her mother daughter of the parson. It would be hard to find a more solidly middle-class base. But then Heidi is a solid and middle-class book, for all its praise of simple peasant virtues.

We thanked our small guide. He bowed courteously and disappeared back to school. We left Hirzel and drove on into Zürich, where I'd arranged an appointment at the Children's Book Foundation. The children looked eagerly out of the windows for gnomes. They spotted at least three hunched among the thick leather upholstery of the long silver limousines that oozed past Bertha. Slightly flustered by the city traffic, she bumbled towards a parking space. At last I found a meter in BeethovenStrasse. A smart and sniffy lady looked critically at our wheels and shook her head disapprovingly.

'I think she means you've got to get exactly between the lines,' offered Tom.

'No problem,' I replied, reversing Bertha with panache, and steering her in again.

'You're still over the line on my side.'

A shade less patiently, I reversed again, and re-entered the space. It had evidently not been laid out with campervans in mind.

'Nearly,' said Tom, beginning to enjoy himself. 'I'll get out and wave you in.'

Swearing under my breath, I put Bertha into reverse again, and jammed my foot down on the accelerator. Then I swept triumphantly into the gap and looked out at Tom for approval. He was walking towards the window with a grey look to his face.

'You've put a socking great dent in the van behind us.' I looked out of the back window. There was a bumper-shaped mark set squarely across the doors of the small commercial vehicle on the other side of the street. I hadn't felt a thing. Feeling vaguely sick, I wrote a long apologetic letter to the van's owner, setting out meticulously the details of our green card, the name of our insurance company, and my own name and address. I added that I was extremely sorry, and that I would be back at the van in two hours time. As I tucked it under the windscreen, I thought wistfully of the famous joke: 'The people who are watching me think I am leaving my name and address on this piece of paper . . .' This would probably mean days of delay, loss of our no claims bonus and all sorts of other nuisances. We set off, a very subdued little party, to the Book Foundation. There we were very kindly received by the librarian, and the children looked round an exhibition of variorum texts of *Little Red Riding Hood* while I examined a thousand and one variations on the theme of *Heidi*. *Heidi Detective* and *Heidi in Tokyo* were only the most surprising of the many sequels. But my mind kept wandering back to a saucer-shaped dent and an unforgettable expression on Tom's face.

We tried to do Zürich justice. We had a ride on a tram, we visited the famous pastrycooks, we strolled along the riverside and browsed in bookshops. We were impressed to see women driving buses, working on building sites, and sweeping the streets as well as stepping smartly out among the financiers in their executive high heels. But hanging over our heads all the time was the retribution to be faced when we returned to the van. Steps dragging, we turned the corner of BeethovenStrasse and prepared to face the music. There was Bertha, stickers thick on her back window, Pinocchio and Ellie's favourite bear peeping out of the sink, the usual litter of childish pursuits spread across her seats and table. In Lucca we had embellished her with huge postcard views of the city; Pisa had added a garish night scene of the famous tower; a large relief map of Europe showed our route so far in purple magi-marker. The van with the crumpled door had disappeared. We never heard anything more about our misdemeanour. Perhaps its driver just couldn't be bothered to wait around. I prefer to think it was Bertha who charmed him into overlooking it.

Enormously relieved, but still rather shaken, I found myself thinking nostalgically of Oxford for the first time in six weeks. The most powerful of all the emotions expressed in *Heidi* is the claustrophobic homesickness that the plucky little girl feels when she is trapped among the buildings of Frankfurt. Was that inspired by Joanna's memory of a childhood visit to Zürich to stay on her own with an elderly cousin? Or was it an expression of her feelings on settling down to married life in the city? There is no evidence that she felt anything but wholehearted enthusiasm for the cultural and artistic life she led as wife of Zürich's town clerk, the friend of such contemporary notables as Swiss author Conrad Meyer and composer Richard Wagner. Richard Wagner – how odd to find the author of *Heidi* keeping the same company as mad King Ludwig.

Tragedy hit Joanna Spyri four years after the publication of *Heidi*. In 1884 her only child Bernhard died, and a year later her husband followed him to the grave. With one niece as companion, she moved out of Zürich society to a quieter house, and lived a very secluded life, devoting herself entirely to writing books for both children and adults. None of them had the staying power of *Heidi*, which has been so relentlessly reprinted, imitated and translated that one of the best-known historians of children's literature, Bettina Hürlimann, described it as 'a clear danger' for the future of children's literature in Switzerland.

> These new tales created their effects from real life, a thing which few German books were doing at that time. Above all, religious and social questions figured in these tales, and they were based on the actual experience of Joanna Spyri, who was the daughter of a country doctor. Almost everything she describes could have taken place . . . The result was that the Swiss writers pounced on the salient features and would not let go of them. What in Joanna Spyri had been new and unique now became a general Swiss style, only a little modified or changed.

Frankly, I think Hürlimann underestimates *Heidi*'s human appeal – she certainly doesn't spend very much time on what is after all one of the best-loved of European children's classics. The essence of *Heidi*'s charm is the triumph of rural simplicity over city conventions, and there could be no clearer way of grasping that point than by contrasting our night on the Alm with our harassing time in Zürich.

A final postscript to our hunt for *Heidi* came after we returned home. When I was scanning catalogue entries under *Heidi* in the humble 'works of secondary academic interest' catalogue in the Cambridge University Library, I was brought up short by an unlikely title. 'Heidi and Shirley Temple' read the card enigmatically. Even more enigmatically, the book was out – gone missing several years before. The Bodleian in Oxford had unaccountably failed to claim its copyright copy of this gem, but I was lucky enough to come across a video copy of the actual film in our local hire-shop. I rushed it round to some friends that very evening, and we sat down together to see how Shirley Temple interpreted the role.

I'm not sure that Spyri herself would have approved of the hectic improvisation of the scriptwriter. Peter's role is ruthlessly reduced to a walk-on, or rather smirk-on, part. Fräulein Rottenmeier becomes a psychopath who kidnaps Heidi, and the Alm Uncle comes to Frankfurt to save her in a one-horse open sleigh. Finally the Zürich police chase him wildwest-style round the streets and back up into the mountains. Despite, or possibly because of, all this, we found it enthralling. Hollywood, for once arguably improving on an original, had scrapped all the moralising and educational improvement that might weary modern young readers in the book, but had left its straightforward heroine improved on rather than debased – to our surprise we found Shirley Temple's dimpled determination, although admittedly rather unSwiss, was absolutely right for Heidi.

Late on Friday afternoon we left Zürich and headed up country. The mountains grew steeper, the houses turned into picture-book Swiss chalets with carved balconies and geranium-filled window-boxes. Crowded together on the steep valley sides and monotonously well-maintained, they looked like models in a souvenir shop window. I felt like lifting their roofs to listen to their tunes. The weather became abominable – driving rain that we could hardly see through, but we could hardly grumble. We were heading for the banks of Lake Lucerne to relive William Tell's dramatic escape from the bullyboy Austrian overlord Gessler during a mighty storm. To the Swiss, of course, Tell is no children's legend but their greatest national figure, a symbol of democracy, justice, and freedom from tyranny. But Tell was part of my childhood – I had a misty memory of a gripping television serial back in the 1950s with a signature tune that invited its listeners to 'Come away, come away, with William Tell, Come away to the land he loved so well' and a storyline that seemed to owe a good deal to Robin Hood. The two men were virtually contemporaries, but I had always assumed Tell was more real than Hood. One of the surprises of this part of the journey was to discover that he was if anything less real – he even owed something to the Robin Hood legend for his own existence.

Not that the Swiss admit this willingly. The official Tell canon is detailed and authoritative. In the thirteenth century the people of the Forest Cantons stood under the protection and supervision of the Emperor, who used to send his bailiff from time to time to judge criminals and collect the imperial taxes. Towards the end of the century the Dukes of Hapsburg Austria tried to extend their dominion to the Forest Cantons. When Albert of Austria became Emperor he sent his own Austrian officials to the Forest Cantons instead of the imperial bailiffs.

One day, an Austrian bailiff called Gessler decided to find out what people thought of his rule. He had an Austrian hat suspended from a pole in the village of Altdorf and issued an order that every man who passed by should bare his head out of respect to the hat. William Tell and his son Walter from the village of Burglen happened to pass that way without paying due reverence to the hat. Tell was seized and taken to Gessler who knew he was reputed to be a famous crossbowman. To humiliate him, he decreed that Tell could have his freedom if he shot an apple from his son's head. Poor Tell offered his own life rather than risk that of his child, but Gessler declared that if he refused or missed at the first attempt, both he and his son would have to die. Tell had no alternative. He took aim and the arrow struck the apple right through the centre, to wild applause from the assembled crowd, who sympathised with Tell. Gessler, however, had noticed that Tell had put a second arrow into his quiver, and asked what it was for. Tell replied evasively that it was a custom among crossbowmen, but Gessler was not satisfied. He promised to spare Tell's life if he told him the truth. Tell then told him that if he had missed the apple with the first arrow, he would have killed Gessler with the second. Livid with fury, Gessler broke his promise of freedom, and ordered Tell to be taken to Küssnacht and imprisoned for the rest of his life.

An Arrow Escape

The whole party including Gessler set sail across Lake Lucerne for Küssnacht. But Tell had friends in high places – a tremendous storm blew up and threatened to sink the boat. The terrified crew insisted that Tell, as fine a steersman as he was a crossbowman, take the helm. Once freed, he steered straight for a rocky ledge on the eastern shore of the lake, the Axenstein, grabbed his crossbow, made a gigantic leap ashore, and kicked the boat back into the raging waters.

The storm subsided, but Tell had not finished with Gessler. He raced across country to Küssnacht and ambushed Gessler on his way up from the lake, killing him with the ominous second arrow he had saved in Altdorf.

At Brunnen we reversed Bertha right up to the waterfront so that we could see up and down the length of the great boomerang sweep of Lake Lucerne. A paddle-steamer waddlepattered past, painted snowy white with gilded baroque curlicues on her bow. A bivouac of Swedish windsurfers was recovering from the storm, their sails tipped together into informal tents, telling sagas of epic leaps to the sound of a small guitar. Despite the drizzle, the girls played around on the shore, jumping from rock to rock and luring in the swans with biscuit crumbs. Tom cooked up a feast of veal, cream and pasta, and I sat back with a drink and listened to the local cowhorn band practising for the intercanton contest later that month.

The rain fell all night and all the next morning. We abandoned our original plan to walk from Brunnen along the shore of the lake to Fuellen via the Tell Chapel, although the 'eight-mile ramble' enjoyed by the American traveller Weldon F. Heald and his wife sounded an idyllic one for better weather:

We pass picturesque chalets and weatherbeaten barns, and farmers haying on the steep grassy hillsides. Across the lake rises a row of towering peaks, culminating in the glittering, glacier-hung summits of the Uri-Rotstock and, straight ahead, at the lake's end, is the giant pyramid of the Bristenstock.

We lunch on potato soup, Emmentaler cheese, French bread and a big salad bowl beneath a trellised vine at the little inn above Tell's Chapel. Then after descending to the steep lake shore, we hit the road and thread the long tunnels of the Axenstrasse, hewn out of solid rock, with windows giving superb views of the lake and mountains. Late in the afternoon we take the boat from Fuellen back to Lucerne and, maybe after a grand sunset over the lake, we approach the lights of the city in the dark of a soft summer night.

We all liked the idea of that return by paddlesteamer, but in the pouring rain the eight-mile walk was out of the question. Instead we drove to Axenstein, climbed down the 157 steps to Tell's chapel and admired the frescoes that celebrate the legendary leap to freedom. They have an Old Testament grandeur about them, full of epic gesture and wild romance, and quite out of keeping with their frame, a humble open porch on the very brink of the lake. The girls practised leaps on the nearby steamer pier and decided that Tell must have had very long legs indeed. At the souvenir shop above the chapel, Ellie bought a horn-handled knife in a leather sheath which has remained her most treasured memento of the trip. I think it gave her a comforting feeling of hidden power, even though its uses were limited to chopping up the lunchtime salads and spreading butter on the picnic rolls.

The rain began to lift a little, and the lake suddenly sprouted sails large and small; stout cabin yachts and sleek Lasers keeling over dramatically to leeward, rainbow-tinted windsurfers with their masts bent back almost horizontally to windward. Fuellen, at the southernmost tip of Lake Lucerne, is a sailor's mecca, and my boomhand was getting distinctly itchy-fingered. But windsurfing, I had discovered on the odd occasions on the trip when I did hire a board, was not great spectator sport for the family. Time passed like lightning for me – skidding over the waves, adjusting to wind shifts, trying out new manœuvres that tested my rather mediocre skills to the utmost. To them it was a tedious toing and froing to no apparent purpose. Whenever I was within hailing distance they yelled 'Mummmeeeee' across the water like banshees, tolling me back from my sole self to the mundane requirements of lunch or tea.

'Why do you keep falling in?' they asked when I returned, hungry for appreciation of my semi-mastery of the duck-tack. I contented myself with fantasising about another holiday with just one keen windsurfing friend – Jane (without Sarah), or Louise, whom I'd taught to sail in Wellington boots on Port Meadow last February. Hopping from lake to lake with our boards on the roofrack and a tent in the boot. This fantasy, embroidered by every new sailing location we passed, had become rather more fun than actually sailing. I didn't even suggest hiring a board at Fuellen. We stopped at the excellent supermarket there, bought strawberries and cream cheese, hazelnut pâté and a rich malted loaf, and picnicked in the van.

After lunch Daisy and Tilly put together an impromptu musical show on the boulevard behind the van. We watched the final performance through the back window. So too did a large uninvited audience – just as the cabaret began, a train shunted slowly past and stopped. The girls were unperturbed, marching up and down under a white umbrella in their rainbow-hued boots, singing and joking in the rain. They had lost all their early self-consciousness and inhibitions about what foreigners might think of them. But were they more civilised? What would Mrs Ross-Browne think of them? I found I didn't really care. What seemed much more important now was their initiative and self-confidence.

We washed up and tidied Bertha into Swiss respectability, then headed up the valley to the heart of Tell country – Altdorf, witness of the famous apple incident, and Burglen, traditional home of Tell. Despite the rain, the statue of William Tell at Altdorf was all that could be desired. Tell's massive legs are the width of an average torso, his jaw puts Desperate Dan's to shame, and his sturdy son, hardly able to clasp his father round the waist, looks adoringly upwards at the heroic bulk of his father. Behind the great bronze is a painted Swiss homeland, a little jaundiced now, but an ancient postcard bought in a bookshop nearby showed its former blue and green glory. The card also showed a tramcar parked beside the monument, with a bevy of prim white-clad schoolgirls spilling out of it and peering earnestly up at Tell's bulging thews. Today the square was deserted, the convent girls replaced by a woman policeman in a formidable ankle-length fluorescent orange mackin-tosh, studded with reflector stickers, and topped by a snowy white topee. Familiarity had bred contempt of Tell's legs: all her attention was concentrated on directing the traffic.

We had parked the car in a carpark. As we walked back to it, Tom noticed a strange building at the end. It was a sports hall, judging from the notices outside it, but it was built right into the mountain. I suddenly remembered an article I had read about Switzerland's nuclear shelter programme. Every Swiss citizen has somewhere to go when the big bang comes, and most of the shelters are used as sports halls. This was evidently the Altdorf bunker, and very capacious and well-appointed it seemed to be. Latter-day William Tells will play pingpong while Europe burns.

After all this hard evidence, it was disconcerting to discover, in the exquisitely arranged little William Tell Museum at Burglen, that the Swiss themselves knew little more about William Tell than I did. For it appears he has no foundation in history at all. He is pure myth.

The museum is housed in the Wattigwyler Tower, once part of the twelfth-century convent of Frauminster. 'Most of the exhibits in the Museum are self-explanatory,' announces its Short Guide with disarming frankness. We admired the numerous absolutely self-explanatory portraits, busts, statuettes and drawings of Tell, Gessler and the boy Walter in every imaginable pose, dress, material and language. Some sort of image of Tell was evidently once as pious a necessity to the Swiss as Abe Lincoln was to the Yankees, Queen Victoria to the British or Mao Tse-tung to the Chinese.

'We can only direct your attention to some objects of note,' the Guide continued. Most notable of all the objects is the famous White Book of Sarnen. Written in 1470, and based on an even earlier manuscript, it is the first known description of the story of William Tell, illustrated by a historic woodcut showing a short chubby Walter looking trustingly across at his far-away father. Tell waves a crossbow vaguely towards him, his eyes raised to heaven in saintly misgiving. In 1585 the government of Uri, Tell's home canton, commissioned an itinerant French artist called William Tugginer to paint a portrait of Tell, and copies of this official likeness were spread all over Europe as the 'true portrait of Tell'.

But although the historical records of the Tell story date back to the fifteenth century, it was not until the eighteenth-century playwright Friedrich Schiller wrote his play, turned into an opera by Rossini, that the myth of Tell, nicely calculated to appeal to the romantic revolutionaries of the late eighteenth century, swept Europe. Then a foolhardy academic wrote a book pointing out how apocryphal the whole story was. Tell, he revealed, owed much to Scandinavian myths, something to Robin Hood and Yorkshire's Clym of the Clough, but nothing all to Swiss history. The book was publicly burnt on bonfires all over Switzerland.

The girls were not particularly worried about the veracity of the Tell legend. They thought he sounded a splendid character, the sort of father you could really depend upon. Tilly's favourite picture was an ingeniously angled affair that changed the scene depicted as you walk past it. Daisy liked a stained-glass version best. Ellie fondled one of the many wooden statuettes, wondering whether to become a woodcarver when she grew up. Susie was predictably most interested in the spirited rendering of Tell in old age, nobly sacrificing his own life to save a baby whose cradle had been carelessly allowed to fall into a mountain torrent. 'And outside', the lady at the checkout told us, 'you can see that very stream.'

We crossed over the road and had a look at it. Turbulent boiling water. No wonder no one else would jump into it. A worthy end for a great hero. Why quibble over details? I remembered Elizabeth Jennings' haunting call for the revival of faith – 'Myths are the memories we have rejected, and legends need the freedom of our minds.' We had come to Europe to look for magic – I had begun to realise that finding it or not was a matter of inclination and mood, almost of whim. On a bad day, when one or all of us were tired, grouchy or nervous, the most exotic of settings could seem banal. On a good one, when our heads were full of adventure and enterprise, the most ordinary of situations could be tinged with romance. Our journey was not dependent on the places we found, but on how we chose to see them.

15
Snow and Svisits

'I have had the most terrible experience that can occur to
anyone,' said the Shadow. 'Only think of it – to be sure, a
poor shadow's brain isn't equal to the strain – only think,
my shadow has gone mad! He believes that he is the man
and that I – just think of it – am his shadow!'
'That is awful,' said the Princess; 'I hope he is shut up?'
'Indeed he is. I'm afraid he'll never get the better of it.'

(Hans Christian Andersen, *The Shadow*)

The real business of Switzerland, international wheelerdealing
apart, is with mountains. The Austrian Alps had been impressive,
but we had only glimpsed them afar in that long day's dash across
the Brenner Pass, our tongues hanging out for Italian icecream.
Maienfeld's peaks had been a shade domestic, Zürich's views too
tamed. We decided to turn Bertha's substantial engine uphill and
head for a traditionally English climbing and walking paradise, the
Bernese Oberland. We drove round the banks of Lake Lucerne,
swinging southwards to Sarnen just before we reached Lucerne
itself, and crossing the Brünigpass into the country between the
lakes.

The chalets grew more intricate – often linked together by
wooden walkways, their balconies carved in fantastical shapes. The
scent of tourism was in the air. Here the Hotel Milan, there Mon
Repos, and there – disgracefully misleadingly, we thought in a
rather superior way, knowing what we did – was a Heidi-Shop,
selling zany bright-eyed Peters and flaxen Heidis with a fine
disregard for Spyri's description of her heroine as having short,

dark curly hair. Even Shirley Temple had had the grace to damp down her blonde curls for the part.

Had it been high summer we could have massed with other tourists and watched the drama of William Tell, the Tellspiele, being retold for the nth time at Interlaken, but happily it was too early in the year to be tempted to do any such thing. My mind was beginning to boggle at the vision of costume dramas being performed all over Europe for the benefit of the tours in search of the picturesque. One detail I would have liked to confirm. A friend who has seen Tellspiele at Interlaken told me that a cunning distraction is launched just as Tell shoots the arrow at his son's head – a team of galloping horses enters the arena from the other end. When the spectators look back, there is an arrow pinioning the apple neatly . . .

Interlaken no doubt has its charms, but it looked too built-up, too crisscrossed by railways and motorways, for our taste. Every flat inch of Switzerland is put to efficient use. Consequently much of it is an aesthetic nightmare: ancient timber farmhouses are huggermugger with concrete bungalows; armies of pylons stalk aggressively through any available valley.

We wound up into the mountains to Lauterbrunnen, from which a rack-and-pinion railway takes visitors year in year out to the highest railway station in Europe, the Jungfraujoch. The usual patient queue of Swiss drivers tailed behind us. In Italy they would have been roaring past on the hairpins with no more formality than a casual crossing of their breasts. Here the large yellow motoring posters advising 'Fairness towards All' were scrupulously observed. The only time we had to watch out on Swiss roads is when we heard the jaunty siren of one of the postbuses, small bright yellow coaches which deliver passengers and mail all over the mountains, and whose drivers regard tourist traffic as of no greater moment than a seasonal migration of toads.

Set in a deep gorge, with curtains of water tumbling a thousand feet or more all around, Lauterbrunnen was evidently a superb base for walks and climbs. We parked Bertha and looked around for somewhere to eat. Attracted by a pretty waitress who grinned out as us as we peered in, we chose a log cabin eatery, a cross between the home of the Seven Dwarfs and a McDonalds. A large rowdy party in national costume sat at the next table – the Lauterbrunnen Lions, to judge from their air of professional complacency and benevolent bonhomie. They too twinkled a welcome to the girls, and soon the storms and prangs of the last two days were forgotten. Snow-White brought over a menu, and very soon the girls were gobbling up generous kinder portions of wienerschnitzel and chips. I chomped through a large peppered steak, and Tom wrapped himself round gooey fondue. Washed down with apple juice and a hearty Pinot Noir, and followed by enormous icecream sherbets all round, it was the best blow-out we had had since Legoland. Up in the mountains, the brisk successful fussiness that plagues the Swiss in towns seemed to disappear. They were never exactly laid back, but they did make an attempt at holiday mood.

We moved Bertha into the enormous campsite. There were hundreds of vehicles parked there, but they were dwarfed by their setting, veiled by silver birches and larches. Caravans, campervans, coaches, even, to the children's delighted recognition, the English doubledecker bus we had seen in Sababurg, looking like dinky toys against the sheer backdrop of the rockface. Permanent vans were disguised as tiny chalets by timber shells. The central buildings of the site were fringed with balconies, the camp office lined with challenging books of mountain walks, and charts of alpine flora and fauna. We had meant to stay only one night at Lauterbrunnen – we ended up staying three, even then finding it hard to tear ourselves away from such a lotusland.

Next morning the clouds had vanished. We woke at half past seven to brilliant sunshine, and Tom and I ambled over to the camp office to register and find out the train times for our ascent of the three giants of the Bernese Oberland – the Monch, the Eiger, and the Jungfrau. The news that we could save £20 by catching the ten past eight train rather than a later one at nine galvanised us into action. We rushed back to the van, urged the children into their warmest clothes, and packed a picnic breakfast as we drove through the village to the station. Not since the ten past seven ferry from Svendburg had so much been achieved so fast. As it turned out, our efforts were a false economy. Tom dropped us at the station and disappeared to park Bertha. Unfortunately, in a hurry and less conscious than I was of her 2.65 metre height – he hadn't after all queued for three hours with the lorries at Rødbyhavn – he opted for the nearby multi-storey carpark.

Either the roof of the van was too high or the ceiling of the carpark too low. There was a soft scrunching of metal – fortunately he had been driving very slowly – as the tip of her cab made contact with a metal pipe casing which underhung the carpark roof. With

James Bondlike sangfroid he reversed back rapidly, parked illicitly in the coach park and raced away from the gathering crowd to leap on to the train. Oblivious of his adventures, the girls and I had been getting increasingly worried that he would miss it. We couldn't understand why he didn't look more triumphant as he settled down beside us for the uphill grind.

Fortunately the day we spent on the roof of Europe was so perfect that even the prospect of insurance and police complications at the end of it could not spoil it. The train was a fine gathering of nations. Our immediate neighbours were an elderly couple from Bombay taking a holiday weekend in the mountains with their son who worked in Munich. They were impressively equipped with duvet jackets and moonboots. My feet were already feeling damp and cold, and I began to wonder if we had kitted ourselves out adequately. Two silver-haired English ladies, obviously stray extras from *The Lady Vanishes*, sat behind us in white cotton sun-hats and stout walking boots, talking of walking down past banks of aconites and gentians. Further down the carriage some students from Hong Kong were chatting merrily to a family of French-Canadians. Outnumbering everybody were the Japanese, craning out of the windows with their cameras clicking like machine-guns. Frowning, they framed, clicked, reframed, clicked again, until it was time to sink down exhausted and change film. I don't think they can have looked at the glaciers, the snowy peaks, the drifts of incredibly varied flowers, with their naked eyes at all.

We changed trains at Kleine Scheidegg, a collection of chalets nestling at the foot of the sheet steel north face of the Eiger. The last leg of the 3,500 metre train ascent was through solid rock, with picture windows cut at intervals to show the untrodden glaciers and cloudlaced valleys. After nearly an hour we arrived at the Jungfrau-joch, the saddle between the Jungfrau and the Monch. After the darkness inside the mountain, the glare of the snowfield all around was blinding. We could see the Sphinx Observatory's silver dome glinting above us, a panorama of white peaks stretching out to every horizon below us. Daisy looked out at it, completely captivated.

'I don't believe this; it just can't be true,' she said quietly, half to herself. We had failed to experience the legendary magic of the summit of the Brocken – but this made up for it with interest.

Very cold indeed by now, despite the brilliant sunshine, we retreated to explore the 'ice-palace', a grotto of tunnels and rooms furnished with cunningly lit ice statuary cut in the heart of the glacier.

'It's like the Snow Queen's palace,' said Susie, who had so taken to some of Hans Andersen's stories that she knew them from memory.

'Do you remember Kay sitting there with the pieces of ice, on the frozen lake that was like a giant jigsaw puzzle? The Snow Queen says he can go if he can spell out the word Eternity from the letters. She said he could have the whole world and a pair of skates.'

'That's right. She called the lake the mirror of intellect – the best place in the whole world.'

'But he can't make the word until Gerda comes, and her tears melt the ice splinters in his heart, and then the pieces of ice dance for joy and end up saying the right word.'

I began to feel dizzy with what I thought was the cold and the glare. Maybe it was the Snow Queen gunning for me – maybe it was just altitude sickness. Whatever it was, I fainted dramatically. I came to slowly in the cafeteria with the aid of some black coffee laced with aquavit. Then a sign on the wall made me forget all weakness.

FRITZ AND GEORGE'S SKI SCHOOL
Learn to ski on Top of Europe.
12 Francs an hour, including ski equipment.

We set off through a warren of tunnels to the other side of the mountain where a tiny ski school had been set up in a vast untrodden bowl of powder snow, fringed by the 4,000 metre peaks all around us. Fritz and George kitted the girls and me out with boots, skis, and gloves. Tom decided to applaud from the sidelines. I'd skied twice before, once as a child and once in Norway just after we got married. Like riding bicycles, the knack came back easily enough. But this was the first time for all of the girls, and an interesting revelation of character.

Susie quickly grew impatient of her disobedient legs and refused to move – but she so charmed Fritz that he swept up to her at intervals, gave her a quick slide down the slope between his legs and then carried her up the T-bar lift back to Tom. Ellie, impatient and ambitious, tumbled and howled and demanded aid, but finally mastered long sideways traverses. A jaunty Australian in a bright yellow T-shirt who skied with no sticks obviously began to admire her gumption – he made a point of waiting by the lift to give her a ride up with him. Daisy jammed her sticks hopefully into the snow and swept away, only to find herself stranded in a far away downhill corner, totally unable to turn or ascend. She stomped furiously up the hill and retired – for the time being. Tilly, methodical and graceful, with a natural sense of balance, listened studiously to George's advice and was soon skiing down and riding up the bar with some verve. Too busy with Ellie to take much notice of anyone else, I suddenly heard a shout of triumph from Daisy. She had returned to the challenge, and had managed, with Fritz's occasional encouragement, to make some respectable progress.

The whole highly technicoloured scene became like a Carry-on film as our train acquaintances caught up with us. The plump parents from Bombay spread out a large green rug on the snow under the indigo sky and sat down crosslegged to watch their son's efforts critically. The prettiest of the students from Hong Kong never mastered the T-bar, so she spent her entire hour standing at the bottom of the slope, very picturesque in a pale pink puffa jacket, being photographed by eager Japanese. Ellie's Australian swerved through the stumbling beginners, whooping with glee. And Fritz and George glided slowly among the fallen bodies with surrealistic grace, tutoring their inept pupils with patient courtesy.

The hour we spent there was a generous one – more like two, I realised when I looked at my watch. Tilly and I were both feeling dizzy by now, and we had run out of money. Fritz pinned enamel badges on to each of the children's jerseys – 'I've skied on Top of Europe' – and congratulated them – especially Ellie.

'She's the champ,' he announced appraisingly. 'They all did well. But she will make a real skier.' I think Ellie's cup was full. She looked rosily content for the rest of the day.

We ate our picnic on some wooden steps in one of the clammy tunnels, wishing we could afford a nourishing hot meal in the restaurant or the cafeteria. In our haste, we hadn't been to the bank that morning so we were having to eke out our last few francs. We queued for the lift up to the base of the Observatory itself, and were eventually pushed in a tangled mass out on to the frail gridiron platform that surrounds it. Susie wriggled out ahead of us, ran to the railing and, as any child would, swung herself over it and back in a neat somersault. Then she went over to have a peek through the telescope. Tom and I, slower-footed, wandered over to the same railing. We looked down at the sheer precipice below. And at each other. Luck had been with us that time. I suddenly felt terribly tired.

Our international fellow travellers were as exhausted as we were. Aggressive couriers massed their groups and, loudly demanding priority, elbowed them into carriages. They were the cosseted sheep, we the unlucky goats, who had to wait for the next train. On the way back fraternity dimmed. Hardly a shutter clicked, heads lolled on weary shoulders. Jolting down in the train was an uncomfortable experience despite the incredible beauty of the alpine flowers that unrolled beside the train window like a never-ending rock garden. A little enviously, I remembered the English ladies we had talked to on the way up, and imagined them striding downhill botanising. Here on the train tiredness was bringing out the worst in everybody, and a gloomy apprehension about Bertha's fate had begun to hover over us.

Our relief at catching a glimpse of her roof as the train entered the station was qualified by the sight of a large yellow clamp pinioning her to the spot. The children were delighted.

'We've been clamped! We've been clamped!' they shouted in triumph.

'I've always wanted to see what they looked like' said Tilly. Ellie began to bounce up and down on the clamp, clinging on to the offside mirror. Susie sat down beside the wheel and started to wrestle with the chains. Tom and I were less amused. I was longing for a cup of tea and a sleep. My eyes were aching with the glare – when I caught a glimpe of myself in the looking glass in the van I saw a beetroot-coloured face and eyes with twin bloodshot stripes running across them. It had been crazy not to take sunglasses with us. We had also realised uneasily that the green insurance card was in my name, and that Tom had left his driving licence in England.

We trudged through the concrete piers of the multistorey carpark to the central office. Slowly and carefully the carpark attendant filled in a long form, drew a tiny diagram to show the exact nature of the 'incident', walked us over to the entrance to describe for the fifth time what had happened, and asked us to sign in triplicate. He was very philosophical about it. No, it wasn't the first time it had happened. In fact, he added, Tom had hit the heating pipes in exactly the same place as an American Winnebago had done in February. Then he walked unhurriedly back to the van with us, unlocked the clamp much to Susie and Ellie's regret, and waved us free.

All next day, and the next night, we dawdled in Lauterbrunnen. I bought Edwardian postcards of English tourists, caught up on letter-writing, dozed and read. Daisy stayed with me, curled up in her nest. Tom and the other three girls went off for a ramble up the valley, and came back full of enthusiasm for its waterfalls and flowers. Travellers returning from the top the next afternoon said there had been a blizzard blowing up there all day – they had seen nothing but cloud and snow. Fortune had smiled on us.

Our final target in Switzerland was the setting of a story quite as down-to-earth as *Heidi* is, but with none of Spyri's moral probity. Mary Plain is as unSwiss a heroine as one could imagine, although her story is set in their capital city and concerns their most famous mascots. Gwynedd Rae was an Englishwoman, and she explains the circumstances of her creation in the introduction to the first of the books.

A few years ago I was obliged to spend most of the winter months at Berne, and I began to look around for some interest. I found it at once in these bears who live in a pit there, and who were, from the very first, an immense joy and amusement to me.

I must explain in a few words their history.

An old legend runs that, as far back as 1191, a certain duke built himself a fortress to protect himself from his enemies, and this same fortress gradually grew into a small fortified town.

One day, hunting near by, he killed a bear, and named the town after it – Berne – now the capital of Switzerland, which still has a bear as its coat of arms.

It was as long ago as 1513 that the Bernese first kept some bears captive in a pit, and ever since, all through the centuries, they have done the same.

They are extremely proud of these beasts, and at all times and in all weathers, you will see an affectionate audience leaning over the wall, feeding them with carrots, biscuits or figs.

There were nine bears when I was there, and they were divided into three pits, which I have called The Den, Parlour Pit and the Nursery. I have also drawn a little plan to make it easier to understand about their home.

I would add that, though I have written this small book, I know nothing whatsoever about the bears' real lives and habits; only, through my many visits to them, they have become my friends, each with their own separate character. So I have written down some things about them, and I feel sure that some of the many children who love bears will agree with me that they might easily be true.

In that last paragraph lies the key to the book's charm. Well-meaning attempts by authors to inform their young readers are usually death to the imagination. Rae makes no effort at all to tell us about the actual habits of bears. She just lets her imagination run riot, and in doing so, creates characters which the children who love her books take to their hearts as true friends. Mary's cousins, Marionetta and Little Wool, her conscientious Aunt Friska, grumpy old Harrods and the formidable Lady Grizzle, were all inspired by the characters of real bears that Gwynedd Rae used to watch in the famous bearpit at Berne. Mary Plain herself is irresistible.

Being an orphan, she had had to bring herself up, more or less, and she had on the whole made a fair success of it. Of course, she was usually in some sort of trouble, but she was quite used to that, and supposed that orphan bears were born different from the rest, so that was why she was always just a little less lucky than the others.

The trouble, as any reader will remember, had nothing to do with luck. Mary, quick-witted and short-tempered, is irrepressibly naughty. Here she is teasing the well-meaning Friska at spelling-time.

'V-I-S-I-T,' spelt out Friskà, 'and when it's more than one visit, what would it be?'

Mary didn't know. 'Yes, come on, you know as well as I do. What does one add on?'

'S,' said Little Wool.

'Good boy. Well, Mary?'

'Svisit,' said Mary brightly.

Friska groaned. 'Mary, Mary, you know as well as I do that's wrong. Think of a word you know – pit. Now, what is it with an S added on?'

'Spit,' said Mary.

'Oh, Mary Plain,' cried the twins in shocked voices, 'what do you mean?'

'This,' said Mary Plain, and spat.

We liked Berne immediately. Even on the map it had looked promising, built in a great loop of the river Aare, with bridges radiating all round it. Beside one of them we saw the magic words: Bear Pit, and aimed Bertha towards it. We parked the van close by the river, and then walked up to the bearpit itself. I had imagined that it would be part of a zoo of some sort, a major site with a formal entrance, so we nearly walked past it. Nothing could be more informal: there is no entrance gate, no charge for leaning over the rail to see the bears go through their paces – scrambling up the ancient pine tree at the centre of each section, cavorting on the edge of the bathing pool, boxing each other good-naturedly.

The bears really are, as Gwynedd Rae described them, much-loved mascots of the people of Berne. Passers-by lean over the railing near their chosen favourite in a mood of benevolent expectancy, just as the Owl Man observed the delinquent Bunch. They look at each bear fondly and toss them the carrots and other wholesome snacks sold at mealtimes from a little central kiosk. It was easy to see how quickly the lonely, slightly bored, Gwynedd Rae would have become caught up in them. We characterised two gruff males in what used to be Mary Plain's nursery, and saw a nurturing mother with two cubs in nextdoor Parlour Pit. One seemed mischievous and aggressive, the other defensively cowered behind a hollow log. In the third part of the pit, the Den, were an older and sleepier pair. That seemed to account for Little Wool and Marionetta as the cubs playing around Friska's feet. Lady Grizzle and the venerable Alpha snoozed in the Den, Harrods and Bunch raced competitively around the largest of the three sections. But of Mary there was no sign. Perhaps she was away on a svisit.

Berne is the home of Lindt chocolate as well as Mary Plain, so we bought a large chocolate bear from the souvenir stall, and a slab of gingerbread topped with a white-iced polar bear. None of the expensive teddy bears looked anything like the brilliant Irene Williamson drawings of Mary, so we weren't tempted by them, but we did fall for a King Nutcracker. I had coveted one ever since we had looked in that Christmas shop in Rothenburg and seen Nutcrackers of every size and every military persuasion. Susie chose a fine squat ugly fellow with a determined chin who will crack nuts for us this Christmas as he has traditionally done for German children for hundreds of years.

We walked over the river to Berne itself, built all of a piece in the fifteenth century, with pale red-tiled roofs and cloisterlike arcades protecting pedestrians from sun or rain; statues and fountains on every street corner, and bears in the most unlikely places. The vegetable market was a work of art, piled with immaculately presented vegetables of the most brilliant quality – shiny white onions, waxy yellow potatoes, gleaming green kohl-rabi. Each stall was a still-life in its own right. At one end a small crowd watched solemnly as two chessplayers manhandled metre-high castles and knights around a board marked out on the pavement. Round the corner was a flower market, a wilderness of clashing pinks and scarlets flourishing in a formal square of government buildings. And in the centre of town was an astrological clock to end all clocks – a monument to Swiss skill in clockmaking. Liveried bears beat drums, dwarfs and ogres grimace, and a gilded cock crows, every hour on the hour.

Under the arcades the shops were full of style. A pair of shoes with toes; a clock powered by tomatoes, another that marked passing minutes by a helterskelter of silver balls. Tom was mesmerised by this, so we decided to buy it for him as an early birthday present. We ate sumptuous warm doughnuts called Berliners for elevenses, then bought smoked ham and long loaves for lunch, with a slab of Lindt chocolate and some peaches to finish up with. In the children's section of a large bookshop, I asked after Mary Plain, but she appears to be completely unknown in her own city. She has never been translated into German, and perhaps that is to be expected. No well-brought-up Swiss child ought to be subjected to such a bad influence.

Nudging our shoulders as we had a last look at the bears was a familiar shadow. Hans Andersen had been to Berne, and visited the bears, on his way from Paris to Italy in 1833. He had heard a story of an old lady, a formerday Gwynedd Rae perhaps, or maybe the original inspiration for the 'Fur Coat Lady' whom Mary svisits so successfully, who loved the bears so much that she left her enormous fortune to them. The will was contested by relatives, but the case of the bears was pleaded so eloquently by the best of Bernese barristers that the bears were made wards in chancery, their inheritance ensuring a supply of carrots and figs in perpetuity.

In a sense we said goodbye to Andersen there. He had been an extraordinarily stimulating guide, leading us to the remotest and most enchanted places of our journey. Of course travelling in his footsteps had not been strictly necessary, even though it had put me under his skin, and opened my mind to a man I had originally found a little absurd. It was by having time to reread his tales to my children that I felt I had got to know and understand him in a totally new way. Characteristics that had once been tedious – his sensitivity to criticism, his bumbling puppylike affection for new acquaintances who might at last admire him as he felt he deserved, his ludicrously childlike enthusiasm for tiny details of experience – didn't annoy me anymore. They made sense as the necessary framework through which a highly original artist could put over far-reaching and insidiously complex messages. Even his inability to win love for himself in his own right ultimately made possible his understanding of the vital role that love does play in the human comedy – or tragedy. How many communicators can win the double audience that the writer of the fairytale, or the classic children's story, achieves? To be read first while a mind is undeveloped and immature, then reread by the same person as an adult with their own children as audience, gives such a story an influence and relevance that is unparalleled by any other art-form. And Andersen himself was quite conscious of this. Our leave-taking of him should be his own words on the subject:

In the whole realm of poetry no domain is so boundless as that of the fairy-tale. It reaches from the blood-drenched graves of Antiquity to the pious legends of a child's picture-book; it takes in the poetry of the people and the poetry of the artist. To me it represents all poetry, and he who masters it must be able to put into it tragedy, comedy, naive simplicity, and humour; at his service are the lyrical note, the childlike narrative, and the language of describing nature.

I will draw a veil over the 360-kilometre drive from Berne to Lyon. In no mood to enjoy the distant snowy peaks or the dramatic views of Lake Geneva, too tired even to take a look at Chillon and dream of Byron and Blondel, we slogged on into Geneva, hitting it at rushhour some months before its ringroad was due to be completed. Misled by motorway signs into thinking they had finished it sooner than our mapbook would have believed possible, we found ourselves sent some thirty miles south to hit what was indeed a motorway, a fine one too – but not one that anyone in their senses would take to get from Geneva to Lyon.

Switzerland had delighted us in many ways. The discovery of Andreas, our own personal Alm Uncle, was for all of us, I think, the high point of the entire trip. The staggering loveliness of our day high on the Jungfraujoch was almost equally unforgettable. And yet we felt strangely displaced there. The premium the Swiss lay on good behaviour and orderly living is something of a strain to those of the casual gipsy persuasion. We had been both lucky and unlucky in our brushes with the authorities, and we had been extremely courteously treated, but the uneasy feeling that we were attending an old-fashioned Great Aunt's teaparty had persisted. The minute we crossed the border and met the casual insouciance of French manners, I felt a load tumble off my shoulders. We stopped in an untidy lay-by around seven in the evening to change drivers. I sat at a bitumen-covered trestle table, glass in hand, and considered the unlovely public conveniences, the overfull wastebins, the lorry-drivers drawing on their Gauloises, with perverse satisfaction.

16

Dulce Domum

This Babar, mad for civilization, is something of an anachronism in our world-weary time; at the same time, however, he is a wonderfully inspiring example. For as an elephant he approaches the achievements of civilization with all the innocence of an animal. The children who take such a delight in the adventures of an enterprising elephant, partake without realising it in the evolution of an ideal society.

(Bettina Hürlimann, *Three Centuries of Children's Books in Europe*, 1959)

Long ago in Oxford, as we were getting into Bertha on May Morning, our French neighbour Martine Moon had come up to me carrying a key. I knew what it was for – the Moon family had a small house in Bagnols, a little village west of Lyon, where Martine herself had grown up.

'Just in case,' she said. 'You might pass near Lyon, and need a break from the van.' Martine also had four children, plus much Gallic common sense.

I thanked her, although at that time our plan was to drive further south and dance on the bridge at Avignon, seek out the Maid of Orleans, follow Hector Malot's *Sans Famille* up the great French canal system to Paris, finally plunging east to Reims to hunt the Jackdaw and breakfast on champagne. But by the time we hobbled out of Switzerland the prospect of a long break from both travelling and the van was very attractive. We rationalised the decision in many ways – kindness to children, rest for us, in-depth rather than cursory exploration of the country, time to digest all that we had seen. All were part-truths. More deeply behind it was an inescapable fact. The lifespan of journeys is variable and unpredictable. 'Who has not known a journey to be over and dead before a traveller returns?' Steinbeck had written in *Travels with Charley*. In effect our quest had run its course by the time we left Switzerland – the little coda that was our week in France was delightful, but it had a sunset quality.

At Bagnols we pottered. On an ancient tiled stove I stirred sun-ripened vegetables in olive oil and garlic. Tom sat in a wooden chair outside the front door, making jottings for the translation of Plato he was working on – his mind had flown ahead of us and was back at work already. Tilly and Daisy lay around reading Pierre and Charlotte's books; Ellie found Adèle had plenty of friends in town, and shy sessions of Anglo-French amity took place with the help of bags of cherries and bunches of wild flowers. Susie found a battered pram in the barn, a life-size babydoll in the attic, and went for proud maternal promenades up and down the quiet village street.

We did make excursions. Tom toured the little vineyards of the region, coming back glowing from wine-tastings, and box after box of Côtes de Rhone was stacked up behind the seats of the cab. Daisy and I went for a long walk to the next little village, past the turrets of a château crumbling in its overgrown domaine, past pigonniers of golden stone and row after orderly row of vines. Village of roses, it was called, but although there were plenty planted, none of them were scented. In its small square there was a bandstand and three patisseries. We treated ourselves to strawberry tarts and carried home a big bag of croissants.

'What stories are we doing in France, Mummy?' Daisy asked me as we strolled back through the sleepy meadows.

'I had lots of plans,' I said. 'But I may have run out of energy.'

'I don't mind,' she said cheerfully.' Whatever we do seems to turn out all right. And I'm looking forward to getting home too. So's Tilly. We want to give our friends their presents.'

I relaxed. Guilt at a task not completed slipped away.

Back at Bagnols, Tom had a large-scale map of the region spread across his knee. He was murmuring a litany of names – 'Chambolles Musigny les Charmes. Fleurie. Mercurey. Nuits St George. Gevrey Chambertin – did you know that Chambertin was Napoleon's favourite wine? He had it bottled specially for him in Sèvres glass bottles stamped with a crowned N. Drank it five or six years old, very diluted with water. What a waste.' I looked at the book open beside him:

Tough and powerful like the greatest of the Cortons, it has the delicacy of Musigny, the velvet of Romanée, the perfume of a high Clos Vougeot. Its colour is that sombre scarlet which seems to imprison in its garnet reflections all the glory of a setting sun. Taste it: feel in the mouth that full firm roundness, that substantial flame enveloped by the matt softness of velvet and the aroma of reseda! Chambertin, king of wines.

Clearly, just as I had lost all desire for romantic adventure, Tom had found his own variety of enchantment. He looked hopefully at me.

'Beaune isn't far. And there are some ruins near it – the Abbey of Cluny. The monks were great winegrowers, apparently.'

'Why not? I've run out of energy.'

'Great. Tomorrow then – or the day after, on the way to Paris . . .'

It took rather longer than that to tear ourselves away from Bagnols. We had got so comfortably spread out about the house, and so used to the gentle pattern of do-nothing days that we kept postponing our departure. Andersen's restless flitting from country to country in search of stimulation no longer held any attraction. Instead, browsing through the children's books on the shelves, I found a set of books that seemed to sum up everything we were gaining from this quiet leisurely time *en famille*.

Huge in format, broken-backed, their pages torn and taped together again, Jean de Brunhoff's stories of Babar, the king of the elephants, were clearly much-read favourites of the Moon children. I started reading them to Susie, but found I soon had an audience of four, not one. Daisy and Tilly had come across one or two of them before, but had never read them all in order as we did then. Babar and Céleste leave the first story in the yellow balloon which is on the cover of the second; Babar's last words in the second – 'I am going to try to be a good king' – predict the subject of the third, *Babar the King*; *Babar at Home* moves from the general governing of a country to the particular governing of a family. I began to realise what a carefully structured and comfortable world they offered.

The first book, *The Story of Babar*, is a proper fairytale. Babar loses his mother, goes on a journey, finds a substitute for her in the Old Lady, matures through education and the civilising experience of the city world, then returns to his home bearing gifts and wealth. But, unlike most children's authors, de Brunhoff tells us exactly how Babar and Céleste lived happily ever after. The five sequels, *Babar's Travels*, *Babar the King*, *Babar and his friend Zephir*, *Babar at Home*, and *Babar and Father Christmas*, provided children – and their parents – with as complete an advice system as a childcare manual. More complete, in fact, than a modern manual, because de Brunhoff was concerned with moral order, good manners and self-discipline in a way which is currently rather unfashionable. 'Remember that in this life we must never lose heart,' says the Old Lady at the end of *Babar the King*. 'The wicked snake has not killed me, and Cornelius is well again. Let us work and play with a will and we shall always be happy.' Fat as the books of advice on our shelves are, few are as positive in their message as this. They tend to be concerned with physical well-being, individual fulfilment and intellectual development rather than considering the child in its social world.

There is an older tradition – courtesy books, etiquette manuals, and volumes of letters of advice from parents to their children – which did concern themselves with such things. When I read more about de Brunhoff after our return, I found one scholar who believes that the Babar books can best be understood in this context. 'Underlying their pure delight, adventurous plots, lively characters, evocative settings and whimsical style is their essentially serious theme: the earnest concern of a father for how his young family should be brought up, a concern for their morals and manners.' In a fascinating essay, Ann Hildebrand suggests that the six classic concerns of courtesy writings – inward grace, outward grace, personal relations, work, recreation, and the nurture of children – are all systematically dealt with in Jean de Brunhoff's books.

Inward grace is represented by Babar's sanguine character, most vividly illustrated in an incredible representation of a dream he has in which elephant angels of love, health, happiness, hope, work, learning, joy, goodness, intelligence, patience, perseverance, and courage drive away the demons of fear, despair, indolence, ignorance, laziness, cowardice, misfortune, sickness, discouragement, stupidity, and anger. Outward grace can be seen in his concern for clothes – the appropriate ones, too, to fit one's station. His subjects are each presented with two sets of clothes – 'beautiful rich clothes for holidays' and 'serviceable clothes suitable for work-days'. Babar is always scrupulously polite, conducting himself with poise and élan even when faced by charging rhinoceroses or hungry cannibals. De Brunhoff's attitude to work is most clearly drawn in *Babar the King*, in the description of the mutual interdependence of all the different trades which 'the elephants who were too old to go to school' take up – even the clown has his place: 'Hatchibombotar kept the streets tidy, Olur mended cars, and when they were tired Doulamor [the musician] played to them. Fandago [the scholar] ate fruit grown by Poutifor. As for Coco, he made them all laugh.'

Children are taken seriously in Babar's kingdom – the school is part of the Palace of Work. 'Sir, this is not a toy,' says the liftboy chidingly as the young Babar rides up and down in the department store elevator for the tenth time. But they are given plenty of fun as well – and so are the adults. 'At Célesteville all the elephants work in the morning, and in the afternoon they can do as they please. They play, go for walks, read and dream.' And *Babar's Children* is almost absurdly precise in the instruction it gives for bringing up babies: 'Every week Dr Capoullousse weighed the babies carefully in his big scales. One day he said to Céleste: "Oh Queen, the babies are not growing fast enough. You must give each of them, in addition to their usual feed, six bottles of cow's milk, and in each bottle you must put a spoonful of honey."'

When I discovered the tragedy that was hidden behind the light-hearted fun of the Babar books, Hildebrand's analysis seemed extremely convincing. Babar was invented originally by Jean de Brunhoff's wife Cécile, for their two sons, Laurent and Mathieu. She used to tell them stories every evening, and King Babar was just one of the characters. De Brunhoff, a painter, contracted tuberculosis when he was still in his twenties, and had to leave his much-loved family for a Swiss sanitorium. The first pictures of Babar were made by him there, and sent home to cheer up his children. His brother Michel suggested he make a book of them. For the next seven years, until his death in 1937, de Brunhoff worked to provide a vision of civilised life for his children. Maybe Hildebrand goes a little over the top, but I like the romanticism of her interpretation:

Brunhoff wanted his children to acquire the experiences and develop the control necessary for *bonheur*. He could not be an enduring model, but he could make one from his own fatherly dreams and hopes. And so the elegantly gallant Babar is the loving, guiding, ideal French father; he is also the *gallant et honnête homme*, the Parfit Knight, the Compleat Gentleman of courtesy literature – the ultimate courtier in an elephant's skin.

Looking at the comfortable pictures of Babar and Céleste sitting beside each other in plump armchairs, crowns tilted casually on their unfurrowed brows, I felt we might have more to learn about civilisation from the French than from anybody. We had run wild long enough in the regions of romance. With Bertha in immaculate order, our clothes washed and ironed for the first time in seven weeks, the cupboards full of small delicacies from French supermarkets, we closed the door of the house at Bagnols for the last time, and headed north for Paris.

We approached it half-heartedly, short of sleep after the most unsuccessful of our nights in motorway lay-bys. Traffic-shy after her long quiet week among the buttercups of Burgundy, Bertha insisted on driving the wrong way down one-way streets, havering at junctions indecisively, wilting at the aggressive hornplay of attacking cars. But Mercury, god of travellers, took a hand. We turned into a sidestreet off the Boulevard St Michel to see the unbelievable sign 'Space reserved for the use of Tourists' beside an empty parking lot. To do justice to the capital city of fashion, the girls put on the prettiest of all the pretty new clothes they had bought. Tilly wore a soft pink and white checked shirt and skirt, with a pink jacket over it; Daisy was in pale apple green trousers and jacket. Ellie and Susie wore their slickest shorts and T-shirts. And out we stepped.

A bus with the right number for the Eiffel Tower purred up behind us, and stopped obediently. We were whisked along the boulevards to the Champs de Mars and the tower itself. It soared up into the sunshine, a web of steel stretching to infinity. Then we too rose to the sky, in a lift that Ellie felt was too frail to be really trustworthy. She was conveniently distracted by the film crew in the lift with us, who were filming the expressionless reaction of a beautiful Japanese girl model to the changing cityscape behind her.

'Who is she, Mummy?' asked Susie.

'She's a model – but they want to show her with Paris in the background. That's why they're photographing her up here.'

'She looks very real. Are you sure she's a model?' asked Susie, looking admiringly at her immaculate mask of make-up, her long scarlet nails, her exquisite turn-out.

'Yes,' said Daisy mischievously. 'She's just a model. Pinch her, and you'll soon see.'

Luckily the lift stopped at that point, and we got out. On a windy day the top of the tower sways several inches from side to side, a guide told us. Ellie looked aghast.

'Not as bad as Pisa, though, Ellie' said Tilly comfortingly. 'And it isn't windy at all today.'

She relaxed visibly.

Below us lay Paris, misty at the edges, its old grey mansion blocks settled and self-confident, the Seine sweeping through it towards the sea and England. Tom pointed to Notre Dame, our final target; I sought out the slim spire of the Sainte-Chapelle. The girls were more interested in a photograph kiosk that offered to snap them with their heads sticking out of absurdly painted boards. Why not, after all, we thought indulgently, and they all pushed their heads into holes and grinned over inappropriately developed bodies. The results were hilarious, worth every penny of the money, and in retrospect easily the best part of our visit to the tower. We had unbuttoned a lot as parents since that first strictly regulated tour of the pump-station museum in Holland. I had found myself imposing less and less on them in the course of the journey; making myself sit back and follow them instead of trying to lead all the time. Looking at the world through the children's eyes made it look a lot less jaded and tired, and a lot more fun.

A taxi took us back to the Boulevard St Michel, and we settled down to a second breakfast of croissants, coffee and hot chocolate. Then we spent an hour in the Cluny Museum on a personal pilgrimage to the six tapestries of the Lady of the Unicorn. Tom and I had bought a copy of one of these fifteen years before, and it is very much part of the children's life. It hangs as the backdrop to a built-in bed – half sofa, half stage – in our family room. They act short dramas in front of it, they balance their heels against it when practising gym, they loll against it to watch TV. Now we could look at the real thing, and try to puzzle out its meaning. Was the set a wedding present, or a mysterious romantic gesture? Did they tell the story of a girl giving up the world to become a nun or were they as unashamedly sensuous as the Song of Solomon?

We sat in the circular room specially constructed for the tapestries and looked at them carefully. Against a rich crimson background, thickly textured with flowers, animals and birds, six blue islands float, each with the same sad-eyed lady, her lion and her unicorn. Five of them seem to be allegories of the senses: in one the girl plays a portable organ, in another the unicorn looks at itself in the reflection of a handglass, in the third a pet monkey sniffs at a carnation, in the fourth it raises a sweetmeat to its mouth, and in the last the Lady gently touches the unicorn's horn.

But the sixth, the central piece, and the original of our own, remains a mystery. Written across the tent in front of which the Lady stands are the words 'A Mon Seul Desir'. A maid is holding out a box of jewels and the lady – well, is she taking that necklace out, or is she putting it back in? Controversy rages over this point; it divides the romantics from the rationalists. Let her take it out and the tapestry becomes the first essential cornerstone in a monument to love: she is accepting the gifts and the hand of the prince. The other five show her wearing the necklace and enjoying the delights of the senses. Let her be putting it back in and the tapestry becomes the end of the story: she is rejecting all the temptations of the world, all passions and sensations, to devote herself to right living – the cast-off necklace becomes the symbol of the renunciation of the passions aroused by the senses when they are not under the control of the will. The choice is yours.

We strolled through the Latin quarter, munching pancakes laced with chocolate, turning over old books and pictures in the stalls on the riverfront. Daisy, Ellie and Susie decided to have chic French haircuts in a bright and cheerful coiffeur, but Tilly refused to part with an inch of her waist-long hair. After lunch we crossed to the brilliant jewelled church of the Sainte-Chapelle: the world of the Lady come to life. Then along the riverside to Notre Dame itself. High in its square towers we could see gargoyles and tourists looking down together over the most civilised city in the world, and we were soon up there beside them. Due to that energy lapse back in Burgundy I hadn't got round to reading the girls the whole story of Hugo's Hunchback, so I cobbled together an abbreviated version of Quasimodo and Esmerelda as we climbed the spiral stairs. But I don't think they were really listening. To them the top of the tower was the view it commanded – and the excellent slide made by the sloping lead roofs.

I remembered the little Lido they had made on Åro, the scaling of Everest at Elbrinxen, the impromptu bazaar created out of chips of stone at Carrara, the pram that had become a pony and trap at Bagnols. Wherever they were, the world had become more than it seemed. Ships' hawsers had been tightropes, swathes of alpine meadow grass huge nests to brood in, Bertha herself transformed by turn into a schoolroom, a café, a shop, or a hairdressing salon, without even the casual flick of a wand that Cinderella's godmother needed to turn frogs to footmen. We'd brought them to Europe with some vague purpose of civilising them, of extending their imaginations to take in how other people lived and thought, of bringing to life their favourite stories. I think we succeeded in all those aims – the unexpected bonus was the new knowledge we gained of them, of their adaptability and competence, their gusto and kindness.

Versailles, intended to be the grand adieu to France and Europe, we never saw. We circled the park and talked of halls of mirrors and the ornate splendours of the Sun King, but the girls were untempted. They were sorting through their souvenirs, deciding which they would give to which friend on our return, then wrapping the treasures up elaborately. So we set off for Le Havre because I liked the idea of leaving Europe as we had arrived, from the mouth of a great river. The Rhine had led us into adventure, the Seine gentled us home. But I had a faint sense of incompleteness – as if I'd left a biscuit half-eaten somewhere. To trail back like this was somehow an anti-climax.

I saw on the map that the Seine made a great loop towards us, and that there was some sort of ruin close to its banks. Nearly mid-day – we could have a picnic lunch before we joined the queue of unbooked vagrants for the ferry at Le Havre. The road wound down a valley, past steep chalk cliffs to a neat little town, Les Andelys. 'To the Château' pointed a sign, and we followed obediently, trusting to fate. The road became narrower and steeper, Bertha puffed and snorted. Then it flattened out and spread into a cliff-top carpark. We stopped the van and sat quite still for a moment, struck by one of the most unexpected and lovely sights of our entire journey. Towering over the Seine was a perfect crusader's castle, its curtain walls laced about a high circular keep. Château Gaillard: Richard the Lionheart's Saucy Castle, built at the gates of Normandy in defiance of the French eight hundred years ago, and still as flamboyant as ever.

The girls raced down into the old moat, then started to scale the hill to the castle itself. Tom and I advanced more slowly, rugs and the picnic in our arms. The great red and gold standard of the Plantagenets flapped lazily above us as we ate lunch. Released from clammy Chillon after Blondel had discovered him, Richard had lost no time in showing the French that the devil, as they called him, was loose – he built a network of defences to control access to

Normandy. Gaillard was the linch-pin, and Richard's favourite residence besides, so impregnable to attack that it was never taken by storm, only by treachery. There are dead stones and live ones: Gaillard is still extraordinarily alive. We split up and explored it. Daisy teetered along the top of a wall, Ellie and Susie disappeared into a dungeon. The elderly custodian chatted amiably to Tom and me, pointed out the old well, the skeletal vestiges of buried buildings. I wandered over to Tilly who was sitting framed in a high-arched window, looking down on trains of barges being towed noiselessly along the river below.

'What about castles next time?' she said. 'Crusaders' castles, in the Holy Land. Daisy suggested it. She thought that Children's Crusade stuff was really interesting. Or are we going to hunt Father Christmas, like you said in Venice? Ellie and Susie would like that best, I suppose. I'd like to see more of France, too. Not now, I mean. We're all tired now. But next time.'

It was the greatest compliment she could have paid me. That assumption that we would be going again, that confidence that they would enjoy it. I felt as pleased as the mother hen in the 'Ugly Duckling' when her brood hatches. I'd hatched a brood too, a brood of travellers. And romantic ones, at that. Real swans.

Bibliography

I like bibliographies that reflect a writer's thinking as well as giving precise information about books mentioned in the text. So I have included books that I haven't specifically referred to, but which are indirectly relevant to the story of the Cart and her adventures. Others are listed because they may lead the interested reader on to deeper and wider adventures in the world of literary travelling than there was time on our journey or space in my book to explore.

Of general interest

Basile, Giovanni Battista, *The Pentameron*, translated by Sir Richard Burton, William Kimbers, London, 1952.

Bettelheim, Bruno, *The Uses of Enchantment: The Meaning and Importance of Fairy Tales*, Thames & Hudson, London, 1976.

Browne, John Ross, *An American Family in Germany*, Harper, New York, 1867.

Campbell, Joseph, *The Hero with a Thousand Faces*, Princeton University Press, Princeton, 1968.

Carpenter, Humphrey, and Prichard, Mari, *The Oxford Companion to Children's Literature*, OUP, Oxford, 1984.

Carter, Lin, *Dragons, Elves and Heroes*, Ballantine Books, New York, 1969.

Connolly, Cyril, *The Unquiet Grave: A Word Cycle by Palinurus*, Hamish Hamilton, London, 1945.

Dinesen, Isak, *Seven Gothic Tales*, Putnam, New York, 1934.

Grahame, Kenneth, *The Wind in the Willows*, illustrated by E. H. Shepard, 1908, reprint, Methuen, London, 1985.

Hazard, Paul, *Books, Children and Men*, translated by M. Mitchell, Horn Book Inc., Boston, 1964.

Hicks, Penny, *Camping and Caravanning in Europe*, AA, London, 1985.

Hürlimann, Bettina, *Three Centuries of Children's Books in Europe*, 1959, translated by Brian W. Aldersen, OUP, Oxford, 1967.

Bibliography

Jung, Carl, *Man and His Symbols*, Aldus, London, 1964.

Lagerqvist, Rune, *Roadbook Europe*, AA, London, 1984.

Michelin Green Tourist Guides to Germany and Italy, Michelin Tyre Co., London, 1982.

Opie, Iona and Peter, *The Classic Fairy Tales*, OUP, Oxford, 1974.

Perrault, Charles, *Old-Time Stories*, translated by A. E. Johnson, illustrated by W. Heath Robinson, Constable, London, 1921.

Rackham, Arthur, *Once Upon a Time: The Fairy Tale World of Arthur Rackham*, introduced by Margery Darrell, Heinemann, 1972.

Ransome, Arthur, *A History of Story-Telling*, T. C. and E. C. Jack, London, 1909.

Steinbeck, John, *Travels with Charley*, Viking, New York, 1961.

Symonds, A. J., *The Quest for Corvo*, Penguin, London, 1940.

Travers, P. L, *About the Sleeping Beauty*, Collins, London, 1977.

Ussher, Arland, and Carl von Metzradt, *Enter These Enchanted Woods: An Interpretation of Grimms' Fairy Tales*, Dolmen Press, Dublin, 1958.

By country

Holland

De Jong, Meindert, *Far Out the Long Canal*, Lutterworth, London, 1964.

De Jong, Meindert, *The Wheel on the School*, Lutterworth, London, 1956.

Dodge, Mary Mapes, *Hans Brinker and the Silver Skates*, 1865, new edition, Dent, London, 1955.

Dumas, Alexandre, *The Black Tulip*, translated by A. J. O'Connor, introduction by Richard Garnett, Methuen, London, 1902.

Denmark

Andersen, Hans Christian, *Fairy Tales and Legends*, illustrated by Rex Whistler, Bodley Head, London, 1935.

Andersen, Hans Christian, *Fairy Tales*, edited by Svend Larsen, translated by R. P. Keigwin, illustrated by V. Pedersen and Lorenz Frölich, Edmund Ward, London, 1958. These four small pocket volumes are the best translations and most attractive presentation of the tales that I have come across.

Andersen, Hans Christian, *The Fairy Tale of My Life*, translated by W. Glyn Jones, British Books, New York, 1955.

Bredsdorff, Elias, *Hans Christian Andersen: The Story of His Life and Work 1805–75*, Phaidon, 1975.

Dahl, Svend, and Topsøe-Jensen, H. G. (ed.), *Hans Christian Andersen, His Life and Work*, Department of Culture, Copenhagen, 1955.

Fifty Years of Play, Legoland, 1982.

Larsen, Svend, *The Life History of Hans Christian Andersen*, Hans Andersen Hüs, Odense, 1984.

Bibliography

Reumert, Elith, *Hans Andersen The Man*, Methuen, London, 1927.

Stirling, Monica, *The Wild Swan: The Life and Times of Hans Christian Andersen*, Collins, London, 1965.

Thomasson, Ed., *Danish Quality Living: The Good Life Handbook*, Forlaget Folia, Copenhagen, 1984.

Germany

Andersen, Hans Christian, *Romantic Rambles in the Harz Mountains*, Bentley, London, 1848.

Browning, Robert, 'The Ballad of the Pied Piper', in *Dramatic Lyrics*, Edward Moxon, London, 1842.

Browning, Robert, *The Ballad of the Pied Piper*, illustrated by Arthur Rackham, Harrap, London, 1934.

Bryce, James, *The Holy Roman Empire*, new edition, Macmillan, London, 1904.

Chamisso, A. V., *Peter Schlemehl*, Whittaker, London, 1824 (first in a series of shadowy obsessions, arguably culminating in *Peter Pan*).

Ellis, John M., *One Fairy Story Too Many: The Brothers Grimm and Their Tales*, Chicago University Press, Chicago, 1983.

Friedmann, Rudolph, 'Struwwelpeter', *New Directions Quarterly*, 1954, reprinted in *The Faber Book of Parodies*, edited by Simon Brett, Faber, London, 1984.

Fryer, Alfred, *Fairy Tales from the Harz Mountains*, illustrated by Alice M. Odgers, Nutt, London, 1908.

Gibson, Evan K., et al., *Heinrich Hoffmann: Der Struwwelpeter Polyglott*, DTV, 1984.

Gould, Sabine Baring, *Curious Myths of the Middle Ages*, 1866, new edition, Longmans, 1901.

Grimm Brothers, *Fairy Tales*, introduced by Sabine Baring Gould, illustrated by Gordon Browne, Wells Gardner, London, 1894.

Hammond, Muriel E., *Jacob and Wilhelm Grimm: The Fairy-tale Brothers*, Dobson, London, 1968.

Heine, Heinrich, 'The Tour of the Harz', in *Travel-Pictures*, translated by Francis Storr, Bell, London, 1887.

Hoffmann, E. T. A., *The Best Tales of E. T. A. Hoffmann*, edited by E. F. Bleiler, Dover, New York, 1967.

Hoffman, Heinrich, *Der Struwwelpeter*, privately published by the author, Frankfurt, 1845.

Hoffman, Heinrich, *The Latin Struwwelpeter*, translated by W. H. D. Rouse, Blackie, London, 1934.

Hoffman, Heinrich, *The English Struwwelpeter*, 12th edition, Friedrich Volkmar, Leipzig, 1860.

Hoffman, Heinrich, *Slovenly Peter*, freely translated by Mark Twain, Harper, New York, 1935.

Bibliography

Hoffman, Heinrich, *Stuuwelpeter-Hoffmann*, Schriftsteller Bürger, Arst, Frankfurt, 1959.

Hoffman, Heinrich, *King Nutcracker, or the Dream of Poor Reinhold*, translated by J. R. Planché, Volkmar, Leipzig and London, 1853.

MacCarthy, Desmond and Guinness, Bryan, *The Story of a Nutcracker*, Heinemann, 1953.

Michaelis-Jena, Ruth, *The Brothers Grimm*, Routledge, 1970.

Our Summer in the Harz Forest, by A Scotch Family, Edmonston and Douglas, Edinburgh, 1865.

Thompson, Sylvanus, *The Pied Piper of Hamelin*, Sette of Odd Volumes, London, 1895.

Treece, Henry, *The Children's Crusade*, Bodley Head, 1958.

Wanley, Nathaniel, *Wonders of the Little World: A General History of Man, with Particular Relation to the Virtues, Vices and Defects of Both Sexes*, Taylor, London, 1678, new edition 1704.

Wilson, Stephen, 'Hans Andersen's Nightingale: A paradigm for the development of transference love', *International Review of Psycho-Analysis* (1980), vol. 7, no. 483.

Italy

Calvino, Italo, *Italian Folk Tales*, translated by George Martin, Pantheon, New York, 1980.

Cambon, Glauco, 'Pinocchio and the Problems of Children's Literature', *Children's Literature*, vol. 2, 1973, pp. 50–60.

Collodi, Carlo, *Pinocchio: The Story of a Puppet*, 1883, translated by M. A. Murray, illustrated by Charles Folkard, Dent, London, 1911.

Donati, Roberto, *Lucca*, Terni, Italy, 1983.

Heisig, James, 'Pinocchio, Archetype of the Motherless Child', *Children's Literature*, vol. 2, 1973, pp. 23–65.

Morris, James, *Venice*, Faber, 1960.

Newman, Cathy, 'Carrara Marble', *National Geographic Magazine*, vol. 162, no. 1, July 1982.

Obici, Marcherita, *Maschere e Travestimenti nella Tradizione del Carnivale di Venezia*, Arsenale, Venezia, 1981.

Shankland, Hugh, *Messer Pietro Mio: Letters of Lucrezia Borgia and Pietro Bembo*, Libanus Press, 1985.

Stisted, Georgiana, *The True Life of Captain Sir R. F. Burton*, written by his niece, 1890, Ward Lock reprint, 1970.

Venice and the Carnival, Edizioni Storti, Venice, 1985.

Switzerland

Heald, Weldon F., *Tell's Country Ramble*, Swiss Tourist Office, 1965.

Rae, Gwynedd, *Mostly Mary*, Marriott, London, 1930.

Bibliography

Rae, Gwynedd, *The Mary Plain Omnibus*, Routledge, London, 1976.

Spyri, Joanna, *Heidi*, first printed 1881, centenary edition illustrated by Marguerite Davis, 1927.

Tritten, Charles, *Heidi Grows Up*, Collins, London, 1939.

Tritten, Charles, *Heidi's Children*, Collins, London, 1950.

France

de Brunhoff, Jean, *Histoire de Babar*, Jardin des Modes, Paris, 1931.

de Brunhoff, Jean, *Le Voyage de Babar*, Jardin des Modes, Paris, 1932.

de Brunhoff, Jean, *Le Roi Babar*, Jardin des Modes, Paris, 1933.

de Brunhoff, Jean, *ABC de Babar*, Hachette, Paris, 1936.

de Brunhoff, Jean, *Les Vacances de Zephyr*, Hachette, Paris, 1936.

de Brunhoff, Jean, *Babar en Famille*, Hachette, Paris, 1938.

de Brunhoff, Jean, *Babar et le Père Noël*, Hachette, Paris, 1940.

Dumas, Alexandre, *The Three Musketeers*, new edition, Paris, 1876, translated by W. Robson, Macdonald, London, 1950.

Gould, Sabine Baring, *In Troubadour Land: A Ramble in Provence and Languedoc*, W. H. Allen, London, 1891.

Hildebrand, Ann M., 'Jean de Brunhoff's Advice to Youth: The Babar Books as Books of Courtesy', *Children's Literature*, vol. 2, 1983, pp. 77–95.

Hugo, Victor, *The Hunchback of Notre Dame*, translated by J. Sturrock, Penguin, 1978.

Malot, Hector, *Sans Famille*, Paris, 1879. (Classic French story of an English boy's adventures in France – unaccountably very little known in England, but a favourite European children's classic. Last published in a complete English translation in 1938. Would make a tour in itself.)

Maurois, André, *Three Musketeers: A Study of the Dumas Family*, Cape, 1957.

Saint-Exupéry, Antoine de, *The Little Prince*, Gallimard, Paris, 1946.

Saint-Exupéry, Antoine de, *Wind, Sand and Stars*, translated by Lewis Galantière, Heinemann, 1970.

Saint-Exupéry: His Life and Times, Cate, Curtis, Heinemann, London, 1970.

Saint-Exupéry, Hachette, Paris, 1963.

Stevenson, Robert Louis, *Travels with a Donkey in the Cevennes*, Chatto pocket editions, 1912.

Thackeray, Anne Ritchie, *The Fairy Tales of Madame D'Aulnoy*, Lawrence and Bullen, London, 1857.

Waddell, Helen, *The Wandering Scholars*, Constable, 1927. (Excellent on the French troubadours.)

Useful Addresses

General

The Haunted Bookshop, 9 St Edward's Passage, Cambridge CB2 3PJ.
Tel.: 0223 312913 – early editions of classic children's stories.

Holland

Duinrel Campsite, Wassenaar. Signposted off A44 Den Haag–Leiden
road. Tel.: 19314. Open all year round.
Skating museum (part of it the Hans Brinker Collection formerly at
Schermerhorn) at Molen de Eendragt, close to the station in Prins
Alexanderstraat, Alkmaar.
Pump station museum: ten miles south of Haarlem at Cruquiusdijk
27/32, usually open 10 a.m. to 5 p.m. Tel.: 023–285704; good teahouse
next door.
Bike hire: contact Tourist Information (VVV) office, or local stations.

Denmark

Legoland Park, Dk 7190, Billund. Tel.: 05-33 13 33. Open 1 May to
mid-September, 10 a.m. to 8 p.m. daily. Winter season open 10 a.m. to
5 p.m. Closed Christmas to New Year.
Billund (for Legoland) Camping, Nordsmarkksvej 2, 7190 Billund. Tel.:
05-33 15 21.
Hans Christian Andersen Museum, Hans Jensensstraede 39–43, Odense.
Ærø: Tourist Information (for ferry times, camping, bike hire etc.)
Torvet, DK-5970 Ærøskøbing. Tel.: 09-52 13 00.
Tivoli Pleasure Gardens, Copenhagen. Open 1 May to 21 September.
Fireworks Wednesday and Saturday evenings, 11.30.
Elsinore: Hamlet's castle: Kronborg, Helsingør. 47 miles north of
Copenhagen. Open all year round. May to Sept 10 a.m. to 5 p.m. Castle
batteries: free access 6 a.m. to sunset.

Useful Addresses

West Germany

German National Tourist Office, 61 Conduit Street, London W1R 0EN: an exceptionally helpful and efficient service.

Wilsede: village without motor traffic on Lüneburg Heath. Carriages from Undeloh, Egestort exit, eastwards off E4 south of Hamburg.

Hamelin: Pied Piper Play: from mid-May to mid-September every Sunday at noon on the terrace of Hochzeithaus.

Lautenthal, near Innerstestaustee: train visit into mine, mining museum. Tel.: 0 53 25/44 44.

Goslar: reconstructed Imperial Palace, Matilda's tomb, old silver mines of Rammelsberg. Tourist Information Office (very efficient, and useful for all the western Harz) tel.: 0 53 21/70 42 16.

Braunlage: cable-car up to summit of Würmberg: good view into Eastern Germany.

Fairytale Road – free map from German Tourist office or direct: Deutsche Märchenstrasse, PO Box 1200420, Humboldstraße 26, D 3500, Kassel.

Sababurg: Sleeping Beauty's castle, alias the Burghotel Sababurg, 3520 Hofgeismar. Tel.: (0 56 78) 10 52.

Kassel: Wilhelmshöhe: picture gallery and waterfalls (switched on at 2.30 p.m. Wednesdays, Sundays and holidays, Ascension Day to September).

Kassel: Brothers Grimm Museum in the Chateau of Bellevue, open 10 a.m. to 6 p.m. except Mondays and holidays.

Struwwelpeter (Heinrich Hoffmann) Museum, Schubertstrasse, Frankfurt.

Bavaria: Mad King Ludwig's Castles: Neuschwanstein (this is the one with the wilderness of turrets, of Chitty-Chitty-Bang-Bang and self-raising flour fame) and Hohenschwangau (less exotic outside but possibly more beautiful inside) are within a mile of each other, two miles east of Fussen, on the border between Germany and Austria.

East Germany

Berolina, 20 Conduit St, London W1R 9TD is the official avenue of approach to the German Democratic Republic. I may have been unlucky in the length of time which it took to process our visa, but I would recommend starting early and being persistent (phoning every day, for example). Otherwise there are no special problems about crossing the border, but it may be wise to aim at offpeak times and backwoods crossing points if long slow investigations are not your idea of fun. We crossed the border at Teistungen, between Worbis and Duderstadt – Göttingen was the nearest West German city.

All the places Hans Andersen visited in the Eastern Harz are close enough to be seen in a short visit to the ring of small towns north of Nordhausen.

Useful Addresses

Qvedlinburg: Matilda's Abbey.

Regenstein: on the north-western outskirts of Blankenburg.

Baumann's Cave: Rubeland, south-west of Blankenburg.

The Roßtrappe (Hoofprint) and Hexenplatz (Witches' Dancing Floor) at Thale.

The Ilsenstein (N.B. there is no through-road to the Brocken at this point) is approached from Ilsenburg, west from Wernigerode.

Italy

Marina di Venezia Camping, Punta Sabbione, Venezia.

Scuola di San Giorgio degli Schiavoni – Carpaccio murals of St Jerome.

Parco di Pinocchio and Villa Garzoni, Collodi, near Pescia, ten miles east of Lucca.

Lucca, duomo and city walls.

Carrara, Marble Quarries (Italian: *Cave*) Colonnata and Fantiscritti.

Switzerland

Swiss National Tourist Office, Swiss Centre, 1 New Coventry St, London W1V 3HG – generous free handouts on Heidi and William Tell.

Heidi: Maienfeld, on the Lichtenstein border, is the gateway to Heidi's country. The Heidihof Hotel, CH 7304 Maienfeld (Tel.: 085/9 11 95) is a good starting point for a walk up to Falknis and the Alm itself.

Hirzel: Heidi Museum, Curator: Jürg Winkler, Brämenhalde, 8816 Hirzel.

Zurich: Swiss Institute for Juvenile Literature.

William Tell: Lake Lucerne is the heart of Tell territory, and most of it can be seen from one of the romantic white-painted paddle-steamers that ply the length of the lake from Altdorf to Lucerne, at the head of the lake, which is where the apple was shot from his son's head. Burglin, a little further into the mountains, has the main Tell Museum, now housed in the Wattigwyler Tower. The Tell Chapel is on the shores of the lake north of Altdorf. Interlaken: Pageant Play of William Tell, open-air performances in July and August.

Jungfraujoch railway: starts in Interlaken, and can be joined at stations on the way, including Lauterbrunnen, which has an excellent campsite.

France

Wine caves: Beaujolais, nr. Rouen; Cotes d'Or, near Beaune. We found 'unknown' villages close to the great names had co-operative caves offering excellent value wine. The butcher in Gevrey-Chambertin is worth a special visit – he bottles his own red, rosé and white.

Useful Addresses

Abbey of Cluny, north-west of Mâcon: museum and guided tours. Once the heart of medieval monastic Christendom, but now a depressing shadow of its old self. All its glories are preserved in

Paris: Musée de Cluny, off the Boulevard St Michel. Also the Lady of the Unicorn tapestries.

Chateau Gaillard, Les Andelys, near Rouen.

Picture Credits

By illustrator – for further details see Bibliography.

Page   7: E. H. Shepard, *The Wind in the Willows*, 1908.
Page 15: 'The Flying Trunk', in *Hans Andersen's Fairy Tales*, 1912.
Page 18: Louis Rhead, *Hans Brinker and the Silver Skates*, 1924.
Page 30: Louis Rhead, *Hans Brinker and the Silver Skates*, 1924.
Page 47: Rex Whistler, 'The Snow Queen', *Hans Andersen's Fairy Tales and Legends*, 1935.
Page 50: Hans Andersen Collection, Odense.
Page 66: Arthur Rackham, 'The Little Mermaid', *Fairy Tales by Hans Andersen*, 1932.
Page 73: 'The Top and the Ball', *Hans Andersen's Fairy Tales*, 1912.
Page 74: Sketch by Hans Andersen, Odense Museum.
Page 82: 'The Stork's Story', *Hans Andersen's Fairy Tales*, 1912.
Page 84: Woodcut from Sylvanus Thompson's *The Pied Piper of Hamelin*, 1895.
Page 93: Arthur Rackham, *The Ballad of the Pied Piper*, 1934.
Page 98: Arthur Rackham, *The Ballad of the Pied Piper*, 1934.
Page 102: Harz District Map from Heine's *Travel-Pictures*, 1887.
Page 104: 'The Old House', *Hans Andersen's Fairy Tales*, 1912.
Page 127: William Kermode, *Moscow Has a Plan*, 1931.
Page 131: A. M. Odgers, *Fairy Tales from the Harz Mountains*, 1908.
Page 141: Wanda Gag, *Tales from Grimm*, 1973.
Page 145: Rex Whistler, 'The Shadow', *Hans Andersen's Fairy Tales and Legends*, 1935.
Page 153: From the Catalogue of Hoffmann Museum, Frankfurt, 1959.
Page 154: Bryan Guinness, *The Story of a Nutcracker*, 1953.
Page 160: Arthur Hughes, *Poems of Christina Rossetti*, 1893.
Page 166: E. H. Shepard, *Dream Days*, 1930.
Page 174: Arthur Rackham, *Cinderella*, 1912.
Page 182: Charles Folkard, *Pinocchio*, 1883.
Page 191: 'The Shadow', *Hans Andersen's Fairy Tales*, 1912.

Picture Credits

Page 210: Marguerite Davis, *Heidi*, 1927.

Page 213: Joanna Spyri's School, from the Heidi Museum, Hirzel.

Page 228: Arthur Rackham, 'The Snow Queen', *Fairy Tales by Hans Andersen*, 1932.

Page 233: Irene Williamson, *Mostly Mary*, 1930.

Page 234: Bryan Guinness, *The Story of a Nutcracker*, 1953.

Page 236: Hans Andersen, self-portrait, from the Hans Andersen Museum, Odense.

Page 247: Rob Sykes, Sketch of Château Gaillard, 1986.

Acknowledgements

Firstly to the girls and Tom, without whom none of this could have taken place: may they forget the pits and remember the peaks. Secondly to Jane, David, and Sarah Jones, for sterling support and light relief respectively. Thirdly to all the well-read friends whose brains I picked and books I borrowed; especially Julia and Robin Briggs, Humphrey and Mari Carpenter, Stephen Wilson, Chris and Ria Schueller, Robert and Martine Moon, Gillian Crampton Smith and Phil Tabor, Bob and Frances Campbell, Michael Black, Liz Crawford. Fourthly to the libraries, without which I would be nothing: the London Library (best of all, because it allows unlimited browsing and never charges fines), the Bodleian Library, Oxford, the Cambridge University Library, and the British Library. Fifthly to Gill Coleridge and David Godwin for having faith in a wild plan, and arranging the wherewithal to carry it out; and to Sally Gough for her care in putting the finished work together for the printers. Finally to all the hundreds of anonymous but friendly citizens of Europe who welcomed us to their countries, and helped us civilise our savages: thank you.

About the Author

Christina Hardyment read History at Newnham College, Cambridge. While her children were growing up she lived in Marlborough, Wiltshire, where her husband, Tom Griffith, taught Classics. She now lives in Oxford.